Strange Bedfellows

How do advocates for the poor gain influence in American policymaking? *Strange Bedfellows* argues that groups representing low-income populations compensate for a lack of resources by collaborating with diverse partners in their lobbying efforts. This study develops a theory of coalition influence that explains the mechanisms and conditions of coalition formation and influence and provides support for the theory through an analysis of one of the most significant social policy changes in recent history. The analysis shows that in the years preceding the federal welfare reform of 1996, advocates collaborated with diverse partners to influence policymaking, coalitions were used as a tool for pooling different types of resources and communicating information, and groups collaborated selectively across issues. Through rigorous theory and rich qualitative analysis, *Strange Bedfellows* sheds new light on lobbying and influence in policymaking while offering a theoretical framework for understanding the broader role of coalitions in American politics.

Robin Phinney is Research Associate in the Humphrey School of Public Affairs at the University of Minnesota. She received her Ph.D. in Public Policy and Political Science from the University of Michigan, where she received awards including the Ford Fellowship Award, Rackham Predoctoral Fellowship, and Mary Malcomson Raphael Fellowship. Her research and teaching focus on American politics and public policy, with an emphasis on organized interests, the policymaking process, social policy, and the well-being of low-income families. She brings an interdisciplinary perspective to her scholarship, which has been published in leading journals of political science, public policy, and social work.

Strange Bedfellows

Interest Group Coalitions, Diverse Partners, and Influence in American Social Policy

ROBIN PHINNEY
University of Minnesota, Twin Cities

CAMBRIDGE
UNIVERSITY PRESS

CAMBRIDGE
UNIVERSITY PRESS

University Printing House, Cambridge CB2 8BS, United Kingdom

One Liberty Plaza, 20th Floor, New York, NY 10006, USA

477 Williamstown Road, Port Melbourne, VIC 3207, Australia

4843/24, 2nd Floor, Ansari Road, Daryaganj, Delhi – 110002, India

79 Anson Road, #06–04/06, Singapore 079906

Cambridge University Press is part of the University of Cambridge.

It furthers the University's mission by disseminating knowledge in the pursuit of education, learning, and research at the highest international levels of excellence.

www.cambridge.org
Information on this title: www.cambridge.org/9781107170360
DOI: 10.1017/9781316756287

First published 2017

Printed in the United States of America by Sheridan Books, Inc.

A catalogue record for this publication is available from the British Library.

ISBN 978-1-107-17036-0 Hardback

For Chris

Contents

Tables

Figures

Acknowledgments

A great number of people provided exceptional advice and encouragement on this project. I am particularly indebted to my advisors at the University of Michigan – Elisabeth Gerber, Rick Hall, Sheldon Danziger, Chuck Shipan, and Mary Corcoran.

I began working with Liz Gerber early in my graduate studies. It was a privilege to learn from her how to apply scholarly insights and methods to actual policy problems. Liz always offered sound advice and guidance on topics ranging from research design and method to data analysis and writing. Among the many things I admire about Liz is her ability to hone in on the most important problems – as well as the strengths and contributions – of a research project. All aspects of this project are stronger as a result of her mentorship. Sheldon Danziger provided an opportunity for me to gain substantive expertise in the area of social policy and introduced me to the community of scholars working on domestic poverty issues. This community has been integral in my knowledge of social policy and in the development of my own research agenda. Not only is Sheldon an incredible poverty scholar, but he is also an amazing mentor. I am grateful for all of his timely responses, extensive comments, and professional advice and support.

In addition to helping me grasp the intricacies of interest group scholarship, Rick Hall challenged me to think deeply about the larger theoretical contribution of the work. Indeed, it was Rick who helped me see potential extensions of the theory beyond the social policy realm. His approach to scholarship provides a model that I seek to emulate in my own research. Rick's enthusiasm for the project was also contagious, and I always left our meetings with a renewed excitement and commitment to the project. Chuck Shipan went above and beyond in providing insightful comments and advice as the project evolved from prospectus to dissertation and finally to book manuscript. He helped me untangle some of the project's thorniest empirical issues and always provided helpful guidance regarding how to translate the project and its findings to different professional audiences. In addition, his support for the project has extended beyond my time at Michigan, and for that I am extremely grateful. Finally, Mary Corcoran, as the director of my graduate program, provided unwavering encouragement and candid advice. At some of the more difficult stages of the project, her many supportive comments provided the motivation to move forward. I am so thankful for her support.

During my time at the University of Michigan, a large number of individuals, including Rebecca Blank, Tony Chen, Michael Heaney, Ken Kollman, Ann Lin, and Cara Wong, offered valuable advice on the project. I am indebted to participants from the Center for Political Studies, the Interdisciplinary Workshop in American Politics, American Sociological Association meetings, Midwest Political Science Association meetings, and American Political Science Association meetings for comments and suggestions on early versions of this project. Friends and colleagues from the University of Michigan, especially Sarah Marsh, Pam Clouser McCann, Alex Resch, Kristin Seefeldt, Katie Drake Simmons, Olesya Tkacheva, and Roger Michalski, also provided encouragement and comments on the project.

Over the course of my graduate studies, my research was supported by generous grants and fellowships from the following organizations: the Department of Political Science at the University of Michigan, the Ford School of Public Policy at the University of Michigan, the Center for the Education of Women (UM), the Nonprofit and Public Management Center (UM), the National Science Foundation, the Horace H. Rackham School of Graduate Studies (UM), the American Political Science Association, and the Association for Public Policy Analysis and Management.

I would also like to thank friends and colleagues at MDRC – especially Chuck Michalopoulos, Tom Brock, and Sharon Rowser – for providing valuable feedback at an early stage of the project. In addition, colleagues at the University of Minnesota, including Liz Beaumont, Ezra Golberstein, Sarah Gollust, Andy Karch, Howie Lavine, Nancy Luxon, Kathryn Pearson, Dara Strolovitch, and Joan Tronto, provided advice and encouragement as the project transformed into its final form.

I would like to thank my editor at Cambridge University Press, Robert Dreesen, for his continued support and enthusiasm for the project, as well as the editorial staff. I am also grateful for the thoughtful feedback provided by three anonymous reviewers for Cambridge University Press. Their insightful comments and suggestions greatly improved the quality and contributions of the final project.

I am indebted to a great number of friends and family members for supporting me throughout this project. My family – Paul and Suzanne Phinney; Karen and Bobby Hammer; Anne, Bridget, and Carolyn Roberts; Harold and Deane Phinney; and Andrew and Sophia Lipinski – deserve special thanks. Each in his or her own way taught me to appreciate knowledge and education, work hard and see things through, believe in my own contributions, and balance the hard work with relaxation.

Finally, I am beyond thankful for the support of my husband, Chris Roberts. His contributions to my life (including Finn and Radley!) are too many to count, but I am especially grateful for our many conversations about this project around the lakes, and as well as the adventure and balance that he brings to my life. His unwavering enthusiasm and support for this project helped me see it through to the end, and it is to him that I dedicate the book.

I

Interest Group Coalitions and Influence in Social Policy

Can low-income populations gain political influence in the United States? According to a large body of political science scholarship, the answer is a resounding *no*. Those living in poverty encounter numerous obstacles to political activity. Low-income individuals often lack the time, money, and civic skills that enable political participation, and many are isolated from the networks that engage citizens in public affairs (Rosenstone and Hansen 1993; Verba et al. 1993). In addition, organizations that lobby on behalf of the poor represent only a small percentage of organized interests in Washington (Schlozman, Verba, and Brady 2012). The groups that do exist face considerable resource constraints, lacking the large budgets and membership bases that facilitate political influence (Baumgartner and Leech 1998; Berry and Arons 2003; Hays 2001; Strolovitch 2007).

Limited political activity by and on behalf of the poor has consequences for the extent to which the interests of low-income Americans are represented in the national policymaking process and in legislative policy choices. In a system in which members of Congress are held accountable through the electoral system, legislators have few incentives to respond to individuals or groups that can neither promise electoral rewards nor threaten electoral punishment. Perhaps as a result, legislators' voting decisions seldom correspond to the interests of their low-income constituents (Bartels 2008). The policies that emerge from Congress more often reflect the interests of the wealthy than the interests of the poor (Gilens 2014).

And yet policies for the poor *are* enacted, sometimes in the face of strong opposition. American history is punctuated by periods of significant social policy expansion, including the New Deal programs of the 1930s and the Great Society programs of the 1960s (Patterson 2000). While more recent years have witnessed declining government support for low-income populations, some social welfare programs, including the Earned Income Tax Credit, Medicaid, and the Supplemental Nutrition Assistance Program (or Food

Stamps), have been expanded or have withheld considerable efforts to scale back their scope (Hacker 2002; Haveman, Blank, Moffitt, Smeeding, and Wallace 2015).

The fact that low-income populations do achieve meaningful policy victories introduces a disconnect between scholarship that predicts the absence of influence by and on behalf of the poor and the reality that legislators do at times respond to the interests of less-advantaged Americans in the policymaking process. If low-income populations do not participate and their advocates have few resources for lobbying, how do such victories occur? How do the interests of the poor gain traction in the legislative policy process?

This book engages the topic of the political influence of the poor through an analysis of the lobbying strategies of the organizations that advocate on their behalf. Building on a rich body of scholarship on interest group lobbying and influence in Congress, I develop and demonstrates empirical support for a theory that explains how such organizations gain influence on behalf of individuals who are otherwise marginalized in the American policymaking process.

In the following chapters, I argue that to understand how organizational advocates for the poor gain influence in the policy process, it is necessary to understand how *coalitions* of advocates gain influence. Lobbying coalitions are common among groups representing low-income populations, as well as groups representing other types of public and private interests (Hula 1999; Strolovitch 2007). Yet to date, most theories of interest group influence have focused attention on the individual group as the actor capable of influencing legislative decisions. The theory developed in this book departs from typical approaches by focusing attention on coalitions rather than individual groups. In doing so, it contributes to a burgeoning body of work that looks beyond the individual group as the theoretical and empirical focus (Heaney and Lorenz 2013; Mahoney and Baumgartner 2015; Nelson and Yackee 2012).

The book develops a theory of coalitional formation and influence in the legislative policymaking process, which I refer to as the *theory of diverse coalitions*. The theory's central premise is that a coalition gains influence through its diversity, which is defined as differences in the interest or interests that a group represents. Coalitions that unite diverse actors, I argue, draw together different informational resources and have the ability to engage in a broad range of lobbying tactics to communicate that information. In addition, when different types of groups work together, the heterogeneity of their voices and the costs associated with collaborating enhance the credibility of the information they provide. By drawing varied forms of credible information to a lobbying effort, a diverse coalition addresses the informational needs of a large number of legislators and in doing so helps a set of groups gain influence in the policy process.

Yet issue contexts create different opportunities and incentives for groups to collaborate with diverse partners. Thus while diverse coalitions can help groups gain policy influence, only certain issue contexts will be associated with diverse coalition formation. Building off the logic of a simple signaling game, my theory predicts that diverse coalitions will be more likely to emerge on issues characterized by high levels of salience, uncertainty, and strong opponents.

To examine the empirical support for the theory, I conduct an innovative analysis of collaborative activity among organized interests in the two years preceding the passage of the Personal Responsibility and Work Opportunity Reconciliation Act of 1996, or welfare reform. This policy represented a profound shift in the nation's approach to the problem of poverty, and many types of groups mobilized to influence its direction. My analysis of collaboration during welfare reform provides considerable support for the theory's central premises – namely, that in certain issue contexts, diverse coalitions enhance the informational lobbying capabilities of a set of groups. In this way, diverse coalitions reduce legislators' uncertainty regarding the consequences of policy change and help groups gain influence in the policy process.

Because the *diversity* of a coalition rather than the overall level of resources acts as a coalition's critical mechanism of influence, the theory explains how groups that advocate on behalf of low-income populations exert pressure in policymaking despite their limited resources. In doing so, the book reconciles research that predicts a lack of influence among organizational advocates for the poor with the reality that organizations with limited means do at times achieve their policy goals. Moreover, the theoretical mechanisms underlying a diverse coalition's influence are not unique to the social policy realm. Indeed, an interest group has strong incentives to work collaboratively with diverse partners, whether that group is rich or poor. Thus there a strong reasons to suspect broader applicability of the theory across issues and policy domains.

In the remaining pages of this chapter, I introduce and situate my project within the existing scholarship on the political activity of low-income populations, mobilization and advocacy on social policy issues, and interest group lobbying and influence in Congress. In the first section of the chapter, I describe the rich body of cross-disciplinary work on the political influence of the poor. This section highlights the increasing presence of interest group coalitions, particularly in the social policy domain, in order to motivate the book's focus on coalitions.

In the second and third sections, I provide an overview of the theory of diverse coalitions and detail my empirical approach. This approach relies on a unique data collection design to analyze the characteristics and activities of interest group coalitions. In the fourth section, I review the case that forms the basis of my empirical analysis, the Personal Responsibility and Work Opportunity Reconciliation Act of 1996 (PRWORA) and highlight the key empirical findings. The fifth section explains the project's contributions and the final section details the plan of the book.

THE POLITICAL INFLUENCE OF LOW-INCOME POPULATIONS

Political Participation among People Living in Poverty

Low-income populations in the United States face considerable barriers to political influence. Activities such as voting, contributing to campaigns, protesting, and joining political organizations require time and money, as well as organizational and communication skills (Brady, Verba, and Schlozman 1995). Such resources are unevenly distributed across the population, with fewer resources concentrated among those living in poverty. Compounding such resource problems, many low-income individuals are removed from the networks that mobilize people for political action, such as door-to-door contacts by campaigns or appeals from community or church leaders (Rosenstone and Hansen 1993). Low-income Americans are also less likely than other Americans to report belief in their political efficacy, an important predictor of political engagement (Verba, Schlozman, and Brady 1995).

In addition to individual-level barriers, formal laws restrict the political participation of marginalized populations such as the poor. More than 15 states require a citizen to show photo identification before being allowed to vote (National Conference of State Legislatures [NCSL] 2015). In addition, nearly all states restrict the voting rights of incarcerated felons, while more than half also disenfranchise parolees, probationers, or all ex-felons (Manza and Uggen 2006). Such laws disproportionately impact individuals of low socioeconomic status, who are less likely than other individuals to possess a driver's license or state identification card (Barreto, Nuno, and Sanchez 2009) and more likely to come in contact with the criminal justice system (Western and Pettit 2010).

Individual and societal barriers have consequences for political activity through established political channels, including voting, contacting elected representatives, and contributing to political campaigns. In their analysis of national survey data from 2008, Schlozman, Verba, and Brady 2012) found that individuals in the lowest socioeconomic status (SES) quintile were less likely than other individuals to contact a government official, participate in campaigns, or work with fellow citizens to solve a community problem.[1] Moreover, the percentage of individuals reporting two or more political acts (of five) was 33 percent in the lowest SES quintile compared to 71 percent in the highest quintile. Such statistics clearly illustrate that less economically advantaged Americans have lower levels of political participation than their higher-income counterparts.

Low levels of participation among the poor have consequences for the extent to which the interests of the poor are represented in the national policymaking process. Because legislators are held accountable through the electoral system,

---

[1] The measure of socioeconomic status used in this study gives equal weight to the family income and educational attainment of the interview respondent.

members of Congress have few incentives to champion the concerns of groups with low participation rates (Arnold 1992; Mayhew 1974). Bartels (2008) shows that across a range of issues, legislators' votes are highly responsive to the preferences of affluent constituents, yet unresponsive to the preferences of low-income constituents. Such differences carry over into public policy choices. Gilens (2014) finds that the opinions of low-income Americans are rarely reflected in public policy, unlike those of high-income individuals. Furthermore, such representational inequalities persist across numerous issues and policy domains.

When established political channels are closed, politically marginalized groups may seek to influence policy through broad mobilizations and social movements that operate outside political institutions and processes. Throughout American history, low-income individuals have mobilized in an attempt to secure policy concessions from the government. For example, unemployed workers in the 1930s and welfare recipients in the 1960s mobilized to press for public relief (Piven and Cloward 1979). Yet the circumstances under which such movements arise are bounded by what social movement scholars refer to as the "structure of political opportunity." This term encompasses aspects of the political context, including the openness of political institutions, the health of the economy, the stability of electoral alignments, and the level of elite support and public support for groups such as the poor(Amenta and Caren 2007; McAdam 1982; Tarrow 1991; Tilly 1978).[2]

At times, characteristics of the political context create opportunities for large-scale mobilization. For instance, the presence of elite allies and public support can inspire and legitimate mobilization efforts, while electoral instability may lead political candidates and parties to reach out to marginalized groups pursuing policy change (Imig 2006). However, features of the political context can also be interpreted as constraining the emergence of movements for the poor. In the absence of elite allies, public support, and electoral instability, marginalized populations may find limited opportunities to effectively mobilize (see Amenta et al. 2010 and Giugni 1998 for a review). Indeed, as I argue in the final chapter, features of the political context likely constrained broader mobilization efforts in the case analyzed in this book.

Organizational Advocacy on Behalf of Low-Income Populations

Given low levels of political activity through established political channels as well as limited opportunities for large-scale mobilization, much of the routine

---

[2] Political opportunity structures are a central component of political process theory, which offers an explanation for the emergence of social movements. Political process theorists posit that features of the political context interact with mobilizing structures (formal and informal networks of mobilization) and collective frames (shared understandings that inspire collective action) to shape the likelihood of movement emergence.

representation of low-income Americans occurs through lobbying by organized interests (Hays 2001). Indeed, social policy scholars frequently identify organizational advocates for the poor as important actors in the policymaking process (Patterson 2000; Pekkanen, Smith, and Tsujinaka 2014; Winston 2002). Many types of groups lobby on behalf of those living in poverty, including social welfare organizations, citizen groups, nonprofit service providers, public interest law firms, research organizations, intergovernmental groups, and labor unions. Some of these groups resemble the business and professional interests that dominate Washington politics with respect to their mission and political activities. Yet others differ in that they are organized for reasons other than lobbying, encounter unique constraints on their political activity, and engage in different patterns of advocacy.

Social welfare organizations are among the most active in lobbying on behalf of the poor. Social welfare organizations are membership-based groups that seek selective benefits for individuals who are unable to represent their own interests, including the poor, children, non-naturalized immigrants, and institutionalized populations (Schlozman and Tierney 1986).[3] For example, the National Coalition for the Homeless is a social welfare organization that lobbies on behalf of the homeless and seeks to end the problem of homelessness for society as a whole. Such groups represent an extremely small percentage of all lobbying organizations, despite the fact that nearly 14 percent of Americans live below the poverty line (Proctor, Semega, and Kollar 2016). In 2001, social welfare organizations represented less than 1 percent of groups in the Washington lobbying community (Schlozman et al. 2012).

Most scholars view social welfare organizations as a type of citizen group, which is a membership group mobilized around an interest other than the vocation or profession of its members (Berry 1999; Imig 1996; Schlozman and Tierney 1986). Although citizen groups, such as the National Organization for Women, are not as prevalent as business and professional groups in Washington politics, they are active participants in the policymaking process and are often perceived as highly credible sources of information (Berry 1999). Not all citizen groups are concerned with issues involving poverty, yet groups representing civil rights, women's issues, and children's issues have at various times acted as allies to social welfare organizations in the policymaking process (Strolovitch 2007).

Nonprofit service providers such as the United Way are arguably the most appropriate representatives of the poor. Through close contact with those living in poverty, service providers have a strong sense of the needs of low-income Americans. Such organizations, however, face distinctive limits on their

---

[3] This definition combines Schlozman and Tierney's (1986) definition of advocacy group and social welfare organization (45–48). In this project, the term "social welfare organization" refers to an interest group representing a particular type of population, rather than a nonprofit organization with the IRS designation of 501(c)4 (which is also referred to as a "social welfare organization").

lobbying activities. Because charitable service providers offer services to needy populations, they are granted special federal tax exemptions that allow them to receive tax-deductible donations. In exchange, they are prohibited from legislative lobbying and contributing to political campaigns (Berry and Arons 2003).[4]

Yet research suggests that many providers "act like" interest groups in their interactions with government officials, especially at state and local levels (Berry and Arons 2003; Pekkanen, Smith, and Tsujinaka 2014). For example, such organizations participate in government commissions, provide testimony on public policy issues, help draft regulations, and provide public education. Political activity is particularly prominent among large service providers with greater resource capacity (De Vita, Mosher-Williams, and Stengel 2001; Mosley 2011, 2014; Salamon and Geller 2008; see Almog-Bar and Schmid 2014 for a review). Thus, despite formal restrictions on their lobbying activities, many charitable service providers are active in advocating on behalf of low-income populations.

In addition to citizen groups and nonprofit service providers, low-income populations also find representation through nonmembership organizations such as public interest law firms, research organizations, and intergovernmental groups. Public interest law firms, such as the National Housing Law Project, are organizations that pursue non-vocational interests but emphasize legal strategies for influencing policy outcomes, while research institutions, such as MDRC (formerly the Manpower Demonstration Research Corporation), seek to influence policy through the creation and dissemination of research (Schlozman and Tierney 1986). These institutional actors lack the resources that derive from a large and politically active membership base, but they may have significant financial resources in the form of federal funding, foundation grants, and donations (Imig 1996; Weaver 1989).

Intergovernmental organizations, or groups that represent subnational governments and government officials, have become increasingly active on the issue of poverty over the past 50 years (Cammisa 1995; Imig 1996). The lobbying activity of intergovernmental organizations on social policy issues has grown alongside an increase in the number of federal social welfare programs administered by state governments as well as the expansion of authority for such programs at the state and local levels (Cammisa 1995). Intergovernmental organizations such as the National Governors Association and the U.S. Conference of Mayors provide a vehicle through which state and

---

[4] Technically, nonprofit 501c3 organizations are prohibited from "substantial" lobbying of national and state legislators, but the IRS has never explicitly defined this term. These organizations have the option of becoming "H-electors" – a designation that essentially allows them to ignore the limits on legislative lobbying. Few 501c3 organizations become H-electors, in part because of the fact that many are unaware that this option exists (Berry and Arons 2003).

local officials can voice their views on social welfare programs and offer an important form of expertise to national policymakers.

Finally, low-income populations have at times found their interests represented by labor unions, which are organized for collective bargaining purposes; professional organizations, which represent the interests of individuals in a particular profession; and religious groups (Imig 1996; Nownes 2006; Schlozman and Tierney 1986). Yet because they are not mobilized around the issue of poverty, the extent to which these organizations will ally with antipoverty advocates on a particular issue is mediated by their own organizational needs and those of their membership base. Labor unions, professional organizations, and religious groups must first and foremost consider the interests of their members or organization. Only after those interests are addressed will they consider allying with advocates in related issue areas (Imig 1996).[5]

Like the individuals they represent, many of the organizations that advocate on behalf of people living in poverty encounter considerable obstacles to political influence. Relative to business and professional organizations, citizen groups mobilized around social policy issues have fewer members and smaller budgets, spend less on lobbying, and engage in fewer political activities (Schlozman et al. 2012; Strolovitch 2007). Such groups are often funded by foundation and government grants, making them vulnerable to shifting preferences among private donors and political actors (Imig 1996).

Organizations that provide services to the poor are organized around service provision rather than advocacy and, as discussed earlier, are prohibited from contributing money to political campaigns and engaging in substantial legislative lobbying (Berry and Arons 2003). In addition, research organizations that study social policy and intergovernmental actors that administer welfare programs lack an active membership base and thus have few electoral resources to exchange for favorable political attention (Hays 2001; Salisbury 1984).

The fact that organizational advocates for the poor encounter barriers to political influence has implications for the lobbying tactics that such groups employ. Specifically, such barriers create incentives for advocates to pursue strategies of influence that do not rely on the resources of any individual organization, such as collaborative lobbying strategies. Existing research on social policy advocacy shows that rather than lobby exclusively on their own, organizations that represent the interests of low-income populations frequently collaborate in their efforts to influence policy (Sandfort 2014; Strolovitch 2007).

---

[5] For example, during the Regan administration, labor unions – traditional allies of the poor – were unable to assist advocacy groups in lobbying against government cuts to poverty-related programs because organizational resources were devoted to defending the immediate concerns of labor unions rather than the concerns of low-income populations (Imig 1996).

In the following section, I situate my study within a burgeoning literature on collaborative lobbying in Congress. The section highlights the prevalence of collaborative lobbying among advocates for the poor, but it also recognizes the ubiquity of coalitions beyond the social policy domain. As the section makes clear, collaborative lobbying is not only common for groups that represent the poor but has also emerged as a dominant tactic of influence across policy domains.

INTEREST GROUP COALITIONS IN WASHINGTON

Interest group collaboration is widespread in Washington. Nearly all groups engage in some type of informal networking, and participation in formal coalitions is common (Baumgartner et al. 2009; Hojnacki 1997; Hula 1999; Schlozman and Tierney 1986). Collaboration serves many purposes, such as allowing groups to monitor policy developments, providing opportunities for networking and social engagements, and helping organizations work together on issues of shared concern (Hula 1999; Loomis 1986; Schlozman and Tierney 1986). This book focuses exclusively on coalitions that unite a set of organizations working together in pursuit of shared policy goals. Following Hula (1999), I refer to these coalitions as *policy coalitions*.

Across policy domains, policy coalitions take a variety of forms. Some have a formal structure and are organized around long-standing issues. For example, the American Tort Reform Association, formed in 1986, is a coalition of nonprofit organizations, corporations, and trade and professional associations working toward reform of the civil justice system (American Tort Reform Association 2013). Some coalitions are more informal, organized for a short period of time around a discrete policy issue. Better Health Care Together, for example, is an ad hoc coalition that united business leaders in 2007 with the goal of elevating health care reform onto the political agenda in 2008 (Halperin 2007). Still other coalitions are so informal that the partnership itself remains unnamed. For example, on October 11, 2013, the U.S. Chamber of Commerce, the AFL-CIO, and the United Way cosigned a letter to President Barack Obama and members of Congress, urging an end to the federal shutdown.[6]

The Rise of Collaborative Lobbying in Washington

Across issue areas, policy coalitions have become an increasingly common strategy for influencing the policy choices of legislators. Writing in 1986, Schlozman and Tierney found that 90 percent of Washington interest groups

---

[6] Letter to President Obama and Members of Congress, U.S. Chamber of Commerce, AFL-CIO, and the United Way, October 11, 2013. Accessed December 10, 2013, www.unitedway.org/page/-/Files/Chamber%20AFL%20UW%20letter%20on%20shutdown%20%2010%2011%202013.pdf.

reported entering into coalitions as a strategy for exercising political influence, with 68 percent reporting increasing use of collaborative strategies over the previous decade (Schlozman and Tierney 1986: 148–55). More recently, Baumgartner and colleagues (2009) report that on average, Washington interest groups use coalition building as a tactic of advocacy more frequently than other commonly used tactics, such as testifying at congressional hearings, working with agency or White House officials, or holding press conferences or issuing press releases.[7]

While policy coalitions are common for all types of groups, research focusing on political advocacy for marginalized populations highlights the prominence of coalitions as a tool for gaining political influence in the arena of social policy (Bass, Abramson, and Dewey 2014; Delgado 1986; Mosley 2014; Piven and Cloward 1979; Sandfort 2014; Staggenborg 1986; Strolovitch 2007; Warren and Cohen 2000). Strolovitch (2007: 185), for instance, finds that more than 96 percent of Washington-based interest groups mobilized around issues related to poverty and economic justice report using coalitions as a strategy of political influence. Collaboration is also pronounced among groups organized for purposes other than advocacy. De Vita, Nikolova, and Roeger (2014) find that among nonprofit organizations active in Washington, D.C., 48 percent engaged in both independent and collaborative advocacy, while 44 percent conducted all advocacy efforts in coalitions.

Scholars attribute the increase in collaboration across issue areas to growth in the lobbying community, which refers to the community of organized interests attempting to influence elected officials (Hula 1999; Loomis 1986; Salisbury 1990). Between 1981 and 2006, the number of organized interests in Washington grew by 106 percent (Schlozman, Verba, and Brady 2012). Growth in the number of interest groups increases the opportunities for collaboration by expanding the pool of potential allies, but it also has the effect of giving each group less power in the political system (Hula 1999; Loomis 1986; Salisbury 1990). In an increasingly crowded lobbying community, policy coalitions provide a way for organizations with similar policy goals to exhibit strength and demonstrate consensus in a political system in which legislators can effectively choose which interests to listen to and which to ignore.

Institutional changes in Congress have also encouraged the use of collaborative strategies (Hojnacki 1997; Hula 1999). The level and scope of policy activity in Congress have increased since the 1960s. The expanding reach of the federal government has been accompanied by an expansion in the subcommittee system, in terms of both the absolute number of subcommittees

---

[7] Approximately 39 percent of organizations reported conducting "outreach or coalition building" in Baumgartner and colleagues' (2009) analysis. The lower reported use of this tactic relative to the reported incidence in Schlozman and Tierney's study likely reflects the fact that Baumgartner and colleagues asked respondents to report on tactics used on a single issue, rather than tactics used by the organization in general.

and the jurisdiction of such committees (Deering and Smith 1997). More policy decisions are being made, and more members of Congress are making decisions, on any given issue. This decentralization of authority creates incentives for all types of interest groups to work together to reach relevant legislators. As Schlozman and Tierney (1986: 306) note: "the organization and structure of Congress no longer permit even the most resourceful of organized interests to press a policy issue singlehandedly." In today's political environment, even the wealthiest groups typically lack the resources to independently determine the fate of congressional legislation.

Existing Research on Interest Group Coalitions

Interest group scholars have long recognized the ubiquity of collaborative lobbying strategies. A rich literature generates valuable insights regarding the increasing use of collaborative strategies (Baumgartner et al. 2009; Loomis 1986; Salisbury 1990; Schlozman and Tierney 1986), the behavior of interest groups within coalitions (Hojnacki 1998; Hula 1999), and the conditions of coalition formation (Hojnacki 1997; Holyoke 2011; Levi and Murphy 2006; Mahoney 2007; Mahoney and Baumgartner 2004).

Research investigating whether and how coalitions influence policy decisions in Congress, however, is only beginning to emerge. The studies that do exist draw attention to the characteristics and resources of formal and informal partnerships, identifying how these characteristics and resources matter for gaining political influence. Nelson and Yackee (2012), for instance, demonstrate that consensus within coalitions is associated with increased policy influence in federal rulemaking, while Baumgartner and colleagues (2009) show that aggregate resource disparities between opposing "sides" of policy debates help explain which side achieves policy success in the short term.

While scholars have begun to investigate the mechanisms and circumstances of coalition influence, the vast majority of research on interest group influence focuses attention on interest groups as independent actors in the policymaking process. For example, numerous studies trace the activities of individual groups as they lobby for their preferred policy goals or examine the effect of groups' campaign contributions or lobbying tactics on legislative votes (see Hojnacki et al. 2012; Smith 1995 for a review). While the extensive body of work in this tradition forms the foundation for much of what scholars know about interest group influence, such an approach is necessarily limited in its ability to assess how *sets of groups* achieve influence in the policy process.

In part, the predominance of research on individual groups reflects a conception of groups as acting autonomously in their efforts to influence legislators. In this view, competition for legislators' attention creates incentives for organized interests to develop unique identities and areas of competence. Cultivating a distinct purpose and area of expertise enables groups to establish credibility and gain access to legislators, as well as build and solidify a membership base. Such incentives lead groups to pursue strategies that enhance their distinctiveness and autonomy (Berry 1977; Browne 1990; Wilson 1973; see Hojnacki 1997 for a review). The emphasis on individual groups in research also reflects practical considerations. As Mahoney and Baumgartner (2015: 205) note: "the tendency to study single lobbyists in isolation rather than as part of a collective is due to the difficulty in gathering data on those collectives." Examining the impact of coalitions requires gathering data on the partnerships themselves, many of which are informal in nature and thus difficult to observe empirically.

The sheer prevalence of collaborative strategies, however, suggests that scholars must continue to prioritize research that considers how groups achieve influence together, particularly in the policymaking process. Indeed, recent research suggests that looking beyond the individual group as the unit of analysis can yield powerful insights regarding the determinants of political activity, influence, and outcomes. Mahoney and Baumgartner (2015), for instance, show that the aggregate resources of a set of groups aligned behind a particular policy recommendation is a more powerful predictor of government activity than the resources of any individual group.

This book is situated within the growing body of research that draws attention to the way in which sets of organizations gain influence in the policy process (see Baumgartner et al. 2009; Heaney and Lorenz 2013; Mahoney and Baumgartner 2015; Nelson and Yackee 2012). It builds from theories of interest group influence that view interest group information as a critical resource in the lobbying process (Ainsworth 1993; Austin-Smith and Banks 2002; Esterling 2004; Hall and Deardorff 2006; Kollman 1998). Yet rather than focus attention on the informational resources of individual groups, I focus theoretical and empirical attention on resources and activities of informal and formal coalitions. In the next section, I provide an overview of the theory that I develop to explain how and when interest group coalitions gain influence in Congress. I refer to this theory as the *theory of diverse coalitions*.

A THEORY OF DIVERSE COALITIONS

My theory begins with the observation that interest groups have two goals when they join policy coalitions: to pool resources and signal political strength. This observation, drawn from existing research, represents an important starting point by offering a framework for understanding *why* groups collaborate. Yet it leaves many questions unanswered. If coalitions help interest groups pool resources for joint political activity, which resources are the most important? Why do organizations with more resources, and presumably less need to collaborate, join policy coalitions as frequently as those with fewer resources? With respect to signaling strength to policymakers, do coalitions signal strength across constituent groups, as much of the literature assumes? If so, how is it possible to understand coalitions that form between groups that have no members, such as corporations or nonprofit organizations? And what makes a signal of political strength credible to a legislator?

The theory of diverse coalitions answers such questions by drawing attention to the characteristics of coalition partners. The theory posits that whether the goal of a coalition is to combine resources or signal political strength, it is the *diversity* of a coalition's organizational members that enhances its effectiveness. By diversity, I mean differences in the interest or interests that a group represents.

When groups that represent different types of interests collaborate, I argue, they are able to draw on diverse information from a wide variety of sources and engage in varied lobbying tactics. This in turn enhances the ability of groups to provide valuable information to legislators wary of the consequences of their policy choices. In addition, by providing heterogeneous cues from diverse groups and evidence of costly lobbying efforts, diversity enhances the credibility of the information that groups provide, which reduces legislators' uncertainty about the consequences of policy choices. Yet because collaboration is costly, groups are unlikely to collaborate with diverse partners in all issue contexts. The theory predicts that diverse coalitions are likely to form on issues characterized by uncertainty, salience, and strong opponents.

The theory is grounded in a rich body of theoretical work that emphasizes the informational properties of lobbying and political influence. Such theories draw attention to the role of interest groups in providing information that addresses legislators' uncertainty over the electoral and policy consequences of their actions. For instance, organizations provide information about constituents' policy preferences, technical expertise about policy, and political information about the alignment of support and opposition for a policy across interested actors (Arnold 1990; Esterling 2004; Krehbiel 1992; Wright (2003 [1995]). When such information helps legislators assess the consequences of their policy choices, existing research concludes that interest groups are able to gain influence in the policy process.

EMPIRICAL ANALYSIS OF THE 1996 FEDERAL WELFARE REFORM

Examining the support for the theory of diverse coalitions requires an empirical approach that positions a coalition, rather than an individual group, as the empirical object of inquiry. Given the difficulty of collecting and analyzing data on coalitions for any single issue, let alone multiple issues, my research design focuses on an in-depth analysis of collaborative activity by organized interests in the two years preceding the passage of the federal welfare reform of 1996. This approach has multiple advantages, which are described in greater detail in the third chapter. Analyzing a single case allows me to observe coalitions that operate as distinct organizational entities as well as coalitions that remain informal in nature. Such an approach also allows me to focus on the mechanisms linking diverse coalitions and political influence as well as refine predictions about the types of diversity likely to generate policy influence.

The Personal Responsibility and Work Opportunity Reconciliation Act of 1996 (PRWORA), or welfare reform, represents an ideal case to analyze. Introduced by President Bill Clinton in his 1992 campaign and reenergized by congressional Republicans in early 1995, legislative proposals to reform the welfare state were broad in scope and represented a significant departure from the status quo. A large number of antipoverty advocates considered the proposals to be salient to their interests, as did a range of other actors who found their interests either challenged or supported by welfare reform proposals. The fact that welfare reform activated a large and diverse set of interests provides an opportunity to examine the numerous instances of collaboration that emerged between different groups with similar policy goals. In addition, the fact that welfare reform involves numerous issues allows me to analyze how diverse coalition formation varies alongside features of the issue context.

The study utilizes an innovative approach in which I collect data on the informal and formal coalitions that were active in the two years preceding the passage of PRWORA. My analysis of congressional hearings testimony, newspaper articles and other media reports, archival records from select organizations and the Clinton administration, and a wide range of secondary sources from academics and policy scholars finds strong support for the theory of diverse coalitions.

First, the analysis demonstrates that both informal and formal coalitions drew together diverse actors. Groups with active membership bases worked with think tanks, groups representing the recipients of government programs collaborated with the administrators of those programs, health groups allied with education groups, and a subset of conservative interests allied with liberal groups. Second, the data show that such diversity allowed coalition members to unite the informational resources of different organizations and engage in a wider range of advocacy activities than would have been possible alone.

Third, the analysis reveals that diverse coalitions routinely drew attention to the heterogeneity of their partnership in their statements to members of Congress and the media, suggesting that the groups viewed their differences as a salient characteristic of their collaborative effort. Moreover, evidence suggests that such groups incurred costs to work with diverse partners. The fact that coalition members highlighted diverse voices within their coalitions and experienced costs to work together lends support to the theory's premise that diversity enhances the credibility of information by providing heterogeneous signals and evidence of costly lobbying efforts and, in doing so, reduces legislators' uncertainty about the consequences of policy changes.

Finally, an analysis of four distinct issues within welfare reform reveals that groups collaborated selectively across issues, with diverse coalitions most likely to form on issues that were salient in scope and uncertain in their implications. In addition, although coalitions emerged on both sides of the welfare policy debate, they were more prominent among groups facing strong opponents – specifically, groups representing the interests of the poor. This evidence provides support for the argument that collaborative decisions are strongly shaped by features of the issue context. Namely, diverse coalitions are more likely to emerge when issues are salient, uncertain in their implications, and on which opponents are perceived as strong.

CONTRIBUTION

Together, the theoretical and empirical analyses presented in this book contribute to two rich bodies of scholarship. First, the book contributes to research on the political influence of marginalized populations such as the poor. Within the political science literature, little is known about how groups representing disadvantaged populations attempt to gain influence in legislative settings, in part because these groups are underrepresented in interest group populations. The rich body of interdisciplinary research that focuses on lobbying on behalf of the poor yields important insights regarding the nature and circumstances of advocacy but lacks a unifying theory to explain how advocates for low-income populations influence legislators given their resource limitations. By developing a theory that focuses on informational resources and collaboration, this book provides a theoretical framework for understanding how interest groups gain influence on behalf of marginalized populations and sheds light on lobbying in an understudied policy domain.

Second, by focusing attention on interest group coalitions, this book contributes to a growing body of research on the collaborative activity of interest groups in Washington. Although existing scholarship recognizes the growing presence of coalitions, a limited number of theories explain how or when coalitions gain influence in the policy process. With a few notable exceptions, most research on interest group influence views influence as deriving from an individual group acting autonomously rather than a set of groups acting collaboratively. This book develops a theory that identifies both the mechanisms and the conditions of coalitional influence. Moreover, the empirical analysis provides support for the theory and helps refine its central predictions. Although the empirical analysis is limited to the social policy domain, there are reasons to suspect broader applicability of the theory. The ubiquity of collaborative activity suggests that future research that considers both the mechanisms and conditions of coalitional influence may help scholars answer long-standing questions regarding interest group influence in policy.

PLAN OF THE BOOK

The remaining chapters of the book develop and analyze the empirical support for the theory of diverse coalitions. In the second chapter, I develop the theory itself, which is situated within the literature on informational lobbying and uncertainty in Congress. In this chapter, I argue that diversity within coalitions matters because it allows organized interests to pool disparate resources, while providing a credible signal to legislators of the consequences of their policy choices. The chapter describes a set of empirical predictions regarding the presence of coalitions, the nature of group partnerships, the activities of informal and formal coalitions, and the conditions of collaborative activity.

The third chapter provides an overview of my empirical approach, which centers on an analysis of interest group activity in the two years preceding the passage of one prominent social policy. This chapter discusses the advantages of pursuing a case study design, the value of the welfare reform case in particular, and the generalizability of the empirical findings. I also describe my data collection and analysis strategy, which differs from standard approaches by focusing empirical attention on formal and informal coalitions rather than individual groups.

In the fourth chapter, I present background on the welfare program to provide context for understanding the magnitude of the changes that were proposed at the start of the 104th Congress (1995–1996). This chapter also highlights the emergence of national organized interests as the welfare program evolved. The fifth chapter introduces the types of organizations that attempted to influence welfare policy choices in 1995 and 1996. Using House and Senate hearings data, this chapter describes the types of organizations active in lobbying on welfare reform in the 104th Congress and identifies the dimensions along which they differed. This chapter also presents an analysis of participation by formal coalitions relative to participation by organizations acting independently.

The sixth and seventh chapters analyze the empirical support for the premises that diverse coalitions allow groups to pool different types of resources while enhancing the credibility of a political signal. In the sixth chapter, I show that organizations on all sides of the welfare reform debate engaged in diverse collaboration as a strategy for pooling resources. Organizations worked with partners that possessed different *types* of resources – for instance, membership-based "traditional values" groups worked with a conservative think tank with technical expertise. Organizations also worked with partners that possessed different forms of the same type of resource – for example, a research organization with expertise on child support programs worked with a research organization with expertise on the cash welfare program. Consistent with theoretical expectations, this diversity in resources allowed groups to leverage their unique informational resources to access different legislators and engage in varying lobbying tactics.

The seventh chapter views diverse coalitions through the lens of political signaling. In this chapter, I show that coalitions that united groups with diverse policy domains and ideologies actively communicated the diversity of their partnerships to legislators. Moreover, in some instances, the diversity of a coalition was contested by organizations opposing the coalition, suggesting that groups prioritized diversity as an important characteristic of coalitions. This chapter also examines the extent to which organizations incurred a cost to participate and argues that in providing evidence of policy and resource costs, the data provide support for the premise that diversity communicates costly lobbying activities.

In the eighth chapter, I examine diverse collaborative activity across four issues within the larger welfare reform legislation: program structure, welfare to work, child disability, and child exclusion issues. The issues were characterized by varying degrees of uncertainty over the consequences of legislative action, salience to organized interests, and strength of opposing policy sides. I find that coalitions did not emerge for all issues, even though the issues involved a similar set of groups. Rather, diverse coalitions were active on issues that were uncertain in their implications, salient to organized interests, and on which opponents were perceived as strong.

In the final chapter, I conclude by arguing that interest groups can and do attempt to influence legislators by leveraging the power of diverse coalitions. The book demonstrates that during welfare reform, diverse partnerships between groups with similar policy goals utilized the different capabilities and specialties of the member organizations. Collaboration was not simply about increasing the size of support or opposition to a policy but was rather about bringing different types of resources to bear on the policy debate. Diverse collaboration thus represented a particularly important lobbying activity for advocates for low-income populations as they attempted to prevent large-scale changes to the American safety net. The final chapter argues that the ubiquity of this strategy, and its likely extensions beyond the social policy realm, suggests that citizens, scholars, advocates, and policymakers must begin to think more seriously about the extent and consequences of diverse collaboration in the policymaking process.

2

A Theory of Diverse Coalitions

INTRODUCTION

Within and beyond the social policy domain, interest groups increasingly turn to policy coalitions as a strategy for influencing legislative policy choices. Whether long-standing or formed only for a brief period of time, policy coalitions represent a strategic response to the expansion and decentralization of policymaking in Congress, as well as the growth of the Washington lobbying community. Yet while the ubiquity of collaborative lobbying is widely recognized within political science scholarship, theories that specify *how* coalitions gain policy influence are only beginning to emerge. In this chapter, I build on existing theories of informational lobbying and interest group influence to develop a theory that identifies both the mechanisms of coalitional influence and the conditions under which certain types of policy coalitions will form. I refer to this as the *theory of diverse coalitions.*

The central insight of the theory is that it is the diversity of coalition partners that leads to legislative influence. By diversity, I mean groups that represent different types of interests – public and private, for example, or liberal and conservative. I argue that coalitions that unite diverse actors expand informational lobbying capabilities, while providing credible information to legislators about the consequences of their policy choices. In offering heterogeneous and credible information to a large number of legislators, diverse coalitions address legislative uncertainty and in doing so, help groups gain influence in the policymaking process. Yet diverse coalitions are unlikely to emerge in all issue contexts. My theory predicts that issues that are salient to a wide range of actors and characterized by uncertain policy outcomes, and issues that involve strong policy opponents are more likely than other issues to witness collaborative lobbying by diverse actors.

Although the theory aims to address a puzzle relating to advocacy and influence on behalf of the poor, the theoretical mechanisms identified by the theory are not unique to the social policy domain. Indeed, groups across policy domains encounter similar incentives and opportunities to work collaboratively with diverse partners. As there are reasons to expect that the theory has broader applicability, I pursue a general approach to theory building in this chapter. While select examples are drawn from the social policy domain, the chapter also incorporates examples from other policy domains. It is my hope that developing a general theory of coalitional influence will allow scholars to apply and test the theory's predictions in a wide range of policy areas.

In the first section of the chapter, I situate the theory of diverse coalitions within the political science literature on informational lobbying and legislative influence. The second and third sections identify the mechanisms of diverse coalition influence in Congress; the fourth section identifies the conditions of diverse coalition formation. In the final section, I review the key insights of the theory of diverse coalitions.

INFORMATIONAL THEORIES OF INTEREST GROUP INFLUENCE IN CONGRESS

Within political science, a rich body of literature focuses on the informational properties of interest group lobbying (Ainsworth 1993; Austin-Smith and Banks 2002; Austin-Smith and Wright 1991, 1994; Esterling 2004; Goldstein 1999; Kollman 1998; Lohmann 1993; Wright 2003 [1995]). Research in this tradition conceives of interest group lobbying as an attempt to persuade legislators to adopt group-friendly positions through the provision of information, rather than campaign contributions.[1] In this view, legislators face considerable uncertainty when making policy decisions (Arnold 1990; Wright 2003 [1995]). Interest groups use their knowledge of constituents, policy, and politics to address legislators' uncertainty about the consequences of policy action and thus gain influence in the policymaking process.

Legislators encounter three types of uncertainty in the policymaking process, which correspond to three categories of interest group information. First, members of Congress face uncertainty over their future electoral prospects (Arnold 1990; Fenno 1978; Mayhew 1974; Kingdon 1989; Wright 2003 [1995]). As reelection seekers, legislators must assess the consequences of their policy actions on their electoral goals. Doing so requires determining what their constituents' policy preferences are and the likelihood that these

---

[1] Political scientists have classified interest group influence in Congress as a process of exchange, persuasion, and subsidy. Some scholars argue that interest groups trade campaign contributions for votes, and that lobbying is essentially an exchange relationship (e.g., Lowi 1969; Synder 1992). Others understand lobbying as form of persuasion, emphasizing the strategic transmission of information from interest group to legislator (e.g., Ainsworth 1993; Austen-Smith and Wright 1991, 1994; Kollman 1998) or represent the relationship between lobbying and legislator as one in which a group subsidizes the resources of legislators with similar policy goals (e.g., Hall and Deardorff 2006).

preferences will influence vote choice (Arnold 1990; Kollman 1998). Establishing the direction and salience of constituents' policy preferences is a complicated endeavor, however. Although individual policy preferences are relatively stable (Page and Shapiro 2010), the political relevance of constituents' preferences can change rapidly in response to a crisis or disaster, media coverage, or selective framing of an issue (Kollman 1998). Legislators therefore seek out electoral information that provides insight into constituents' policy preferences and the relevance of these preferences for voting behavior.

The technicalities of policy are a second source of uncertainty in Congress. To legislate effectively, members require substantive information about the problem that necessitates government involvement, the goals or outcomes that a policy intends to achieve, and the likelihood that policy alternatives will produce those outcomes (Esterling 2004; Hall and Deardorff 2006). As Esterling argues: "policies that entail too much uncertainty risk failure and those that are ambiguous may result in unintended consequences" (Esterling 2004: 8–9). Policy information, which consists of technical information about policy problems and solutions, reduces uncertainty about how a policy will work, as well as the likely consequences of policy choice. Policy information also provides support for alternative definitions of a problem, draws attention to potential unintended consequences of government intervention, and offers insights into the hypothesized causal relationship between a policy and its intended outcome (Esterling 2004; Rich 2004).

A third and final source of uncertainty pertains to how an issue will travel through the legislative process (Wright 2003 [1995]). Will a bill move smoothly through both chambers of Congress? Will it become entangled in controversy in committee or floor debates? For some issues, legislators have limited incentives to invest scarce time and resources in pushing forth a policy that has little chance of passage (Kingdon 1989). For other issues, legislators may be hesitant to move an issue forward that has the potential to divide partisan or organized interests. Political information about the preferences and anticipated behavior of relevant actors such as interest groups, legislators, political parties, and members of the administration helps legislators assess how an issue will move through the legislative process as well as the likelihood of policy passage.[2]

For members of Congress, interest groups represent an important source of information about constituents, policies, and politics.[3] As representatives of

---

[2] The extent to which legislators value each type of information varies across issues. On some issues, electoral information dominates and technical information about the likely policy impacts is irrelevant; the intended policy outcome may be so popular or unpopular that legislators feel compelled to vote for or against it. In contrast, research suggests that substantive information is important on issues that are technical and complex and have the capacity to generate gains for society as a whole (Esterling 2004).

[3] Interest groups are only one source of information for legislators, who also receive information from other members of Congress, political parties, congressional staff, and the media. Interest

groups of constituents, organized interests possess "channels of communication" with constituents (Hansen 1991) and are able to assess the direction and electoral salience of their members' policy preferences with relative ease and efficiency (Goldstein 1999; Kollman 1998). Many interest groups invest substantial resources in developing policy expertise. These groups can help legislators by synthesizing the state of current research, offering policy analysis and recommendations and drafting legislation (Esterling 2004; Hall and Deardorff 2006). As specialists in particular policy domains, interest groups also have a strong sense of the preferences and likely actions of other actors operating within their issue area, or they can gather this information at relatively low cost (Kingdon 1989; Schlozman and Tierney 1986). Because interest groups possess specialized knowledge of constituents, policies, and politics, legislators routinely rely on them to address uncertainty about the consequences of policy choices.

Informational theories of interest group influence posit that groups gain influence through the skilled use of their informational resources. By calling on members to call or send letters to members of Congress, for example, an interest group communicates electoral information about voter support for policy change. In presenting technical analysis in hearings testimony, an organization provides evidence pertaining to the substantive impact of policy change. By mobilizing its allies to participate in a collaborative lobbying effort, an interest group provides political information regarding the policy preferences of a set of organized interests. When such information reduces legislators' uncertainty about the consequences of legislative policy decisions, informational theories hypothesize that interest groups are able to gain influence in the legislative policy process.

The theory of diverse coalitions builds on the informational lobbying literature by positing that policy coalitions help groups gain influence because they enhance the informational lobbying capabilities of a set of organized interests. Yet viewing coalitional lobbying through an informational lens clarifies that it is the *diversity* of coalitional partners that enhances informational lobbying and reduces legislative uncertainty, thereby leading to influence in the policymaking process.

The theory proposes two sets of mechanisms through which diversity works to reduce uncertainty, which are elaborated in the following two sections. The first mechanism holds that diversity within policy coalitions allows groups to pool different types of information and utilize varied tactics for communicating this information. I refer to this mechanism as the *resource mobilization mechanism*. The second set of mechanisms holds that diversity

---

groups compete with these other actors for the attention of legislators. Hansen (1991) argues that legislators will grant access to interest groups when interest groups provide information more effectively and efficiently than other actors, and when legislators expect particular groups, issues, and circumstances to recur.

enhances the *credibility* of information by communicating heterogeneous support for a policy position and providing evidence of costly lobbying efforts. I refer to these mechanisms as the *political signaling mechanisms*. Together, the resource mobilization and political signaling mechanisms indicate that diversity increases the scope of informational lobbying and enhances the credibility of interest group information, thereby helping groups reduce legislative uncertainty and gain influence over policy decisions.

The circumstances of diverse collaboration are, however, context dependent and diverse policy coalitions are unlikely to emerge on all issues. The theory therefore identifies a set of predictions regarding the conditions of diverse coalition formation. In the final section of the chapter, I utilize the logic of informational signaling to identify the issue-level predictors of collaboration. The final section highlights salience, uncertainty, and opposition strength as necessary conditions for the formation of diverse coalitions.

DIVERSE COALITIONS AND RESOURCE MOBILIZATION

The first part of the theory builds from the observation that policy coalitions allow groups to pool the resources necessary for a lobbying effort. A set of organizations working collaboratively can cover more ground – delivering more lobbyists and devoting more hours to lobbying – relative to an organization lobbying alone. As Hula (1999: 27) notes: "A hallmark of coalition strategies is that membership enables the workload to be spread out." In a legislative environment that necessitates broad lobbying efforts, coalitions allow groups to pool the resources necessary for reaching the many legislators who share authority in any given policy area (Hula 1999).

Yet while all policy coalitions permit resource sharing, the theory posits that it is only diverse coalitions that will be able to translate these resources into legislative influence. Diverse partners draw heterogeneous resources to a lobbying effort, which in turn allows groups to incorporate multiple types of information into their lobbying efforts and to utilize a range of tactics when communicating this information. A diverse policy coalition is consequently better able to address the informational needs of multiple legislators with authority in a given policy area.

Informational and Tactical Diversity

To understand how diversity expands access to information and lobbying tactics, consider the many types of resources that interest groups use in their lobbying efforts. Groups possess resources related to their organizational structure (membership or nonmembership), personnel (leaders, experts, and staff), finances, and position within a network of similar actors. Each of these resources relates to a particular type (or types) of information as well as tactic (or tactics) for communicating information.

In terms of organizational structure, a membership-based group such as the Sierra Club or professional association such as the American Medical Association is composed of individuals or organizations that can contribute dues, staff support, and direct political activity toward the group's political goals. Membership groups have information about members' policy preferences and can communicate this information through outside lobbying tactics, which aim to influence a legislator indirectly through the mobilization of constituents (Goldstein 1999; Kollman 1998). For example, a membership group such as the AARP can mobilize its members to call or send emails to members of Congress, hold press conferences, or demonstrate in support of a particular policy position. In contrast, an institutional (or nonmembership) group such as a corporation or research organization lacks the resources – and hence the information –that derive from individual or organizational members.

Leaders, experts, and staff also serve as resources for an organization. Such actors possess particular types of information and are able to engage in specific types of lobbying tactics. Well-known and respected leaders have both policy expertise and political knowledge stemming from long-standing involvement on an issue. Perhaps for this reason, leaders are cited as the most important organizational resource for approximately 20 percent of groups in Schlozman and Tierney's study of interest groups in Washington (1986). A strong and well-known leader is likely to be adept at using inside lobbying tactics, or tactics in which a group communicates with a legislator directly, such as testifying at congressional hearings or working with congressional staff to draft legislation.

With respect to experts and staff, groups may employ individuals with specialized policy expertise or knowledge of legislative processes. Some organizations invest substantial resources in hiring policy experts and developing technical expertise, stating that such expertise helps them gain political access and influence (Esterling 2004; Rich 2004; Schlozman and Tierney 1986). Policy experts communicate their knowledge in particular ways – by testifying at congressional hearings or drafting legislation and issuing reports that help legislators evaluate proposals or existing programs (Hall and Deardorff 2006; Rich 2004). Hiring former government employees as lobbyists is also common: LaPira and Thomas (2014) estimate that approximately 52 percent of active lobbyists have some prior federal government experience. Former government employees possess political knowledge as well as contacts within government, which may enhance access to a particular set of legislators (Baumgartner et al. 2009; Hula 1999).

A group's position within a larger community of organizations, or network, also serves as a resource and has implications for the information that the group can offer legislators. Relative to a group that operates on its own, a group that occupies a central position in a policy network is likely to have greater knowledge of the policy preferences of other groups and thus can better assess the strength of support for or opposition to a particular policy. Such information is valuable to legislators wary of expending scarce resources or political capital on an issue that may become entangled in controversy or surprising forms of opposition in the legislative process (Kingdon 1989; Schlozman and Tierney 1986). A group that is centrally located within a network may also be better able to mobilize other organizations to lobby on a particular issue. Perhaps for this reason, Heaney (2006) finds that groups that connect other groups, or act as "brokers," are more likely to gain influence in legislative settings.

Financial resources, which have perhaps garnered the most attention within the interest group literature, are not necessarily associated with a particular type of information or lobbying tactic, but they do enable interest groups to engage in a wider and more varied array of political activities. With ample financial resources, a group can poll constituents, hire policy experts, conduct research, and hire lobbyists to monitor political developments, thereby increasing the electoral, policy, and political information that the group has to offer. Large budgets also allow groups to utilize multiple lobbying tools, such as talking with legislators directly, running issue advertisements, drafting legislation, submitting amicus briefs, and making campaign contributions (Schlozman, Verba, and Brady 2012; see Smith 1995 for a review).

Organizational resources related to structure, personnel, network position, and to a lesser extent finances thus have implications for the type of information that a group possesses and the types of lobbying activities in which it can engage. Moreover, organizations typically specialize in particular types of resources and information – a single group rarely possesses all the information relevant to policymaking on a particular issue (Wright 2005 [1995]). For instance, a group might focus on information about constituents or technical policy analysis, but not both.

I theorize that when organizations that are diverse work together, they are able to draw a varied set of resources to the collaborative lobbying effort and utilize a broad array of lobbying tactics. Because individual groups specialize in particular types of information, a diverse coalition is better able to address the varied informational needs of a greater number of legislators, relative to a group lobbying alone.

Diverse sources of information and varied lobbying tactics are important in legislative settings for several reasons. Because policy authority is distributed across chambers, committees, and subcommittees, many legislators are responsible for making decisions in any given policy area. An interest group seeking to shape the content or fate of legislation must lobby legislators from both chambers, monitor developments within different committees and subcommittees, and employ an array of tactics to influence legislators accountable to different constituent and partisan interests. Even the wealthiest groups lack the ability to undertake such a lobbying effort on their own, creating strong incentives for groups to work collaboratively with similarly minded groups whose resources complement, but do not mirror, their own

(Baumgartner et al. 2009; Hula 1999; Loomis 1986; Schlozman and Tierney 1986).

The critical point – and one not theorized in existing scholarship – is that diversity within coalitions matters because it gives a set of organizations access to different types of information and enables varied tactics for communicating information. This informational and tactical diversity in turn allows a coalition to reach the large number of legislators who share authority in a given policy area. By addressing the informational needs of multiple legislators, diversity helps organizations gain influence in the policymaking process. Thus the first posited mechanism of influence, which I refer to as the *resource mobilization mechanism*, identifies informational and tactical heterogeneity as the mechanism through which diversity of coalition partners leads to influence in legislative settings.

An Example: Informational Lobbying and Tax Credits for Low-Income Workers

To provide an example from the social policy domain, imagine that a congressional committee is considering whether to expand a federal program that provides tax credits to low-income workers. An extensive lobbying campaign by a relatively well-financed association of state governmental actors may fail to persuade a committee member from a wealthy district who is concerned with the reaction of her higher-income constituents to the proposed expansion. Even if a national membership-based organization mobilizes its members to communicate that higher-income voters support such an expansion, a different committee member from a relatively less-advantaged district may want information about the likely reaction of lower-income constituents who are the intended recipients of the expansion. Still another committee member concerned with the effect of the expansion on businesses employing low-income workers may be unwilling to enact the policy in the absence of technical information assuring that the policy will not harm such actors.

Armed with information about state-level interests and constituent interests as well as policy expertise, a diverse coalition of groups representing government administrators, constituents, and policy experts is capable of addressing the informational needs of the multiple committee members. At the same time, the coalition can engage in a broad range of lobbying tactics: it can mobilize members to call or email legislators in support of the tax credit program, provide technical analysis at congressional hearings, or meet with congressional staff to draft legislative language to expand the tax credit program. Because the set of organizations has diverse informational resources and can undertake varied lobbying tactics, it is better positioned to influence multiple legislative committee members, relative to a group acting alone or a coalition representing only a single type of interest.

DIVERSE COALITIONS AND POLITICAL SIGNALING

The second part of the theory builds from the observation that coalitions function as signals that convey information to legislators about underlying support for policy change (Hula 1999; Mahoney 2007). Although elected officials rely on interest groups to provide electoral, technical, and political information, it is not always apparent whether they should take this information at face value. Interest groups sometimes have incentives to misrepresent information – for example, by overstating the salience of constituents' policy preferences or manipulating policy research to indicate support for a favored policy alternative. It is not simply the content of information that helps groups gain influence but also the credibility of that information (Ainsworth 1993; Austin-Smith and Banks 2002; Austin-Smith and Wright 1992, 1994; Grossman and Helpman 2001; Lohmann 1993; Potters and Van Winden 1992).

Groups devote considerable time and resources to establishing their credibility, from building a reputation for being trustworthy to demonstrating the accuracy of the information they are providing (Esterling 2004; Hansen 1991; Kersh 2007). Organizations specialize in narrow policy areas or provide concrete evidence of constituent opinion by mobilizing letter-writing campaigns or engaging in demonstrations (Goldstein 1999; Kollman 1998). Legislators, for their part, also structure interactions with interest groups to discourage the latter from offering inaccurate information. For example, legislators may impose a cost on lobbying to ensure that groups do not misrepresent their information, such as directing lobbyists to register or requiring additional evidence that an interest group is providing accurate information (such as letters from constituents) (Ainsworth 1993).

I theorize that interest groups enhance the credibility of information they provide legislators by engaging in collaborative lobbying efforts with diverse partners. Within the interest group literature, scholars have theorized that heterogeneous and costly signals from organized interests make interest group information more credible to legislators. Diverse policy coalitions, I argue, contain heterogeneous cues from different types of interests and provide evidence of costly lobbying efforts. Diverse coalitions therefore signal that information communicated by the coalition is credible and, in doing so, help interest groups gain influence in the policymaking process.

Heterogeneous Signaling

The first way that diverse policy coalitions enhance credibility is through heterogeneous signaling. The logic of heterogeneous signaling derives from formal theoretic research on legislative uncertainty and information in Congress. Scholars including Epstein (1999), Gilligan and Krehbiel (1989), and Krehbiel (1992) show that heterogeneous committees, or committees in which legislators have different preferences over policy, reduce uncertainty regarding the consequences of legislators' policy choices. The authors show that under certain conditions, members in heterogeneous committees have incentives to provide confirmatory signals (or say the same thing) about the consequences of a policy choice. When committee members with different underlying preferences provide confirmatory signals, the information provided is perceived as credible because the members do not usually agree. While these conclusions are based on formal theoretic methods, the logic is straightforward: "Committee specialists from opposite sides of a policy spectrum are collectively more informative than specialists from only one side of the spectrum" (Krehbiel 1992: 84). Thus the authors argue that heterogeneity works to reduce uncertainty in Congress.

I theorize that in much the same way, diverse policy coalitions contain heterogeneous cues that can provide credible information to legislators about policy preferences of constituents and interests, the policy under consideration, and the alignment of support and opposition in the political environment. A coalition containing different types of membership groups is able to communicate the preferences of a broad mix of constituents, thereby creating "an aura of legitimacy" for democratic policy decisions (Hula 1999: 29). If a legislator can point to multifaceted support for her decision, she may be better able to defend herself against challengers who seek to use that decision against her in the next election. A signal of diverse organizational support is likely to be particularly compelling when the organizations have different underlying preferences, such as liberal or conservative orientations.

Diverse policy coalitions may also provide heterogeneous cues that help legislators evaluate the substantive effects of a policy. Different types of organizations possess expert information about different aspects of policy. For example, research organizations and think tanks summarize and draw inferences from existing research, professional organizations speak to the immediate needs or preferences of those who implement or receive benefits from the policy, and governmental entities or nonprofit organization have knowledge of implementation. Actors who are engaged in different areas or stages of a policy but collectively support or oppose a given policy provide credible evidence that a policy will have a particular set of impacts, thereby reducing legislators' uncertainty about the substantive impacts of a policy.

Finally, diverse coalitions may signal that a set of interested actors collectively supports or opposes a piece of legislation, providing evidence that an issue is likely to progress through Congress with minimal disruptions. Collaborative behavior also has the potential to provide a legislative subsidy. Hall and Deardorff (2006) theorize that interest groups "subsidize" the activities of like-minded legislators by providing information, policy analysis, or policy proposals. By forging agreement across actors, collaborative behavior may lessen the work that a legislator must do once a policy arrives on the legislative agenda. Such cues reduce legislative uncertainty regarding how an issue will progress through the policymaking process.

The theory posits that the heterogeneity of informational cues within a diverse policy coalition enhances the credibility of interest group information, whether electoral, policy, or political. While this argument is similar to that presented in the first part of the theory, there are important differences. Specifically, the resource mobilization mechanism discussed in the first part of the theory posits that diversity matters because it expands a coalition's access to information and enables a wider array of lobbying tactics. This allows a diverse policy coalition to reach more legislators because different legislators respond to different types of information. The second part of the theory argues that coalitions that contain diverse partners enhance the credibility of the information that the coalition provides. In the latter sense, diversity is important because it makes a coalition's information more believable to a single legislator.

To build off the tax credit example introduced in the previous section, the alliance between state governmental actors, constituent groups, and policy experts in support of the expansion not only allows groups to reach more legislators (by uniting diverse information and enabling multiple tactics) but also reduces uncertainty about the consequences of expanding the tax credit program (by providing credible evidence that diverse actors support the expansion).

Costly Lobbying

The second way that diverse coalitions enhance credibility is through the mechanism of costly lobbying. Existing scholarship theorizes that interest group information is perceived by legislators to be more credible when groups engage in costly lobbying activities, for example, by mobilizing constituents to contact members of Congress or running media advertisements (Ainsworth 1993; Austin-Smith and Banks 2002; Austin-Smith and Wright 1992, 1994; Lohmann 1993; Potters and Van Winden 1992; Wright 1995 [2003]; see Grossman and Helpman 2001 for a review).[4] When lobbying is without cost, an organization has an incentive to use its informational resources to persuade legislators to act in its favor, regardless of the accuracy of its claims. However, when there is a cost to lobbying, organizations that seek to misrepresent information will be deterred from lobbying. Because a group does not lobby

[4] The theory of diverse coalitions builds from a body of formal work that views costly lobbying as facilitating information transmission between interest groups and legislators, especially those theories that focus on endogenous cost lobbying, in which the costs of lobbying are not fixed but rather vary according to preferences and effort level of organizational actors (Ainsworth 1993; Austin-Smith and Banks 2002; Austin-Smith and Wright 1992, 1994; Lohmann 1993; Potters and Van Winden 1992; see Grossman and Helpman 2001 for a review).

unless it is presenting accurate information, legislators can be assured that the information they receive is credible (Ainsworth 1993).[5]

I theorize that in much the same way, collaboration across diverse actors provides evidence of costly lobbying efforts and signals that the information provided by a group of organizations is credible. Collaboration is costly in terms of resource expenditures, lost opportunities, policy goals, and reputations. Such costs are likely to be higher, I argue, when coalitions are diverse with respect to the interests that are represented by coalition members.

In general, coalition building is costly whether members are diverse or represent similar types of interests. With respect to resources such as time and money, coalition founders must provide the initial capital and labor to organize and host a coalition, provide administrative support, and direct its early activities. Coalition founders must also devote resources to gathering information on the preferences and likely activities of potential allies and opponents, and to ongoing coordination and maintenance efforts (Hula 1999; Levi and Murphy 2006; Loomis 1986).

Collaborating also entails substantial opportunity costs. In an increasingly crowded interest group environment, competition creates incentives for groups to develop distinctive identities and occupy specific policy niches. An organization that cultivates a unique identity gains a "marketable good" to exchange for legislative access and influence (Browne 1990). By collaborating with other groups, an organization trades an opportunity to differentiate itself for a chance at increased policy influence.

An organization also incurs policy costs if participation in a coalition requires the group to modify its preferred policy position – either in terms of the position advocated or the strategy employed. Organizations that collaborate may also face reputational costs. An organization's reputation is among its most important resources, and groups may alienate funders, members, or allies by collaborating with other organizations (Schlozman and Tierney 1986).

Diversity increases the costs of collaboration in several ways. Diversity with respect to the professional identity of a group can increase costs because groups mobilized around different professional interests tend to have different organizational structures that may impede collaborative lobbying efforts. Membership organizations such as citizen groups and professional

[5] The conclusions of this model depend on the assumption that the net benefits of lobbying (i.e., the benefits of successful lobbying minus the costs) differ for organizations providing credible and non-credible information (Ainsworth 1993). Specifically, when lobbying is costly, an organization that provides credible information will gain more than it loses from a successful lobbying effort, while an organization that provides non-credible information will lose more than it gains by lobbying. The net benefits of lobbying may differ as a result of differences in the benefit of a policy win or differences in the cost of lobbying. In the model proposed by Ainsworth (1993), the conclusions stem from the fact that the payoff of a policy "win" differs for each type of organization.

associations are constrained by the preferences of their members, while institutional actors such as government agencies, corporations, or nonprofit service providers are not so constrained (Salisbury 1984). Membership and nonmembership organizations also tend to adopt different types of lobbying strategies. Nonmembership organizations often prefer inside lobbying strategies in which they interact directly with decision makers, rather than using public strategies. In contrast, membership-based citizen groups that receive funding primarily through dues have an incentive to pursue highly visible and often confrontational public strategies to demonstrate activity and effectiveness to their members (Gais and Walker 1991). Such differences may make it more difficult for diverse coalition partners to agree on the coalition's lobbying strategy, thus requiring groups to devote more resources to collaborative efforts.

Organizations that operate in different policy domains or represent different professional interests within a given domain also prioritize issues differently. For example, two "green energy" companies are likely to agree that climate change is an important problem and that organizational resources should be spent advocating for government support for renewable sources of energy. It may be more difficult (and hence more costly) to convince a health organization to expend resources to lobby on this issue because the organization focuses on a different set of policy issues, which may or may not be related to climate change. Similarly, organizations representing different professions within a given domain – green energy companies and municipal power districts, for instance – speak for different interests and thus may face difficulty collaborating on issues of shared concern.

In addition, organizations focused on similar issues are more likely to have what Hula refers to as intergroup links or group interlock, both of which facilitate coalition building (Hula 1999). Intergroup links refer to the connections that develop when staff members move from one organization to another, while group interlock results when one person works simultaneously for two organizations (Hula 1999: 55). Such links facilitate the flow of information about organizational preferences, strategy, and resources. In doing so, they lower the informational costs – and, by extension, the resource costs – of coalition building. In addition, groups that are similar are more likely to have a history of shared collaborative behavior, which can also mitigate resource costs by facilitating information transmission between groups (Heaney 2004).

Finally, partisan or ideological differences can increase costs. Organizations that are ordinarily on different sides of the ideological spectrum risk alienating their members or damaging their reputations if they work together on a specific issue on which their preferences align. Organizations that typically oppose one another in the political process for other reasons – for example, energy companies and consumer groups, or health insurance agencies and patients' rights groups – may similarly face backlash from members, funders, or corporate boards when collaborating with opponents even in the presence of preference alignment on a particular policy.

To summarize the second part of the theory, legislators need information to reduce various forms of legislative uncertainty. Interest groups, with their direct lines to constituents, substantive expertise, and knowledge of policy communities, possess such information or can gather it at relatively low cost. However, the extent to which groups' informational advantage will translate into political influence depends on the credibility of the group and of its informational resources. Groups that are not able to demonstrate that their information is credible are unlikely to gain influence regardless of the extent of their informational advantage.

The *political signaling mechanisms* of the theory of diverse coalitions hold that one way that groups demonstrate the credibility of information is by engaging in lobbying efforts with diverse partners. Coalitions enhance the credibility of an informational signal by providing evidence of heterogeneous signals (the heterogeneous signaling mechanism) and costly lobbying activities (the costly lobbying mechanism). Because they demonstrate that information is credible, diverse coalitions help groups gain influence in the policy process.

THE CONDITIONS OF DIVERSE COALITION FORMATION

The third and final part of the theory identifies the conditions under which diverse policy coalitions will form. An important finding from existing research is that collaborative lobbying decisions are strongly shaped by features of the issue environment. Rather than work together on all types of issues, interest groups collaborate selectively in certain issue contexts (Hojnacki 1997; Hula 1999). Although diverse coalitions allow groups to mobilize a wide array of resources and signal credible support for a policy position, the incentives to lobby in partnership and the opportunities for collaboration vary across issue contexts. In this section, I identify three issue-level characteristics that are associated with the formation of diverse policy coalitions.

A Simple Signaling Model of Coalition Formation

Like many researchers of interest group lobbying and influence, I turn to the logic of formal theory to identify the conditions of lobbying and influence. A rich body of political science research employs formal theoretic methods to better understand the mechanisms and conditions of interest group influence in Congress (Ainsworth 1993; Austen-Smith and Wright 1992, 1994; Denzau and Munger 1986; Hall and Deardorff 2006; Helpman and Persson 2001; Mitchell and Munger 1991; Persson and Tabellini 2000; see van Winden 2003 for a review). Although formal theoretical models require considerable abstraction, they allow scholars to simplify complex relationships by isolating key interactions and mechanisms of influence.

Rather than create a new model of coalition formation, however, I build off the framework of a standard signaling game to identify the conditions under which diverse coalitions will emerge (Spence 1973). Signaling models are particularly useful for identifying the conditions of diverse collaboration formation because they highlight informational asymmetries between groups and legislators. Such models assume that an interest group has information that a legislator values but does not have, such as information about constituent preferences or likely policy outcomes. Signaling games help scholars isolate the conditions under which interest group lobbying communicates credible information despite the fact that an interest group sometimes has an incentive to misrepresent its information to a legislator.

A typical signaling game has two players: a sender of information (in this context, the interest group) and a receiver of information (the legislator) (Ainsworth 1993; Kollman 1998; see also Spence 1973). In the game, the interest group would like the legislator to enact a particular policy change, called policy p. The legislator, however, is not positively inclined to adopt policy p. She will only do so if there is credible evidence that the benefits of policy p outweigh its costs. To convince the legislator to adopt the policy, the interest group sends a signal to the legislator – for instance, by testifying at congressional hearings, organizing a letter-writing campaign by constituents, or lobbying collaboratively with other interest groups. This signal contains information about the consequences of enacting policy p. The legislator views the signal sent by the interest group and attempts to deduce whether the benefits of adopting policy p actually outweigh its costs. If the signal convinces the legislator that this is so, then the legislator accepts policy p. If the reverse is true, then the legislator rejects policy p.

Signaling games typically conceive of an interest group as one of two "types": a low type or a high type. Different signaling games have different definitions of what constitutes low- and high-type groups. For the purposes of this theory, a low-type group exists in an environment in which no other groups support policy p, whereas a high-type group exists in an environment of strong support for policy p across a diverse array of organized interests. The environment in which each group operates thus distinguishes its type. Both types of interest groups would like to see policy p enacted. As a result, both groups would like to signal that the policy enjoys strong support rather than low support, or that the group is a high type rather than a low type. The question is whether the signal sent by the group allows the legislator to correctly deduce the group's type.

A solution to a signaling game establishes the conditions under which the group's signal, such as a lobbying effort to mobilize constituents, allows a legislator to correctly infer the group's type. One way this happens is if only one type of group sends a signal. For example, if a high-type group sends a signal that it is a high type by mobilizing a diverse set of constituents but a low-type group is unable to, then the legislator knows on seeing that particular signal that she is dealing with a high-type group. In a signaling game, this is referred to as a "separating strategy" – so named because the low- and high-type interest groups "separate" in terms of their actions, with one type of group sending a signal and the other type of group abstaining.

The diverse coalition is the "signal" sent by the interest group. This signal contains information that many types of groups support the adoption of policy p. Recall that only the high-type group actually exists in an environment of broad support for policy p. In theory, however, both types of groups could build a diverse coalition to communicate broad support. If this were to happen, the low-type group would simply be misrepresenting the true level of support in the environment. If both types of groups build a diverse coalition, then the legislator is unable to tell the difference between the high and low types. However, if the groups separate in their lobbying strategies, then the presence of a diverse coalition provides information to the legislator about the group's true type – specifically, that she is dealing with a high- rather than a low-type group.

The two types of groups may separate in their lobbying strategies if the costs of coalition building differ for low- and high-type groups.[6] Specifically, if the costs of building a diverse coalition prohibit the low-type but not the high-type group from doing so, then the legislator can infer that the group is a high type on seeing a diverse coalition. In other words, the presence of a diverse coalition communicates to a legislator that the group is a high type, or that there is strong electoral, policy, and political support for policy change. At the same time, the fact that the signal will impact the legislator's support for policy p provides an incentive for the high-type group to pay the costs to collaborate with diverse partners.

An Example: Informational Signaling and the Tax Credit Program

The tax credit example presented in previous sections will help illustrate the signaling framework just described. Again, imagine that a legislator is considering whether to expand the program providing tax credits to low-income workers. The legislator is uncertain about the electoral, policy, and political consequences of this policy change. How will the tax credit expansion affect her reelection prospects? Will the policy reduce poverty among low-income families? Does the tax credit program have the support of advocates, nonprofit service providers, and state and local governmental actors? If the policy change enjoys diverse popular, technical, and political support, then the legislator would like to accept the expansion. If support for the expansion does not exist, then the legislator would prefer to reject the expansion. If the

---

[6] Previous formal theoretic research notes that the two types of interest groups may pursue different actions if the costs of signaling differ across groups. For instance, if the low type finds it exceedingly costly to signal but the high type does not, then the high type may signal while the low type abstains (see Ainsworth 1993; Kollman 1998). Again, if only the high type signals, then the legislator can be confident that she is dealing with a high-type group and can accept policy p.

legislator does not know whether support is high or low, then she does not know whether to accept or reject the proposed expansion.

Now imagine that a leading antipoverty advocacy group can provide information that will answer the legislator's questions. The advocacy group has gathered data on constituent opinion, conducted studies on the impact of the tax credit, and engaged in policy discussions with other organizations. The advocacy group knows whether there is popular, technical, and political support for expanding the tax credit program. Because it knows what type of environment it is operating in, it knows whether it is a low- or a high-type group. Yet as a representative of the poor, the advocate always favors expanding the program, regardless of the level of support in the broader political context. The group therefore has an incentive to tell the legislator that the policy enjoys a high level of electoral, policy, and political support even when that is not true. As a result, the legislator does not know whether or not to believe the advocacy group's claims that the policy enjoys wide support.

To convince the legislator to expand the tax credit program, the advocate that exists in an environment of strong support for policy change (the high-type group) will build a diverse coalition with other proponents of the expansion. Collaboration is costly, but because the advocate and its potential partners are united in their support for the tax credit expansion, these costs are not prohibitive. By contrast, the advocate that exists in an environment in which no other interests support the policy or consider it to be salient (the low-type group) has few potential partners. To build a diverse coalition, an advocate would need to devote considerable resources to identifying groups with similar preferences and convincing those groups of the importance of the policy. The large costs associated with changing the policy preferences of other interested actors effectively prevent collaboration with diverse partners for the low-type group.

This means that when an advocate exists in an environment of broad support for expanding the tax credit, or is a high-type group, it has the ability to build a diverse coalition to communicate this support to the legislator. When this support does not exist, or when the group is a low type, the advocate is unable to build a diverse coalition. Because the only advocate capable of collaborating with diverse partners is the one that exists in an environment of support for policy change, the legislator can be confident on seeing a diverse coalition that she is dealing with a high-type group. In such instances, the legislator will accept the tax credit expansion, providing an incentive for the high-type group to lobby collaboratively with diverse partners rather than lobby alone.

Diverse Collaboration across Issues: Salience, Uncertainty, and Opposition Strength

The signaling game framework draws attention to several issue-level characteristics that lead to diverse coalition formation: salience, uncertainty, and opposition strength. First, in the game described earlier, the two group types reflect different levels of salience in the broader political environment. Specifically, the low-type group exists in an environment where few groups support the proposed policy change, whereas the high-type group exists in an environment of broad support for policy change. The interest group's information (or signal) therefore pertains to the salience of the issue to different types of interest groups with similar preferences for policy change. In addition, the game implies that diverse collaboration is only possible when an issue is salient to a wide range of organized interests, or when the group is a high type. If a policy does not enjoy widespread attention or support, then a group does not have partners with which to ally and the costs of collaboration are prohibitive. This means that diverse coalitions will only emerge when an issue is salient to many different types of groups with similar preferences for policy change.

The hypothesized relationship between salience and collaboration finds support in existing research. In her analysis of interest group collaboration in the United States and the European Union, Mahoney (2007) finds a positive relationship between an issue's salience to the public and interest group collaboration. Similarly, Mahoney and Baumgartner (2004) find that groups in the United States are more likely to collaborate on issues that are salient to actors inside Washington.

Second, the signaling game highlights the fact that the legislator is uncertain about the interest group's type. This uncertainty provides an incentive for the interest group to build a diverse coalition to communicate information about the underlying support for policy change. Here, again, the tax credit example is instructive. If the legislator already knows how much support exists for the tax credit expansion, then the advocate has no reason to collaborate to reveal its true type to the legislator. Lobbying alone is less expensive than collaborating with diverse partners, and building a diverse coalition is unnecessary if the legislator already knows the group's type. Uncertainty provides the push for the interest group to collaborate with diverse partners. Unlike salience, prior work has not identified uncertainty as an important contextual characteristic. The use of a signaling framework thus helps identify a previously unrecognized feature of the policy context that is likely to impact coalitional activity.

Third, the model assumes that there are two possible policy choices and that the legislator will choose different policy choices in different political environments – accepting the proposed policy change when support for policy p is high and rejecting it when support is low. This implies that diverse collaboration will only occur when there is conflict on an issue, that is, when there are two or more opposing sides to a policy issue. To return to the tax credit example one final time, if there is only one policy choice or if a legislator will always support or oppose the advocate regardless of the level of support in the broader environment, then the advocate lacks an incentive to build a diverse coalition. This means that diverse coalitions are unlikely to emerge in the absence of conflict on an issue.

Existing research highlights the role of conflict in coalition formation: an interest group encountering conflict on an issue has an incentive to work collaboratively with other organizations to defeat a common threat (Gais and Walker 1991; Hojnacki 1997; Whitford 2003). Empirical research on the relationship between conflict and collaboration, however, yields mixed results. Mahoney and Baumgartner (2004) find that the presence of opposing views on an issue is associated with decreased coalitional activity: groups are less likely to collaborate when conflict exists. Hojnacki (1997), however, finds that when groups encounter strong opponents on a particular issue, they are more likely to engage in collaborative behavior. This suggests that it is not the presence of conflict alone that mobilizes collaborative activity but rather the existence of strong opponents alongside the presence of conflict that creates an incentive for groups to work together.

The third part of the theory yields a set of predictions regarding the conditions of diverse coalition formation, which I refer to as the *political context predictions*. These predictions hold that on policy issues involving two or more sides, diverse coalitions will form when high levels of salience, uncertainty, and strong opponents characterize issues.

CONCLUSION

Organized interests have strong incentives to collaborate to influence legislative policy choices. This chapter has presented a theory that explains both the mechanisms of coalition influence and conditions of coalitional formation. The theory draws attention to the role of diversity in collaborative activity and yields three sets of predictions for empirical research. First, the resource mobilization mechanism holds that diversity within coalitions expands access to information and lobbying tactics. Second, the political signaling mechanisms hold that diversity within coalitions provides evidence of heterogeneous support and costly lobbying efforts. Finally, the political context predictions hold that diverse coalitions will emerge on issues characterized by salience, uncertainty, and strong opponents.

As noted in the introduction to this chapter, there are reasons to suspect that the theory of diverse coalitions applies across policy domains. The contextual factors that create *incentives* for groups to collaborate – uncertainty in the policy environment and strong opponents – are not unique to poverty-related issues but rather exist across policy areas. In addition, the factors that create *opportunities* for groups to work together – issue salience to a diverse mix of groups – similarly exist for many types of groups and in different policy areas. Although my empirical analysis will focus exclusively on collaboration in the social policy domain, the theory's implications therefore likely extend across issues and domains. The concluding chapter will elaborate on the generalizability of the theory.

Finally, it is important to note that diversity can present itself in many ways. For example, a coalition might draw together the financial resources of a corporate actor with the electoral resources of a citizen group, as happened in the late 1990s when telecommunications companies united with consumer groups to push for the repeal of the 3 percent federal excise tax on telecommunications (Baumgartner et al. 2009: 190–206). Or, a coalition might unite the electoral resources of groups from diverse economic sectors, as when unions worked with environmental groups to protest the World Trade Organization meetings in Seattle in 1999 (Levi and Murphy 2006). Because there are many types of diversity within coalitions, the theory incorporates only a broad definition of diversity. A central aim of the empirical analysis is to identify the particular *types* of diversity that are salient in the policymaking process.

The following chapters introduce the empirical analysis and examine the support for the implications of the theory. In the next three chapters, I introduce my empirical analysis and case. Specifically, Chapter 3 details my empirical approach, while Chapter 4 introduces the case that forms the basis for my empirical analysis. Chapter 5 provides an overview of organizational activity during welfare reform. In the subsequent three chapters, I analyze the empirical support for the theory of diverse coalitions. Specifically, Chapter 6 examines empirical support for the resource mobilization mechanism, and Chapter 7 examines support for the political signaling mechanisms. Finally, Chapter 8 examines empirical support for the political context predictions.

3

An Empirical Investigation of Collaboration in the Policy Process

INTRODUCTION

In the previous chapter, I developed a theory that identifies the mechanisms of coalition influence and the conditions of coalition formation. In this chapter, I elaborate on my methodological approach and introduce the case that forms the basis for my empirical analysis. In the first section of the chapter, I describe the advantages of pursuing a case study design to analyze support for the theory of diverse coalitions and specify how the results of this particular case study generalize to other types of cases. The second section of the chapter introduces the Personal Responsibility and Work Opportunity Reconciliation Act of 1996 (PRWORA), or welfare reform, and defends the case selection. In the third section, I provide an overview of my data collection and analysis procedures, which focus attention on interest group coalitions rather than individual groups. The final section summarizes the central points of the chapter and concludes.

RESEARCH DESIGN

To examine the empirical support for the theory, I analyze organizational advocacy on a single case. A case study represents a strong empirical approach, for the following reasons. First, a case study allows me to identify and measure multiple indicators of collaboration, thereby achieving a high level of conceptual validity. Second, examining a single case allows me to investigate the mechanisms linking diverse coalitions with policy influence. Third, a case study allows me to explore diversity within coalitions in great depth, thereby offering additional insights about a still developing topic of research. Yet while analyzing a single case has many advantages, it is not without limitations. This section elaborates on the advantages, disadvantages, and implications of pursuing a case study design.

Advantages of a Case Study Design

First, a strength of case studies is that they permit high conceptual validity, which means that they allow a researcher to develop strong measures for a given theoretical concept (George and Bennett 2005: 19). In this project, the central theoretical concept – a coalition – is defined as any informal or formal partnership united behind a common policy goal. Because a coalition can be informal or formal in nature, it was necessary to pursue an empirical strategy that allowed me to observe loose informal partnerships as well as coalitions that operate as distinct organizational entities. While formal coalitions can be identified through lists of registered lobbyists or campaign contribution records, it is more challenging to observe collaboration that remains informal, as such partnerships may crystalize only for a short period of time around a discrete issue or decision. Such informal coalitions can be observed through cosponsored advertisements, cosigned press releases, joint statements before congressional committees, and joint press conferences and protests, to name just a few examples. These types of observations are possible in a case study given the depth of analysis, but not in a project examining a larger number of issues. By allowing me to observe coalitions of varying degrees of formality, a case study therefore permits an analysis of units that are similar in terms of their analytic status but variable with respect to their empirical form.

Second, case studies are well suited for analyzing *how* or *why* variables are related because they offer researchers the opportunity to examine how the mechanisms that connect variables operate in a particular case (George and Bennett 2005; Gerring 2004; Yin 2003). Because this project focuses attention on the mechanisms linking coalitional diversity with policy influence, a case study represents an appropriate approach. The theory developed in the previous chapter hypothesizes that diverse coalitions will lead to policy influence but also identifies several mechanisms through which this influence occurs. Specifically, the theory posits that diverse coalitions will increase access to information and allow groups to use more tools for conveying information, while enhancing the credibility of information. A case study allows me to examine the empirical support for each of these posited mechanisms of influence by examining how the mechanisms operate in a particular context. Delving deeply into a single case therefore provides greater insight into the pathways connecting diversity with policy influence.

Finally, case studies permit a depth of analysis that is not possible in larger, cross-unit studies. This depth of analysis is particularly useful when research is of an exploratory nature, meaning that it seeks to develop new theories rather than confirm or disconfirm existing theories (Gerring 2004). This project is not completely exploratory, as the theory proposes a causal relationship between coalitional diversity and policy influence. Yet while the theory defines diversity in terms of the resources that partners bring to a collaborative lobbying effort, diversity can emerge in a variety of ways. For example, a diverse coalition might draw together the substantive expertise of a research organization with the electoral resources of a labor union, or the Washington contacts of an intergovernmental group with the membership base of a child advocacy organization. By examining lobbying in a single case, I am able to identify the *types* of diversity that are associated with access and influence, thereby refining the definition of diversity and by extension, the theory itself.

Generalizability of Empirical Findings

Despite clear advantages with respect to the measurement of key concepts, investigation of causal mechanisms, and depth of analysis, there are trade-offs associated with pursuing a case study design. Chief among these trade-offs is that an analysis of a single case limits the extent to which the findings apply to a broader range of cases (Gerring 2006). As a result, it is important to specify the range of cases to which any case study analysis applies.

In this project, the empirical findings are intended to generalize to cases involving policymaking on social policy issues. As the fifth chapter discusses, interest group activity on social policy issues is somewhat distinct from activity on other policy issues. Specifically, the business and professional interests that dominate Washington politics have a much smaller lobbying presence in the social policy domain, relative to domains such as the energy or health policy. Because this project was motivated by an interest in understanding the influence of advocates for the poor, it was appropriate to select a case involving social policy, rather than a set of cases representative of a broader set of issues. This choice, however, means that the findings are not intended to generalize to a broader class of cases involving other policy domains.

In addition, both the analysis and the generalizability of the findings are limited to the decision-making stage of the policymaking process. During welfare reform, this stage began when the Republicans won decisive majorities in the House and Senate in the midterm elections of 1994 and ended when President Clinton signed the welfare reform bill into law on August 22, 1996. My prioritization of the decision-making stage results from a theoretical focus on legislative outcomes; I am interested in the influence of collaborative lobbying on policy decisions, rather than influence in the agenda-setting or implementation stage. Past research suggests that organized interests behave differently in different policymaking stages. Kingdon (1989), for instance, argues the following: "when the issue has a serious chance of legislative or other action, then advocates become more flexible, bargaining from their previously rigid positions, compromising in order to be in the game" (167–68). Because groups are likely to behave differently across stages of the policymaking process, I restrict my focus to the decision-making stage.

Finally, as the next chapter makes clear, the welfare reform case is characterized by defensive lobbying by advocates for low-income populations.

During welfare reform, advocates were in the unenviable position of lobbying in a Republican-controlled Congress where leaders were generally unreceptive to their concerns. While there is some variation across issues, most lobbying during welfare reform involved advocates working to prevent the large-scale dismantling of the welfare state in a highly partisan environment.

The defensive nature of lobbying on an ideologically charged set of issues, while striking at the time, is perhaps less unusual in the contemporary political climate. The current political environment is highly partisan and characterized by a focus on cost cutting and devolution of policy authority. It seems reasonable to infer that in the contemporary climate, advocates often find themselves in the defensive position of lobbying to prevent cuts to existing programs.

In addition, there are few theoretical reasons to suspect that the defensive nature of lobbying during welfare reform significantly shaped collaborative activity. Theoretically, it is not the defensive nature of lobbying that is posited to affect diverse coalition formation but rather the presence of strong opponents. If advocates find themselves pushing forth a policy in an environment characterized by salience, uncertain impacts, and strong opponents, then the theory predicts that they will lobby collaboratively with diverse partners in favor of this policy. Indeed, the strength of a status quo position creates a particularly strong "opponent," creating incentives for groups to collaborate with diverse partners to overturn the status quo. Thus the findings are likely generalizable to a wide set of social policy issues in which advocates lobby proactively as well as defensively.

Like all case studies, the generalizability of the empirical findings is limited. Yet analyzing lobbying on welfare reform offers distinct advantages, which I discuss in the next section. Moreover, I argue in the concluding chapter that there are theoretical reasons to expect broader applicability of the theory across policy domains because the causal mechanisms identified by the theory are not unique to the social policy domain. Yet while there are reasons to suspect that the theory has a broader reach, I do not claim that the empirical analysis generalizes beyond what I believe the data can provide. Whether the theory of diverse coalitions finds empirical support across policy domains remains a question for future research.

THE PERSONAL RESPONSIBILITY AND WORK OPPORTUNITY RECONCILIATION ACT OF 1996

My empirical analysis centers on organizational advocacy in the two years preceding the passage of the PRWORA, one of the most significant federal social policies of the past several decades. The policy ended the long-standing guarantee of federal cash assistance to poor families by replacing the entitlement program Aid to Families with Dependent Children (AFDC) with the block grant program Temporary Assistance to Needy Families (TANF). TANF differed from its predecessor in that cash benefits were time limited and made conditional on employment activities. Many programmatic decisions were devolved from the national to the state level and states were granted increased discretion over issues including work incentives, program time limits, and sanctions for noncompliant behavior.

The PRWORA provides a unique opportunity to analyze the empirical support for the theory of diverse coalitions. Because it included a large number of changes to the social safety net, the proposals to reform welfare activated a large number of groups representing an array of interests and ideologies. Liberal antipoverty advocacy groups and child advocates lobbied against ending the individual entitlement to welfare. Child disability advocates and groups of health professionals challenged proposals to tighten eligibility for the child disability program. Anti-hunger organizations and groups representing food distributors pressured legislators to maintain the existing structure of the Food Stamp program. State government actors sought structural changes that would give states more discretion over the welfare program. And conservative "pro-family" groups lobbied in favor of new rules intended to encourage marriage and discourage out-of-wedlock childbirth.

These organizations brought a diverse array of resources to their lobbying efforts. Some represented professionals within the health policy domain while others represented educators and school administrators. Some had members traditionally aligned with Republican interests; others had members aligned with Democratic interests. Some possessed expertise based on research; others brought expertise based on program administration or service delivery. Different types of organizations at times found themselves with similar positions on specific provisions within the welfare reform legislation. For instance, pro-family groups such as the Christian Coalition and conservative research organizations such as the Heritage Foundation both supported eliminating benefits to children born to mothers currently on welfare. Similarly, membership-based groups representing women, children, and poor families all opposed eliminating the federal entitlement to welfare assistance. Thus the community of interested actors on welfare reform consisted of a diverse array of organizations, each representing different interests and possessing different resources.

In addition, the environment in which organized interests found themselves created strong incentives for collaboration on issues of shared concern, particularly for advocates. Welfare reform proposals were salient to a wide range of interests, creating opportunities for collaboration. In addition, the debate surrounding welfare reform was contentious, and conservative interest groups had considerable access to the Republican leadership in Congress. The heightened conflict and strength of conservative opponents created strong incentives for groups to work collaboratively with diverse partners to influence the shape and content of welfare reform legislation. Thus the circumstances surrounding welfare reform made it particularly likely to witness the type of collaboration proposed by the theory.

Such properties, I argue, make welfare reform an appropriate case to analyze. In selecting welfare reform, I intended to maximize the amount of information that could be gained about advocates' collaborative activities, rather than select a case that would serve as a "representative" case of lobbying in the social policy domain. Atypical cases are often able to provide a greater number of insights about a given phenomenon because they involve more variables and mechanisms of interest (Gerring 2006). The fact that welfare reform created opportunities and incentives for groups to collaborate increases the likelihood of observing coalitions. This in turn provides a large number of embedded units to analyze, both with respect to the characteristics of the coalitions and covariation between coalitional properties, lobbying activities, and policy influence.

It is also true that welfare reform included a number of sub-issues that varied with respect to the strength of opponents, uncertainty, and salience. Initial proposals to reform the welfare program involved changing the structure of cash welfare and child welfare programs from federal entitlement programs into block grant programs, tightening eligibility rules for the child disability program, imposing strict work requirements, denying cash assistance to teen mothers, and enhancing efforts to collect child support. These sub-issues differed in terms of the level of partisan and organizational conflict, salience to organized interests, as well as the uncertainty of policy outcomes. Efforts to enhance child support collection, for example, enjoyed bipartisan support, while provisions denying cash assistance to teen mothers activated both interparty and intraparty disputes. The consequences of ending the federal entitlement to cash assistance were highly uncertain, but work requirements had been tested in several states. The fact that sub-issues varied with respect to conflict, uncertainty, and salience provides an opportunity to analyze whether and how diverse collaborative activity varies based on the features of the issue context.

Thus within the single case of welfare reform are a series of embedded cases that serve as the units of analysis at different points in the book. Chapters 6 and 7 focus on coalitions as the unit of analysis and examine diversity within coalitions and the consequences for lobbying activity. Chapter 8 focuses on issues as the unit of analysis and examines variation across issues with respect to coalitional activity. This issue-level variation allows me to analyze the relationship between issue characteristics and diverse collaboration.

Yet although a case study allows me to analyze the empirical support for the hypothesized relationships in the theory, I am not able to make claims regarding the *frequency* with which groups will work with diverse partners on similar types of issues. Such questions are better explored through cross-case or large-n research designs (Gerring 2006). Yet the fact that welfare reform includes a large number of embedded units (coalitions and issues) makes this policy an ideal choice for analyzing the support for the theory of diverse coalitions.

DATA COLLECTION AND ANALYSIS

My data collection and analysis efforts focused on the informal and formal coalitions that were active in lobbying on the issue of welfare reform during the 104th Congress (1995–1996). Gathering data on the coalitions required a novel data collection design. Specifically, because diversity is a property of a set of organizations, rather than any individual organization, it was necessary to focus empirical attention on coalitions rather than the individual groups that may or may not collaborate. This means that I did not investigate collaborative activity by interviewing group leaders or tracing the activities of a set of interested actors as they decide whether to work in partnership or act alone. Rather, I gathered data on the coalitions to examine the nature of diversity and its role in shaping lobbying activity and legislative influence.

To identify the informal and formal coalitions that were active during welfare reform, I employed a range of primary and secondary source material. First, I collected data from congressional hearings on welfare reform held in the House and Senate during the 104th Congress (1995–1996). Between January 1995 and August 1996, when the PRWORA was signed into law, the House held 11 hearings over the course of 20 days, and the Senate held 14 hearings over the course of 19 days.[1] The hearings data, which are contained in several thousand pages of documents, include testimony from invited participants, question and answer sessions with legislative committee and subcommittee members, and statements submitted for the record by interested actors. Over the course of the hearings, more than 300 organizations testified in person or submitted testimony for the record (see Winston 2002).

Second, I collected articles from the *New York Times* that either mentioned or discussed organizational activity during welfare reform. To generate the list of articles, I searched all articles published in the *New York Times* between November 8, 1994, and August 22, 1996, using the search terms "welfare" and ("Aid to Families with Dependent Children" or "AFDC"). November 8, 1994, was the date of the midterm elections in which the Republican Party gained majority control of the House and the Senate, and August 22, 1996, was the date that President Clinton signed the PRWORA into law. This search generated a list of 747 articles. Of these, I kept only those articles that mentioned an organizational actor or non-governmental policy expert by name. Together, the hearings data and newspaper articles provided a foundation for viewing the informal and formal collaborative activities of interest groups.

---

[1] A list of the hearings is included in the Appendix.

I analyzed the content of all hearings testimony and newspaper articles to identify indicators of informal or formal collaboration. For example, an indicator of informal collaborative activity might be a cosigned statement submitted during congressional hearings, a mention of a partnership in oral hearings testimony, a jointly sponsored protest, or a coauthored editorial, while an indicator of formal collaborative activity might be testimony by a formal coalition. When the initial sources provided evidence of collaborative activity, I probed additional journalistic and scholarly sources to provide greater coverage of the coalition. For example, when a *New York Times* article identified a press conference jointly sponsored by several advocates for children and families, I collected additional data on that event from other media outlets, including the *Washington Post* and C-SPAN, as well as the organizational records of one of the groups attending the press conference.

To the hearings and newspaper data, I added data from other media reports, archival documents from the Clinton Presidential Library and NOW's Legal Defense and Education Fund, and select secondary sources. The Clinton Presidential Library contains a welfare reform collection of close to 70 boxes documenting the activities of the administration, Congress, and outside actors on the issue. Archival documents from the Clinton Library collection provide contextual information about the many issues within welfare reform, as well as evidence of organizational activities and indicators of collaborative activity that were not visible from hearings or media sources, such as letters from groups to congressional offices and correspondence between advocates and members of the administration.

To generate information on coalitional activities that occurred behind the scenes, I visited the archives of the NOW Legal Defense and Education Fund (now called Legal Momentum) to gather data on the activities of one prominent coalition (the Child Exclusion Task Force). The archives of NOW's Legal Defense and Education Fund offered a wide range of coalition materials, including meeting notes from the Child Exclusion Task Force's Subcommittee on Legislation and Lobby Corp Subcommittee, which provided valuable data on the lobbying activities of partners as they attempted to influence welfare reform legislation.

For each informal or formal coalition identified by the various data sources, I investigated similarities and differences between partners with respect to the interest represented, policy domain, organizational structure, and ideological leanings. I recorded how organizational representatives described their organizations as well as their partnerships, especially with respect to the similarities or differences between partners. If organizational representatives highlighted group differences, I observed the axes of diversity to which representatives drew attention. I also examined partners' differential resource strengths – policy expertise versus large constituency base, for example, as well as the sources of that strength – expertise deriving from research and analysis versus expertise deriving from program administration, for example. Finally, I investigated the issues on which various coalitions were active.

This data collection and analysis strategy allowed me to observe a set of informal and formal coalitions that were active in lobbying legislators during the 104th Congress. Because I focused empirical attention on *coalitions* rather than individual groups, I was able to observe a wide variety of partnerships as well as analyze the characteristics of coalitions and the issues on which they were active. This in turn allowed me to analyze the empirical support for the arguments that diversity within coalitions enhances access to information, contains heterogeneous cues, communicates costly lobbying efforts, and emerges in different issue contexts.

Limitations

Three limitations of the data collection and analysis strategy are worth noting. First, one limitation is the decision to rely in part on congressional hearings testimony as a primary source of data on interest group activity and collaborative lobbying. It is well established that congressional hearings function as a type of "political theater" in which participants are acutely aware of the public nature of their participation. It is possible that groups will overstate or otherwise misrepresent their coalitions in hearings testimony – for instance, by communicating that a coalition is larger or more diverse than it actually is. In addition, participation in congressional hearings is only one of a myriad of possible lobbying tactics. Interest groups can and do engage in a wide range of activities including direct contact with legislators and legislative staff, talking with the media, releasing organizational statements, and mobilizing constituents.

While these potential drawbacks are important to keep in mind, it is also the case that hearings provide an opportunity to systematically observe the activity of organized interests across a set of issues. This means that in the case of welfare reform, I can compare the coalitions active on welfare to work to the partnerships that emerged on child exclusion issues. Moreover, testifying or submitting written testimony in hearings is a prevalent form of lobbying. Although it is true that groups engage in a range of lobbying tactics, testifying at congressional hearings is frequently one of these tactics (Schlozman and Tierney 1986). Thus lists of hearings participants are likely to provide a relatively comprehensive view of the population of organized interests active on welfare reform (see Winston 2002).

It also seems reasonable to suspect that the public nature of the hearing may guard against some forms of misrepresentation. An organization is unlikely to refer to a partner by name if a partnership does not really exist. Though a coalition may overstate the participation of a member (and in doing so, overstate the salience of the issue to that member), it is unlikely that the coalition would misrepresent the policy preferences or the collaboration of that member. Moreover, my decision to utilize multiple sources to provide information on observed coalitions may also help mitigate this limitation. By using media reports as well as archival documents to provide additional data on the partnership, I am able to observe the partnership in a variety of contexts and from a variety of perspectives. A diverse coalition that emerges in multiple contexts – in hearings testimony as well as media reports of news conferences – provides additional evidence that groups within a coalition are committed to their policy position.

Second, while I attempted to utilize a wide range of existing data sources to identify the coalitions, some likely remained unobserved. Namely, coalitions that operated exclusively behind the scenes and coalitions in which partners met but decided not to act were not observable in my data. I would not observe an informal coalition of organizations that worked together to monitor policy developments by attending (but not participating in) congressional hearings. Similarly, I would not observe a set of organizations that held a series of meetings on welfare reform but decided either not to act or not to act collaboratively. The coalitions that I observed therefore likely represented an underestimate of the collaborative activity that occurred.

Finally, the decision to collect data on coalitions rather than individual groups means that I cannot observe many of the group-level costs associated with diverse collaboration or group decisions to collaborate or work alone. Such group-level data would undoubtedly provide valuable information, particularly with respect to the reasons that diverse coalitions did or did not form during welfare reform. The archives of the NOW Legal Defense and Education Fund provide a window into the group-level calculations that shape collaborative behavior, but in general these calculations are not observable for the vast majority of groups in my data. This is a necessary trade-off given my empirical focus on informal and formal coalitions. Focusing on coalitions simply did not allow me to observe group-level characteristics. However, such a focus provides valuable insights regarding the characteristics of coalitions that shape their activity and influence in the policymaking process – insights that would not be apparent with an empirical focus on individual groups.

CONCLUSION

This chapter has provided an overview of my research design, case selection, and the data collection and analysis procedures. In each section of the chapter, I have highlighted the strengths and weaknesses of the empirical approach in an effort to specify the conclusions that can be drawn from the research. I have argued that the advantages with respect to the case study design, the case selection, and the focus on coalitions outweigh the limitations. While case studies represent a common approach in the literature on interest group lobbying and influence, the focus on social welfare policy and coalitional lobbying distinguishes this project from existing research. Such a focus offers the opportunity to generate insights regarding an increasingly common strategy of political influence in a relatively unexplored policy domain. In the next chapter, I turn to an overview of the welfare policy program to contextualize the activities of organized interests in the two years preceding the passage of the Personal Responsibility and Work Opportunity Act of 1996.

4

Policy Change and Interest Group Involvement on Welfare Issues

INTRODUCTION

The Personal Responsibility and Work Opportunity Reconciliation Act of 1996 (PRWORA), signed by President Bill Clinton on August 22, 1996, represented a profound shift in American social welfare policy. Known popularly as "welfare reform," the PRWORA ended a 60-year guarantee of cash assistance to needy families by replacing the entitlement program Aid to Families with Dependent Children (AFDC) with the block grant program Temporary Assistance to Needy Families (TANF). TANF differed from its predecessor in that benefits to poor families were time limited and made conditional on employment activities. Many programmatic decisions were devolved from the national to state level, and states were granted significant discretion over a wide range of issues.

In this chapter, I describe the evolution of the welfare program from its origin in the 1935 Social Security Act to the passage of the PRWORA in 1996. Although the program experienced considerable change in the decades preceding welfare reform, the proposals introduced in the 104th Congress (1995–1996) represented a striking departure from the past. My goal in reviewing the program's history is not to duplicate the many fine historical accounts of AFDC's evolution, but rather to provide the background necessary for understanding both the participants and proposals of the early 1990s.

I begin the chapter by discussing the evolution of the welfare program to contextualize the policy changes proposed by the Republican Party at the start of the 104th Congress. To provide the background necessary for understanding the groups that were active on welfare issues in the early 1990s, the second section discusses the corresponding mobilization of organizations alongside the welfare program's evolution. In the third section, I describe the welfare reform proposals that were introduced by House Republicans after the party gained majority control of Congress in 1994. The fourth section discusses the progression of the legislation from its introduction in the House of Representatives in January 1995, through two presidential vetoes, and finally to President Clinton's desk in August 1996. The fifth section concludes.

THE EVOLUTION OF THE WELFARE PROGRAM IN THE UNITED STATES, 1935–1994

For nearly 60 years prior to the passage of the PRWORA, cash benefits were provided to needy families through the AFDC program.[1] The program originated in the Social Security Act of 1935, having developed out of a series of state-level pension programs that were designed to provide destitute families (typically widows with children) with a cash benefit that would allow children to remain with their mothers and prevent them from being moved into orphanages or foster care. From its inception, national and state governments shared the cost of AFDC, with states retaining broad authority over program elements such as individual eligibility requirements, benefit levels, and program administration (Patterson 2000).

The welfare program remained largely unchanged throughout the 1940s and 1950s. During these decades, the economy expanded, poverty rates declined, and there was a widespread belief that economic growth could bring an end to poverty (Danziger 2001; Patterson 2000; Trattner 1998). However, among families that remained below the poverty line, less than one-fifth received benefits through federal programs designed to assist low-income families. In the South, many states maintained restrictive rules designed to limit the eligibility of "undeserving" families, such as "suitable home" provisions that denied benefits to unmarried women living with a male partner (Patterson 2000: 76–93). Benefit levels within the AFDC program also varied widely across states and were generally well below the official poverty line. While the poverty line was approximately $3,000 in 1960, the average annual welfare payment for a family of four was $2,150.

By the early 1960s, the average annual decline in the poverty rate had tapered off, and it was clear that the rising economic tide had not lifted all Americans out of poverty. A series of influential writings, including Michael Harrington's *The Other America* and Dwight MacDonald's article "Our Invisible Poor," alongside increased attention to the problem of poverty within African Americans communities, helped elevate the problem of poverty and the federal programs designed to support low-income individuals and families onto the national political agenda (Haveman, Blank, Moffitt, Smeeding, and Wallace 2015).

President John F. Kennedy's administration (1961–1963) took initial steps to address the problem of poverty by enacting modest expansions to the welfare

---

[1] The program was originally called Aid to Dependent Children, or ADC. In the 1960s, the name was changed to Aid to Families with Dependent Children, or AFDC.

program through the Public Welfare Amendments of 1962, which extended eligibility to two-parent families and increased federal funding to welfare offices for services such as job training and placement (Patterson 2000). National antipoverty efforts accelerated under President Lyndon B. Johnson's administration (1963–1968), especially following President Johnson's declaration of a "war on poverty" in 1964. The Economic Opportunity Act (EOA), signed into law in August 1964, allocated $1 billion to support low-income individuals and families. The EOA created the Office of Economic Opportunity to oversee a broad range of federal social welfare programs, which emphasized employment and training programs to enhance the labor market prospects of the poor (Danziger 2001; Haveman et al. 2015; Katz 1989; Patterson 2000; Trattner 1998).

The liberalizing reforms of the 1960s contributed to an increase in the size and cost of the AFDC program (Trattner 1998). The welfare caseload grew from 3 million in 1960 to 10.2 million in 1971, with program costs increasing from $1 billion to $6.2 billion (Weaver 2000). Elected leaders grew increasingly uncomfortable with rising caseloads, costs, and low levels of work activity among program participants. Such changes in the size and cost of the program would become a focal point for reform efforts in later years.

In 1967, lawmakers attempted to arrest the growth of AFDC by enacting policies aimed at moving recipients into the labor market, employing a combination of policy tools that both liberalized AFDC and imposed new work requirements. Reforming AFDC remained on the national agenda through the presidential administrations of Richard M. Nixon (1969–1974) and Jimmy Carter (1977–1980), though attempts at reform during this time were characterized more by failure than success. Nixon's Family Assistance Plan (FAP) aimed to impose a minimum income guarantee alongside work requirements for women with older children, but the legislation failed in the Senate in 1970. Similarly, President Carter's Program for Better Jobs and Income (PBJI) of 1977 proposed an income guarantee to welfare recipients and created public service jobs for those unable to find employment, but the program was never enacted (Danziger 2001; Patterson 2000).

The proposals of Nixon and Ford emphasized programmatic changes to the welfare program that would bolster employment activity among those able to work, although recipients with young children were generally not expected to find jobs. Proposals to increase work activity while providing a minimum welfare benefit or income guarantee reflected changing perceptions regarding how best to address the problem of poverty, emphasizing income-based strategies to address poverty rather than the service-based strategies of the previous decade (Danziger 2001).

During the 1980s, states began to actively experiment in the development and administration of the AFDC program. While Supreme Court decisions of the 1960s had reduced state discretion over the welfare program, several policies allowed states to conduct demonstration programs and apply for waivers to test alternate welfare program designs. The 1962 Social Security amendments contained a provision that allowed states to apply for waivers to test alternative welfare reforms, under which the secretary of the Department of Health and Human Services was granted the authority to approve state waivers. In addition, both the Work Incentives Program (WIN), enacted through the 1967 Social Security Amendments, and the Community Work Experience Program, enacted as part of the Omnibus Budget Reconciliation Act of 1981, allowed states to develop their own demonstration programs to encourage work activity among welfare recipients (Teles 1998).

The Reagan administration (1981–1988) was active in granting states waivers to experiment with their welfare programs. Indeed, most states had received waivers by the time welfare reform reemerged on the political agenda in 1992. Though waivers were initially narrow in scope and focused on welfare-to-work initiatives, over time states began to experiment with proposals that addressed issues related to family structure (namely, teen pregnancy and out-of-wedlock childbirth) as well as dependency on the welfare program (Teles 1998; Weaver 2000).

The 1980s also witnessed a shift in the attention of national policymakers away from addressing the problem of poverty and toward reducing welfare caseloads and costs. The Omnibus Budget Reconciliation Act of 1981 eliminated work incentives that allowed welfare recipients to keep a portion of their earnings before losing benefits and reduced allowable deductions for expenses related to work and child care. Such policy changes resulted in approximately 408,000 families losing eligibility for the welfare program (Danziger 2001; Patterson 2000). By restricting the eligibility of individuals who were working, such changes had the effect of concentrating nonworking recipients on the welfare caseload.

Welfare reform emerged on the national political agenda in the late 1980s, as elected leaders grew increasingly concerned with low levels of work activity among welfare recipients and long-term "dependency" on the welfare program (Weaver 2000). In 1986, less than 2 percent of adult female welfare recipients held full-time jobs while just over 4 percent held part-time jobs.[2] In 1988, Congress enacted the Family Support Act (FSA), a bipartisan act that expanded AFDC while increasing work requirements. The FSA expanded the safety net by extending benefits for two-parent families and instituting child care and Medicaid for families transitioning off welfare. The FSA also required states to participate in the Job Opportunity and Basic Skills Training Program (JOBS), which consisted of employment and training programs for welfare recipients and imposed work requirements and sanctions for noncompliance with program rules (Blank 1997).

---

[2] Statistics available from U.S. Congress, House of Representatives, Committee on Ways and Means, "Background Material and Data on Programs within the Jurisdiction of the Committee on Ways and Means (Green Book)," 1998.

Although the FSA aimed to increase the work activity of welfare recipients, the welfare caseload increased by almost 30 percent between 1989 and 1992 and rates of work activity among welfare recipients remained below 10 percent (Weaver 2000). The work participation requirements within the FSA were relatively modest, with states required to enroll only 7 percent of their nonexempt welfare caseload into the work-oriented JOBS program by 1990. In addition, work-oriented programs emerged slowly because of the limited economic capacity of states following the 1990–1991 recession (Blank 1997; Focus 1988–1989; Patterson 2000). Rising caseloads and stubbornly low levels of work activity led to widespread dissatisfaction with the AFDC program on both sides of the political aisle. Support grew for more significant changes (Heclo 2001).

The welfare program again rose to national attention when William J. Clinton incorporated work-oriented welfare reform into his 1992 presidential campaign platform. Promising to "end welfare as we know it," Clinton proposed a combination of time-limited benefit receipt, work requirements, and job training, alongside an increase in the Earned Income Tax Credit, a refundable tax credit program for low-income working individuals.

Including welfare reform in his campaign was politically expedient, as it allowed Clinton to highlight his past experiences in national policymaking. As co-chair of the National Governor's Association, Clinton had been active in urging Congress to pass the Family Support Act of 1988. This issue also allowed Clinton to capitalize on widespread dissatisfaction with the welfare program that existed by this time and to offer a vision of policy change that resonated with a large share of the electorate. The emphasis on work and individual behavior in welfare reform was consistent with the campaign's New Democrat political project, which was designed to help Democratic candidates amass electoral support beyond typical liberal interests (DeParle 1994b; Weaver 2000).

Although welfare reform was a central aspect of Clinton's campaign, once in office, the administration's efforts to reform the welfare program took a back seat to its focus on health care reform. An interagency welfare task force, consisting of three co-chairs and 32 members, was appointed to translate Clinton's campaign pledges into legislative proposals. However, competing perspectives alongside the multiple commitments and varying interest levels of task force members slowed its progress through the administration's early months (DeParle 1994b).

Clinton's welfare reform bill, called the Work and Responsibility Act of 1994, was ultimately released in June 1994. The act consisted of escalating work requirements alongside education and job training, time-limited welfare receipt, and efforts to strengthen child support payments and paternity establishment.[3] The House Ways and Means Committee held hearings on the

---

[3] *Work and Responsibility Act of 1994*, HR 4605, 103rd Cong., 2nd sess., *Congressional Record* 140 (June 21, 1994): H4779

administration's plan in the summer of 1994. By that time, however, neither party had strong incentives to push the bill forward so close to the November elections. The bill never moved out of committee, but the stage was set for more significant welfare reform policymaking efforts in the 104th Congress (Haskins 2006; Weaver 2000).

ORGANIZED INTERESTS AND NATIONAL WELFARE POLITICS

As the welfare program evolved over the latter half of the twentieth century, so too did the community of organized interests that sought to play a role in the national welfare policymaking process. The mobilization of organized interests coincided with periods of social policy expansion as well as larger national political trends. By the early 1990s, a large and diverse community of groups engaged in welfare policymaking existed at the national level.

Several of most active participants in welfare reform policy debates were service organizations that grew out of charitable relief efforts of the early 1900s. The National Conference of Catholic Charities, for example, was founded in 1910, while the Child Welfare League of America was founded in 1920 (Catholic Charities USA 2015; Child Welfare League of America 2012). Programs and services for the poor were traditionally provided by charitable organizations at the local level. As the federal government assumed a larger role in poverty relief over the course of the twentieth century, charitable service providers increased their involvement in advocacy efforts at the national level (Imig 1996).

Many organizational advocates for the poor were born during the War on Poverty period of the 1960s, when the EOA created an array of social programs that facilitated the mobilization of groups with an interest in poverty. The Community Action Program (CAP), for example, sought to engage poor communities in developing and administering antipoverty programs and permitted community-based organizations to apply for federal funds to help organize the poor. The program contributed to the mobilization of membership-based welfare rights organizations that worked to resolve the individual grievances of welfare recipients and press for enhanced welfare rights and benefits.

The National Welfare Rights Organization (NWRO), a national, membership-based organization of poor people that was established in 1967, grew from local efforts to enhance access to public assistance (Imig 1996; Katz 1989; Patterson 2000; Piven and Cloward 1979). Similarly, the Legal Services program aimed to establish a more generous welfare program with fewer differences across states (Melnick 1994). By 1969, the program employed 1,800 lawyers across 850 law offices (Patterson 2000; Piven and Cloward 1979).

The organized interests that mobilized in response to the federal government's growing involvement in social policy played an active role in expanding social welfare programs. Advocacy by welfare rights organizations, in the form of demonstrations, sit-ins, meetings, and boycotts, contributed to an increase in both the number of families applying for AFDC, and the number of applications that were approved (Piven and Cloward 1979; Trattner 1998). Legal service attorneys brought cases challenging the restrictive state-level requirements that had disqualified blacks from participation in AFDC. This led to a series of court decisions that overturned many state requirements and effectively changed the structure of the program from one that had entitled states to federal funding for the program to one that entitled individuals to cash benefits through AFDC (Melnick 1994).

The 1970s witnessed the emergence of citizen groups and social welfare organizations that would serve as advocates for the poor in subsequent rounds of welfare reform. For instance, the Food Research and Action Center (1970), the Community Nutrition Institute (1970), the Children's Defense Fund (1973), and Bread for the World (1975) all developed during this time. Some of these groups, including the Food Research and Action Center and the Community Nutrition Institute, were aided by federal funding that was made available for research and advocacy during the War on Poverty period. Foundation grants and membership dues facilitated the emergence of groups such as the Children's Defense Fund and Bread for the World (Imig 1996). The growth of citizen groups representing the poor in the 1970s was accompanied by a corresponding decline in membership-based organizations of poor people. The NWRO, for instance, closed its Washington office in 1975 (Piven and Cloward 1979).

In the 1980s, federal support for organizational advocacy on behalf of the poor declined, as did the political activities of antipoverty groups. Cuts in spending enacted under the Reagan administration decreased the financial support available for groups that represented the poor politically, such as the Center for Social Welfare Policy and Law (CSWPL), the Food Research and Action Center (FRAC), and the Community Nutrition Institute. The resulting decline in organizational resources caused groups to curtail political activity or, in some instances, shift focus. For instance, the CSWPL, which had been primarily funded by federal dollars, saw its total income reduced by more than 18 percent between 1981 and 1985. In response, the organization reduced its spending, and its presence, on national political advocacy activities (Imig 1992, 1996).

Whereas most organizational advocates in the social policy realm were aligned with liberal or Democratic causes, the 1970s and 1980s also saw an increase in the political activity of conservative membership-based groups on social policy issues. Aided by a sense of alienation from Washington and strong opposition to the liberal policies of the previous decade, groups such as the Christian Coalition grew in size and became increasingly engaged in electoral politics during this time (Blee and Creasap 2010). Several socially conservative groups that would participate in welfare reform policymaking during the 104th Congress were founded during this period, including the Family Research

Council (founded in 1981), the Concerned Women for America (founded in 1979), and the Eagle Forum (founded in 1972). Although such groups were mobilized around a broader set of concerns related to religion and morality in America, they were united around a view of the welfare system as a causal factor in the moral decline of the country (Weaver 2000).

In addition to service providers, public interest law firms, and liberal and conservative citizen groups, a large number of actors with substantive expertise over the welfare program existed by the 1980s. The welfare reforms of past years had provided funding for evaluation, leading to the growth of a research industry engaged in the analysis of domestic social programs. The Urban Institute, founded in 1969, grew in part through its reliance on government contract support to evaluate the social welfare programs of the earlier decade (Rich 2004). State-level experimentation under welfare waivers provided an opportunity for further evaluation of state programs. The Manpower Demonstration Research Corporation (now called MDRC), for instance, released the results of a rigorous, large-scale evaluation of work and training programs in eight states in 1987 (Cammisa 1995; Weaver 2000).

Growth in the evaluation industry was accompanied by the rise of research organizations with partisan and ideological leanings, particularly on the right. Conservative intellectuals and think tanks would become a considerable force behind the Republican welfare reform proposals of the early 1990s. Scholars including Charles Murray and Lawrence Mead, alongside policy intellectuals at think tanks such as the Heritage Foundation and American Enterprise Institute, increasingly challenged traditional views of the welfare program, viewing it as the source rather than solution to the problem of poverty. By the late 1980s, conservative policy intellectuals had both the ability to articulate a set of policy recommendations for conservative reform and extensive networks for disseminating such recommendations throughout Washington (Toner 1994).

Finally, the role of intergovernmental actors such as the National Governors Association (NGA) and the American Public Welfare Association in national welfare policymaking grew over the 1970s and 1980s. State innovation in welfare policy gave intergovernmental actors considerable expertise regarding the implementation and effectiveness of specialized programmatic reforms adopted under the welfare waiver program. Indeed, the NGA was instrumental in both elevating the issue of welfare reform to the national agenda in the late 1980s and securing passage of the Family Support Act of 1988 (Cammisa 1995).

Thus by the early 1990s, a robust community of organizational actors existed with varied interests and expertise concerning the welfare program. Public interest law firms and social welfare advocacy groups had been active in lobbying on behalf of the poor for decades. These organizations knew the technicalities of existing policy and had knowledge of the relevant actors both within and outside government. Socially conservative groups, many boasting large membership bases, were by this time mobilized and united in a belief that the welfare system was hastening the moral decay of America. Research organizations and partisan or ideological think tanks possessed considerable expertise on both the implementation and the effectiveness of existing programs. State-level actors and charitable groups also had on-the-ground expertise regarding the administration of welfare programs. Many of these organizations had been engaged in previous rounds of welfare reform policymaking and were well positioned to participate in reform efforts once the program reemerged on the political agenda in the early 1990s.

THE PERSONAL RESPONSIBILITY ACT OF 1994

By the early 1990s, reforming the welfare program was a top priority for members of both political parties. Although Clinton's presidential campaign had elevated the issue of welfare reform to national attention, Republicans in the House of Representatives had also been developing their own set of welfare reform proposals. Even before the administration came to office, a group of moderate Republicans was circulating proposals detailing how the party might move forward on welfare reform.[4]

In May 1993, the Republican leadership in the House appointed a welfare reform task force with the aim of developing legislation around which all House Republicans could unite (Haskins 2002). The resulting proposal, given the designation H.R. 3500 when it was introduced in the House of Representatives on November 10, 1993, was cosponsored by 164 of 176 House Republicans. This legislation imposed a two-year time limit on welfare receipt in the absence of work, as well as work requirements accompanied by sanctions for failing to comply with program requirements. H.R. 3500 addressed out-of-wedlock childbirth, an important issue for conservatives, by requiring states to deny welfare payments to minor parents and women who had a child while on welfare, unless the state passed legislating opting out of such requirements. The legislation also imposed spending caps on several prominent social policy programs.[5]

The task group deliberations surrounding H.R. 3500 preceded a more contentious set of negotiations surrounding the welfare reform provisions

---

[4] In 1991, a group of approximately 40 moderate House Republicans released a paper entitled "Moving Ahead: Initiatives for Expanding Opportunity in America." This paper argued that an array of social problems, including welfare dependency, had increased during the 1980s despite continued federal support and included recommendations for testing the impact of mandatory work and time-limited cash benefits (Wednesday Group 1991). A follow-up paper entitled "Moving Ahead: How America Can Reduce Poverty through Work" detailed a set of proposals including increased state-level experimentation and an emphasis on required work activity (Haskins 2002; Shaw, Johnson, and Grandy 1992).

[5] *Responsibility and Empowerment Support Program Providing Employment, Child Care, and Training Act*, HR 3500, 103rd Cong., 1st Sess., *Congressional Record* 139 (November 10, 1993): H9563.

contained within the Republican's Contract with America, a national campaign platform that aimed to unify Republican candidates while energizing select constituencies in the 1994 elections (Balz and Brownstein 1996; Haskins 2006). Introduced to the public with much fanfare in September 1994, the Contract consisted of a set of 10 policies that candidates pledged to enact if elected in the upcoming midterm elections. Third on the list of policy changes was the Personal Responsibility Act (PRA). This act aimed to

Discourage illegitimacy and teen pregnancy by prohibiting welfare to minor mothers and denying increased AFDC for additional children while on welfare, cut spending for welfare programs, and enact a tough two-years-and-out provision with work requirements to promote individual responsibility. (Gingrich et al., 1994)

The PRA reflected a vision of welfare reform focusing on the problems of long-term dependence on government benefits, low levels of work activity among welfare recipients, and perhaps most significantly out-of-wedlock childbirth among poor mothers.

The welfare reform proposal in the Contract reflected months of negotiations in which congressional Republicans worked to develop a welfare reform bill that would both excite the party's conservative base and around which all candidates could mobilize. The dual goals of maintaining conservative support while unifying Republicans proved challenging, as moderate Republicans and Republican governors balked at both the spending caps and the harsh illegitimacy provisions favored by conservative interest groups. The fact that the Contract proposal was more conservative than H.R. 3500 reflected the strong influence of conservative groups such as the Christian Coalition, which were essential to the Republican's reelection efforts but whose favored policies were otherwise absent from the Contract with America (Haskins 2006; Weaver 2000).

In 1994, the Republican Party swept into power at both national and state levels in the midterm elections, gaining 52 seats in the House and 8 seats in the Senate and becoming the majority party in Congress for the first time in 40 years (Balz and Brownstein 1996). This victory shifted the political tides for welfare reform, as policies that had been unlikely under unified Democratic control became a possibility once Republicans gained majority control of Congress (Haskins 2006).

Following their electoral victory, Republican leaders moved quickly to pursue reforms, introducing H.R. 4 (a modified version of the PRA) within the first few days of the 104th Congress (1995–1996). H.R. 4 contained widespread changes to the safety net, including changes to the cash welfare system, food and nutrition programs, child disability program, and child support enforcement program. Most of these changes reduced eligibility or spending on government assistance programs, and some represented a fundamental shift in the government's approach to providing assistance to low-income populations (Weaver 2000).[6]

For example, H.R. 4 imposed spending caps on an array of social programs and included a proposal to allow states to convert AFDC into a block grant program in which grants to states were capped to avoid spending increases.[7] The conversion of AFDC into a capped block grant would eliminate the individual entitlement to welfare benefits that had been established through court decisions of the late 1960s and early 1970s.

H.R. 4 incorporated provisions designed to address rates of out-of-wedlock pregnancy by prohibiting the payment of additional benefits to children born to mothers currently receiving AFDC (called the family cap) and prohibiting states from paying cash benefits on behalf of children born to unmarried mothers under the age of 18 (called the teen-mother exclusion).[8] Known collectively as "child exclusion policies," these provisions reflected the belief that upward trends in marital dissolution, out-of-wedlock childbirth, and teen pregnancy were the result of an overly permissive welfare state (Murray 1984).

With respect to work requirements, the legislation required welfare recipients who had been receiving benefits for two years to work at least 35 hours per week to continue participating in the program, and it required that states move 2 percent of their welfare caseload into work programs by 1996 and 50 percent by 2003 or risk financial penalties. Benefits would be time limited at five years, and states were allowed to enact policies that would terminate benefits at 24 months. The legislation made few accommodations for recipients unable to find work resulting from the lack of available jobs.[9]

Alongside these changes in program structure, program entry, and work activity requirements, the legislation also proposed to eliminate eligibility of legal immigrants for 60 means-tested programs, transform several food and nutrition programs into block grants, and impose drug testing for AFDC recipients.[10]

The significant changes included within H.R. 4 reflected the political interests and influence of several important sets of organized interests: conservative membership-based groups, conservative intellectuals, and Republican governors. Conservative membership groups and intellectuals had actively lobbied for the illegitimacy provisions contained within H.R. 3500 and the Contract with America (Bennett 1994; Brownstein 1994). The family cap and teen mother exclusion policies in H.R. 4 represented concessions to groups such as the Christian Coalition, Empower America, and the Heritage Foundation,

---

[6] *Personal Responsibility Act of 1995*, HR 4, 104th Cong., 1st sess., *Congressional Record* 141:1 (January 4, 1995): H122–123.

[7] *Personal Responsibility Act of 1995*, HR 4, Sec. 301, 302, and 601.

[8] *Personal Responsibility Act of 1995*, HR 4, Sec. 105–107.

[9] *Personal Responsibility Act of 1995*, HR 4, Sec. 202.

[10] *Personal Responsibility Act of 1995*, HR 4, Sec. 401, 501, and 701.

even though such policies were largely unsupported by moderate Republicans and Republican governors and thus threatened to sever Republican unity on welfare reform (Haskins 2006; Pear 1995).

Congressional Republicans also maintained informal contact with Republican governors when crafting the outlines of welfare reform in 1993 and 1994. Discussions became more formal following the elections, as the newly empowered Republican leadership sought to build on the expertise of the governors while enlisting their support in pushing welfare reform through the legislative process (Haskins 2006). On January 7, 1995, half of the nation's 30 Republican governors met with House Speaker Newt Gingrich and Senate Majority Leader Bob Dole to push forward a plan that would transform multiple social welfare programs into block grants to states (Gray 1995). Before the welfare reform bill passed the House, Republican members of Congress and a select group of governors agreed to several modifications to H.R. 4 that would devolve significant policy authority from the national to the state level by transforming multiple entitlement programs into capped block grants (Katz 1995c; Vobejda 1995).

WELFARE POLICYMAKING IN THE 104TH CONGRESS

The analysis presented in subsequent chapters focuses on the period of time between the midterm elections in November 1994 and the enactment of the Personal Responsibility and Work Opportunity Reconciliation Act of 1996. In this section, I provide a brief overview how the legislation moved through the House and Senate in 1995, through two presidential vetoes, through the legislative process once again in 1996, and finally to President Clinton's desk in August 1996.[11]

As noted previously, H.R. 4 was introduced in the House of Representatives on January 4, 1995. The legislation moved quickly through the three House committees with jurisdiction over the various programs targeted by the legislation. The Ways and Means Committee was the lead on welfare reform, as it possessed primary jurisdiction over many of the provisions regarding AFDC, child protection (foster care) programs, and child support enforcement. The Economic and Educational Opportunities Committee and Agriculture Committee also shared authority over provisions involving child protection, welfare-to-work provisions, and child nutrition programs.

In January and February 1995, the three House committees held eight hearings over a period of 16 days, during which time hundreds of witnesses either testified on welfare reform or submitted testimony for the record. The welfare

---

[11] In addition to media reports, committee reports, and existing scholarship on welfare reform, this section draws from the following source: "Welfare Reform, 1995–1996 Legislative Chronology." In *Congress and the Nation, 1993–1996 (Vol. 9)* (Washington, DC: CQ Press, 1997).

reform bills to emerge from the Ways and Means, Economic and Educational Opportunities, and Agriculture Committees on March 15, March 10, and March 14, respectively, were consolidated into a single bill that passed the House on March 24, 1995 (Katz 1995b; Katz and Hosansky 1995).[12]

The Senate held a series of 13 welfare reform hearings between late February and early May. The Senate Finance Committee, Labor and Human Resources Committee, and Agriculture, Nutrition, and Forestry Committee shared authority on the issue, with the Finance Committee acting as the counterpart to the Ways and Means Committee in the House.[13] The Senate was generally expected to act as a moderating force in welfare reform, and advocates for low-income populations increased their advocacy efforts in this chamber (Haskins 2006). Though welfare reform cleared the Finance, Labor and Human Resources, and Agriculture, Nutrition, and Forestry Committees on June 9, June 8, and June 14, 1995, respectively, dissension within the Republican Party over the issues of teen pregnancy and out-of-wedlock childbirth, as well as the allocation of federal funds to the states, delayed progress on the bill until early August. A revised welfare reform bill was introduced in early August, and the legislation passed the chamber on September 19, 1995 (Katz 1995d, 1995e).

In conference, Republican leaders of the House and Senate agreed to a compromise version of the welfare reform legislation. Democrats were largely sidelined from these negotiations. Among other provisions, the conference version included a limited number of block grants and child exclusion provisions that could be enacted by states if they chose. Most of the provisions of the bill were contained within a large budget reconciliation bill that also included unpopular cuts to the Medicare and Medicaid programs. President Clinton vetoed the reconciliation bill on December 6, 1994, as well as a stand-alone version of the welfare reform bill on January 9, 1996. The president's opposition to the bill focused on controversial changes to the Food Stamp and School Lunch programs and limits on immigrant eligibility for public assistance programs (CQ Weekly 1996; Katz 1995f).

After the president twice vetoed welfare reform, Republican and Democratic governors worked to revive the issue in early 1996. At the National Governors Association winter meeting in February 1996, the bipartisan organization agreed to a revised version of welfare reform, which became the basis for revised bills that were introduced in May 1996 (Pear 1996). The prospect of Clinton's signature on welfare reform, however, remained uncertain because the legislation was tied to changes in the Medicaid program. Republican

---

[12] See House Committee on Economic and Educational Opportunities, *Part 1 – Welfare Reform Consolidation Act of 1995*, H. Rept. 104-75 (1995); House Committee on Agriculture, *Food Stamp Reform and Commodity Distribution*, H. Rept. 104-77 (1995); House Committee on Ways and Means, *Welfare Transformation Act of 1995*, H. Rept. 104-81 (1995).

[13] See Senate Labor and Human Resources Committee, *Child Care and Development Block Grant Amendments Act of 1995*, S. Rept. 104-94 (1995).

congressional leaders formally delinked Medicaid and welfare reform on July 11, 1996, and the administration signaled a willingness to sign the bill. The Personal Responsibility and Work Opportunity Reconciliation Act of 1996 became Public Law No. 104–193 on August 22, 1996 (Weaver 2000).

CONCLUSION

The changes proposed by the Republican Party at the start of the 104th Congress represented a stark departure from the welfare reform policies of the past. Among other changes, the provisions included within H.R. 4 aimed to shift authority for welfare programs out of Washington and toward state governments and cap the amount of federal funding in a range of program areas. The legislation included strict behavioral requirements and offered limited supports to aid recipients as they transitioned off welfare and into employment.

As the next chapter shows, the breadth of the proposed changes activated a wide range of actors from different sides of the ideological spectrum, including social welfare organizations and providers; citizen groups mobilized around issues related to women, disability, and families; intergovernmental actors; and research organizations. While many of these organizations were long-standing players in Washington politics, others were relatively new to welfare policymaking.

With control of Congress firmly in the hands of the Republican Party, advocates for low-income populations found themselves at a disadvantage in the legislative policymaking process. Advocates faced the difficult task of defending the unpopular welfare program against large-scale changes and had few allies in leadership positions within Congress.

At the same time, conservative groups and Republican governors enjoyed strong access to the members of Congress tasked with reforming the welfare program. Indeed, many of the favored policies of such actors were already incorporated into legislation introduced in early 1995. In particular, H.R. 4's focus on family structure and devolution reflected the active lobbying efforts of groups including the Heritage Foundation, Christian Coalition, and Empower America, as well as active negotiations with the Republican Governors' Association. Though Republicans were far from united over the strong illegitimacy-related provisions or various devolution provisions, such groups were in a decidedly stronger position than advocates.

The history of the welfare program provides context for understanding the magnitude of the proposed policy changes and the many types of organizations that were active in lobbying on those policy changes. In the next chapter, I use the first set of congressional hearings on welfare reform in the Ways and Means Committee to identify the types of organizations that participated in welfare reform policymaking and to describe the various ways that groups collaborated in their efforts to influence policy decisions in the 104th Congress.

5

Organizational Advocacy and Collaboration in the 104th Congress

INTRODUCTION

At the start of the 104th Congress (1995–1996), the American safety net was under attack. A Republican-controlled Congress had introduced legislation to radically transform a myriad of public assistance programs, including Aid to Families with Dependent Children (AFDC). Among other changes, the Republicans' proposal sought to end the long-standing entitlement to welfare assistance, impose strict work requirements as a condition of receiving aid, and eliminate cash benefits to young, unwed mothers. Such changes represented a fundamental transformation of the system of assistance to low-income families – and a stark contrast from the welfare reform legislation proposed by the Clinton administration just one year earlier.

In this chapter, I introduce the groups that attempted to influence the welfare reform legislation as it moved through the 104th Congress. As the chapter will show, the breadth and magnitude of the proposed changes to the welfare program activated a large number of organized groups with varied interests in social welfare policy. Advocates for the poor actively participated in policymaking debates, as did women's and civil rights organizations, religious organizations, intergovernmental groups, education and health professionals, liberal and conservative policy intellectuals, charitable service providers, and conservative "traditional values" groups. These organizations possessed a wide array of resources, including membership bases of active voters, experience with program administration, and policy expertise, as well as ties to different members of Congress and the Clinton administration.

To describe the types of organized interests that were active on welfare reform, the chapter relies on an analysis of 15 days of congressional welfare reform hearings in early 1995. The hearings, which were held by the House Ways and Means Committee and Senate Finance Committee between January and April 1995, represented the first set of major congressional hearings on welfare reform in the 104th Congress. The hearings covered a wide range of topics including the structural transformation of the Aid to Families with Dependent Children (AFDC) program, the transition from welfare to work, states' perspectives on welfare reform, the problems of teen pregnancy and out-of-wedlock childbirth, and Supplemental Security Income (SSI) program.[1]

The chapter proceeds as follows. In the first part of the chapter, I present data on the types of organizations that participated in congressional welfare reform hearings. This discussion highlights several types of diversity across active interests, including diversity with respect to the professional identity, policy domain, and ideological or partisan affiliation of organizations. The second part of the chapter describes informal and formal collaboration by the organized interests that testified or submitted testimony for the record during congressional hearings. The final part of the chapter summarizes the chapter's key points and concludes.

ORGANIZATIONAL ADVOCACY ON WELFARE REFORM IN THE 104TH CONGRESS

A heterogeneous set of actors participated in the first major set of congressional welfare reform hearings, held before the Subcommittee on Human Resources in the House Ways and Means Committee and the Senate Finance Committee in early 1995.[2] These two committees had primary jurisdiction over most programs targeted by the welfare reform legislation and were the lead actors

---

[1] Although organized interests can and do engage in many types of lobbying tactics, testifying and submitting testimony in congressional hearings represent a common activity for most organizations. While legislators are strategic in selecting witnesses to testify, the hearings analyzed in this section include witnesses who were invited to testify as well as those who were not invited but submitted written testimony for the record. Indeed, the extent of interest in welfare reform prompted legislators to include an additional day of hearings in both the House and the Senate in which additional interested organizations were permitted to testify (see Haskins 2006). As a result, groups did not need to have been invited by Republican leaders in Congress to be included in the data. For these reasons, the hearings data analyzed in this chapter are likely to provide a comprehensive view of organizational interest in welfare reform.

[2] The hearings analyzed in this chapter include: *Contract with America – Welfare Reform: Hearing before the Subcommittee on Human Resources of the Committee on Ways and Means, United States House of Representatives*, 104th Cong. (1995); *States' Perspectives on Welfare Reform: Hearing before the Committee on Finance, United States Senate*, 104th Cong. (1995); *Broad Policy Goals of Welfare Reform: Hearing before the Committee on Finance, United States Senate*, 104th Cong. (1995); *Administration's View on Welfare Reform: Hearing before the Committee on Finance, United States Senate*, 104th Cong. (1995); *Teen Parents and Welfare Reform: Hearing before the Committee on Finance, United States Senate*, 104th Cong. (1995); *Welfare to Work: Hearing before the Committee on Finance, United States Senate*, 104th Cong. (1995); *Growth of the Supplemental Security Income Program: Hearing before the Committee on Finance, United States Senate*, 104th Cong. (1995); *Welfare Reform – Views of Interested Organizations: Hearing before the Committee on Finance, United States Senate*, 104th Cong. (1995); *Child Welfare Programs: Hearing before the Committee on Finance, United States Senate*,

on welfare reform in Congress. Over the course of 15 days, 231 groups and individuals either testified in person or submitted written testimony for the record. Of these 231 groups and individuals, 44 were members of Congress or represented the Clinton administration and 18 were private individuals with no obvious organizational affiliation. The national government actors and private individuals are excluded from the analysis presented here.[3]

The next section categorizes organizational participants in three ways: by professional and nonprofessional interest, by policy domain, and by ideology. Although there are several ways to categorize groups, such as by profession or economic sector represented, these three distinctions correspond to the three types of diversity that emerge as salient to groups' collaborative lobbying efforts during welfare reform.

Professional Diversity among Organized Interests during Welfare Reform

Table 5.1 presents summary data on the types of organizations that either testified or submitted written testimony during the 15 days of congressional hearings. In this table, groups are categorized by their professional identity. This means that I divide groups into those representing vocational and non-vocational interests and then separate vocational groups into various professions (social service provider, intergovernmental actor, union, etc.). This method of categorizing organizations is the most prevalent way to categorize organized interests in the interest group literature (see, e.g., Baumgartner et al. 2009; Baumgartner and Leech 1998; Schlozman and Tierney 1986). Throughout the book, I refer to differences that relate to the professional identity of groups as *professional diversity*.

Table 5.1 shows that of the 169 organizations and actors, approximately 33 percent are citizen groups, a category that includes membership and nonmembership organizations that represent non-vocational interests. Just over one-third of the citizen groups (13 percent of all organized interests) are mobilized specifically around social welfare issues such as poverty or hunger. This category includes organizations of poor people, such as the National Union

---

104th Cong. (1995); *Welfare Reform Wrap-Up: Hearing before the Committee on Finance, United States Senate*, 104th Cong. (1995).

[3] The analysis presented in this section is similar to Winston's (2002) analysis of interest group involvement in welfare reform. In her chapter entitled "The Role of 'Factions' in the National Welfare Debate" (chap. 3), Winston describes the organizations that either testified or submitted testimony for the record during congressional hearings on welfare reform. While my method for identifying the population of interest actors is similar to Winston's, our goals and coding schemes differ. Winston's aim is to use the national analysis as a benchmark for comparing interest group activity across states. My aim is to use the national analysis to provide a broad overview of the type of organizations active in the welfare debate and identify how they differed with respect to the resources they use to influence legislators' decisions. Thus I divide the organizations in a variety of ways to demonstrate how organizations differ with respect to professional interest, policy sector, and ideology.

TABLE 5.1 *Organizational Involvement in Welfare Reform Hearings*

Type of Organization	N	%
Citizen Group		
Social Welfare Focus	22	13.0%
Other Focus	34	20.1%
Social Welfare Service Provider		
Social Welfare Service Provider	23	13.6%
Public Interest Law Firm	8	4.7%
Intergovernmental Group or Individual	30	17.8%
Research Group or Individual		
Research Organization	20	11.8%
Individual Expert	9	5.3%
Professional Organization	7	4.1%
Corporation, Business, or Trade Association	6	3.6%
Union	6	3.6%
Religious Organization	4	2.4%
Total	169	100.0%

Source: The list of organizations is drawn from witness lists from welfare reform hearings held in the House Ways and Means Committee Subcommittee on Human Resources and the Senate Finance Committee between January and April of 1995.

of the Homeless and the Welfare Rights Organizing Coalition, as well as organizations that advocate on behalf of poor people or poverty-related issues, such as the Coalition on Human Needs. The remaining citizen groups (20 percent of all organized interests) are mobilized around other issues or populations including women, children and families, traditional values, and the disabled.[4]

The remaining groups are mobilized around different types of vocational interests. For example, 18 percent of organizations that testified are service providers such as the United Way of America (14 percent of all organized actors) or public interest law firms that provide legal services to the poor, such as the Legal Assistance Foundation of Chicago (5 percent of all organized actors). Approximately 18 percent of organized interests are intergovernmental actors. This category includes agencies such as the California Department of Social Services, as well as professional associations of public employees, such as the National Governors Association and the American Public Welfare Association.

---

[4] Only those organizations with an explicit focus on poverty, hunger, or homelessness are included in the category of "social welfare focus." Organizations that focus on children and families but do not focus exclusively on poor children and families are not included in this category.

Organizations specializing in research, such as the Heritage Foundation and MDRC (formerly the Manpower Demonstration Research Corporation), represent approximately 12 percent of those that testified or submitted testimony, while individual experts represent 5 percent.

The hearings data show that relatively few organizations testified on behalf of unions, religious organizations, private professional interests, and business or trade associations.[5] Business and professional interests active during welfare reform hearings, each representing 4 percent of organizations testifying, include professional groups engaged in the delivery of services to children and disabled populations, such as the American Academy of Pediatrics; for-profit businesses involved in child support enforcement and collection, such as the Child Support Council; and general business interests such as the U.S. Chamber of Commerce. Unions and religious organizations represent 4 percent and 2 percent of organizations that testified, respectively. Such groups include the Service Employees International Union and the Evangelical Lutheran Church of America.

Because many studies of interest groups categorize groups by their professional identity, it is possible to compare the distribution of groups active on welfare reform to the distribution of groups active in Washington. Such a comparison underscores the atypical nature of organizational advocacy in the social policy realm. Specifically, the population of groups testifying during welfare reform does not mirror the larger Washington lobbying community, where corporations, trade associations, and professional interests dominate. A leading study of group participants across a sample of 98 national policy issues found that 35 percent of major participants were corporations or trade associations, 11 percent were professional organizations, 26 percent were citizen groups (many of which do not represent social welfare interests), 5 percent were government associations, 6 percent were unions, and 16 percent were other types of groups (Baumgartner et al. 2009: 13).

In part, the absence of corporations, trade associations, and professional organizations during welfare reform hearings reflects the fact that the Republican welfare reform bill aligned with the interests of many business and professional groups and was unlikely to change significantly given the Republican's control of the House and Senate. In her discussion of organizational involvement during welfare reform, Winston (2002) notes that while some business-oriented groups demonstrated interest in welfare reform, their involvement remained limited. She argues that such groups "were broadly supportive of [welfare reform's] direction ... and they attempted to stay abreast of negotiations about it, but otherwise they invested their resource elsewhere ... With welfare reform going in a conservative

---

[5] The category of "religious organization" includes various congregations but does not include religious-affiliated service organizations such as Catholic Charities USA and the Council of Jewish Federations. The latter are coded as service organizations.

direction, they did need to get very involved" (93). Thus while there is evidence that some business-oriented groups monitored welfare reform hearings, such groups likely did not need to testify because the legislation already reflected their interests (Winston 2002).

Yet the absence of professional and business interests during welfare reform also indicates that social welfare policy programs and issues have traditionally been of limited relevance to many of the business-oriented groups that dominate Washington politics. Even in the 103rd Congress, when Democrats held the majority and the direction of welfare reform was decidedly less conservative, businesses and professional associations represented an extremely small percentage of groups testifying during congressional hearings. Rather, advocacy groups, policy experts, intergovernmental groups, and government officials dominated hearings testimony (Weaver 2000: 142).

As Chapters 6 and 7 show, differences with respect to professional identity have implications for the type of information that groups bring to their lobbying activities. The varied informational resources of groups with different professional identities are clearly evident in hearings testimony, where professional organizations, labor unions, and conservative citizen groups, which are predominantly membership based, routinely highlight the size of their membership, as well as the preferences of their members.[6] This is in contrast to service providers,[7] which call attention to the broader number of individuals served by charitable programs, as well as research organizations,[8]

---

[6] For example, in hearings testimony, the representative for the American Federation of State, County, and Municipal Employee union references "AFSCME's 1.3 million members" in the opening lines of her statement (*Contract with America – Welfare Reform: Hearings before the Subcommittee on Human Resources in the Committee on Ways and Means*, 991), while the representative of the Services Employees International Union introduces himself as "the director of the Public Sector Division of the 1.1 million members Service Employees International Union" (1119). Similarly, the spokesperson for American Academy of Pediatrics states that he is testifying "on behalf of the 49,000 pediatricians who are members of the American Academy of Pediatrics" (1046), and the vice president for domestic policy from the U.S. Chamber of Commerce describes the policy preferences of Chamber members regarding welfare reform in his written statement (1706).

[7] As an example, the president of Catholic Charities states: "Catholic Charities is the Nation's largest private social service network. With 1,400 agencies and institutions, and 272,000 staff and volunteers, our programs serve 10.6 million people a year" (*Contract with America – Welfare Reform: Hearings before the Subcommittee on Human Resources in the Committee on Ways and Means*, 714). The opening statements of the United Way of America Welfare Reform Task Force's chairman and the Child Welfare League of America's executive director similarly draw attention to the professional activities of the groups. The chairman from the United Way of America, for instance, states that the "United Way of America supports and services approximately 1,400 local United Way member organizations across the country," while the executive director of the Child Welfare League of America introduces his organization as "an association of 800 child welfare agencies, public and nonprofit, that serve nearly 2.5 million children" (1021; 842).

[8] For example, the president of the Manpower Demonstration Research Corporation describes the results from an evaluation study of the welfare-to-work program in Riverside County, California – the "best evidence" regarding programs that focus on transitioning welfare recipients into work. Representatives from the Heritage Foundation and Center on Budget and Policy

which demonstrate expertise by synthesizing bodies of work or discussing the results of particular studies.

Domain Diversity among Organized Interests during Welfare Reform

While most studies categorize groups by their professional identity, it is also possible to separate groups according to the policy domain of which the organization is a part. Within the categories of "citizen group," "service provider," and "research group," for example, groups are involved primarily with social welfare programs; with programs related to health, disability, and education; and with issues related to civil rights. Although some scholars categorize groups by economic sector (see, e.g., Gray and Lowery 1996), this method of categorization is less common than the first. However, distinguishing groups by their sector or domain is important in this study because like professional differences, distinctions with respect to domain also have implications for the informational resources that groups possess. Throughout the book, I refer to domain differences between groups as *domain diversity*.

The hearings data provide ample evidence of domain diversity across interested actors. Several of the most prominent policy domains represented include social welfare, education, and health. The data also include organizations mobilized around social groups or issues, including women's interests, civil rights, and conservative values. These sets of actors do not necessarily represent distinct policy domains, but they do represent distinct communities of organized interests as well as specialized sets of policy issues and are therefore included in this discussion.

Examples of groups representing diverse domains include the Consortium for Citizens with Disabilities, a citizen group mobilized around issues related to populations with disabilities; the National Organization for Women, a citizen group mobilized around issues related to women; and the National Urban League, a citizen group mobilized around civil rights issues. The American Academy of Pediatrics is a professional organization that operates in the health domain, while the National Association of Social Workers is a professional organization concerned with social welfare issues.

Such differences stem not from whether a group represents a profession, but rather from the policy community of which a group is a part. As subsequent chapters show, such differences are relevant because groups that represent different domains have ties to different sets of constituents that they may be

Priorities also present (and dispute) data on the cost of entitlement programs and elaborate on the consequences of shifting welfare to a block grant by providing statistics on the allocation of state funding under a hypothetical food stamp block grant (*Contract with America – Welfare Reform: Hearings before the Subcommittee on Human Resources in the Committee on Ways and Means*, 251; 63; 101).

able to mobilize during a given lobbying effort, as well as expertise regarding different programs and policy areas.

Ideological Diversity among Organized Interests during Welfare Reform

A final way to distinguish groups is with respect to their ideological or partisan identification. Although few studies of interest groups categorize them along this dimension, it is clear that some groups typically identify with conservative interests (such as pro-life citizen groups) while others align with liberal interests (such as labor unions). During welfare reform, a large number of groups clearly aligned with either liberal or conservative interests. Throughout the book, I refer to ideological and partisan differences between groups as *ideological diversity*.

A majority of the social welfare citizen groups and service providers active during congressional hearings advocated for enhanced supports for welfare recipients and against many of the provisions contained within Republicans' welfare reform proposals. These organizations were aligned with liberal interests. Yet there were also advocates for more conservative interests. Nine of the 34 citizen groups are "traditional values" groups that advocated for restrictive changes to the welfare program or for enhanced "fathers' rights" (see also Winston 2002). These groups, as well as several research organizations, were aligned with conservative or Republican interests. For example, the Heritage Foundation and the Cato Institute are conservative research organizations, while the Republican Governors Association is affiliated with the Republican Party. Like professional and domain diversity, ideological differences matter because they provide information about distinct sets of constituents. In addition, such differences are likely to be associated with access to different sets of legislators.

The analysis of hearings testimony reveals that the organizations active during welfare reform possessed different professional identities, were drawn from a range of policy domains, and were associated with different partisan and ideological interests. The fact that the groups active during welfare reform represented multiple professions, policy domains, and ideologies means that the *potential* for collaboration between groups with diverse informational resources existed. Chapters 6 and 7 provide more detail on coalitions that were diverse along such dimensions. In the next section, I introduce the various ways that organizations collaborated in pursuit of their shared policy goals.

FORMAL AND INFORMAL COLLABORATION DURING WELFARE REFORM

Interest groups collaborate both formally and informally in the policymaking process. In this section, I illustrate the many ways that organizations collaborated during welfare reform. The analysis of hearings data reveals the participation of formal coalitions that represented distinct organizations, as well as informal coalitions, in which partnerships did not necessarily develop into separate organizational entities. As the section shows, coalitions at times united groups that were not diverse but rather were similar with respect to profession, domain, or ideology. In addition, coalitions were present among both conservative and liberal interests, though far more prevalent among the latter.

Formal Collaboration

I begin by focusing on formal coalitions. In this analysis, a formal coalition consists of any organization or named partnership whose members consist of different organizational entities.[9] This definition includes associations such as the Child Welfare League of America, whose membership consists of a range of groups involved in the administration of child welfare services, but it does not include associations such as the United Way of America, a national social service group, or the ARC, a national disability advocacy group, whose membership consists entirely of local, state, or regional United Way or ARC organizations. In addition, because their membership consists of different groups, trade associations such as the American Rehabilitation Association and business associations such as the U.S. Chamber of Commerce are coded as coalitions.[10] In this analysis, the definition includes organizations with both individuals and organizations as members but excludes organizations whose membership consists entirely of individuals. Therefore, several welfare rights and membership-based antipoverty organizations are not included in this category, despite the fact that the organization's name contains the word *coalition*.

Twenty-three formal policy coalitions testified in person or submitted testimony during welfare reform hearings, representing approximately 14 percent of all organized actors.[11] Most coalitions are citizen groups representing the poor,

[9] To determine whether an organization met the definition of a "coalition," I examined organizational statements in hearings testimony. Most organizations identified the character of their membership immediately in their oral or written statements. For organizations in which the character of the membership was unclear, I examined organizational websites and history. While the categorization was straightforward for a majority of organizations, three organizations could not be categorized.

[10] Though these types of organizations are not typically categorized as coalitions, they are likely to function similarly when they lobby legislators. For instance, for both a formal coalition and trade association, establishing an organizational position is likely to require at least some degree of agreement across member organizations that may be similar in their professional orientation but nevertheless represent distinct organizational entities. In addition, the information communicated by a trade association or a peak business association is similar to the information communicated by a coalition in that the organization communicates policy preference alignment across different types of actors.

[11] The full list of coalitions is American Fathers' Coalitions, Coalition on Women and Job Training, Consortium for Citizens with Disabilities, Council of Presidents of National Women's Rights

women, and children. They include local and state coalitions, such as the Day Care Action Council of Illinois and the Pittsburgh-based Coalition to Stop Welfare Cuts, as well as national coalitions, such as the Adoption Coalition. Some of the formal coalitions had been active in national or state politics for at least a decade. For example, the Coalition on Human Needs, a partnership between organizations concerned with low-income and vulnerable populations, was founded in 1981 in response to President Reagan's proposed changes to human needs programs (Coalition on Human Needs 2012). While many of the formal coalitions represent long-standing partnerships, a small number represent ad hoc partnerships organized to either support or oppose specific provisions of welfare reform. For instance, the Child Exclusion Task Force was an ad hoc coalition formed to oppose the child exclusion provisions in the Personal Responsibility Act. Finally, few formal coalitions – 2 of the 23 – represented conservative interests.

Informal Collaboration

The number of formal policy coalitions that testified or submitted testimony during congressional hearings understates the extent of collaborative activity among organized interests. In addition to formal collaboration, the hearings data provide considerable evidence of informal collaboration, in which a set of organized interests works collaboratively but does not necessarily form a separate organization. For example, an informal coalition can refer to a set of organizations that meets periodically to coordinate policy positions on welfare reform, a set of organizations that cosigns a statement that is submitted during hearings, or a set of organizations that works in partnership to contact and distribute information to congressional offices.

Informal policy coalitions are evident in several ways in the hearings data, reflecting the many ways that groups work informally in partnership. For instance, groups drew attention to joint support or opposition from other organizations in their statements, providing evidence of collaboration behind the scenes. In testimony before the Subcommittee on Human Resources in the House Ways and Means Committee, the president of the Religious Action Center of Reform Judaism (RAC), a Jewish social justice advocacy organization, stated:

Organizations, Day Care Action Council of Illinois, Family Resource Coalition, National Task Force on Violence against Women, National Congress of American Indians, National Indian Child Welfare Association, Adoption Coalition, Child Welfare League of America, Chinatown Resource Center Family Service America, Indian and Native American Employment and Training Coalition, Child Exclusion Task Force, Coalition on Human Needs, Coalition to Stop Welfare Cuts, Public Welfare Coalition, Save our Security Coalition, Work, Welfare, and Families Coalition of Illinois, American Rehabilitation Association, Child Support Council, and the U.S. Chamber of Commerce.

I come to you today on behalf of the Reform Jewish Movement; the Conservative Jewish Movement; the Reconstructionist Jewish Movement; the large umbrella community relations organization in the United States, the National Jewish Community Relations Advisory Council; the North American Association of Jewish Homes and Housing for the Aging; and the Council of Jewish Federations.[12]

In this statement, the RAC president identifies a set of organizations that supports the testimony and stated policy preferences of the RAC – a statement the president is unlikely to have made without first consulting the other organizations. Thus the statement illustrates informal collaboration between a set of religious organizations.

Organized interests also included lists of cosignatories to hearings testimony. While cosigning a document is not necessarily a costly undertaking, it does reflect working together behind the scenes. For example, the United Way submitted a written statement entitled "The Role of Charities on Welfare Reform" and included with the statement a list of cosignatories, which included 11 national service organizations such as the Family Services of America and the YWCA of the U.S.A., as well as more than 150 state and local United Ways.[13] The list of cosignatories represents an informal policy coalition and provides evidence of preference alignment across charitable providers. Similarly, the Council of Presidents of National Women's Rights Organizations included a list of 27 cosignatories to its "National Women's Pledge on Welfare Reform: Principles for Eliminating Poverty" during Senate Finance Committee hearings, representing an informal coalition that coalesced around a specific set of welfare reform goals.[14]

These coalitions provide just a few examples of the informal coalitions that participated in welfare reform; the vast majority of collaborative efforts are described in subsequent chapters. The examples provide evidence of informal coalitions that do not appear in lists of congressional witnesses, while illustrating the many ways that informal coalitions present themselves in the data. Considering informal collaboration is important for this study because diversity within coalitions is theorized to enhance influence regardless of the coalition's level of formality. As a result, it is important to consider informal partnerships as well as formal coalitions.

Diverse Coalitions or Usual Suspects?

As the previous examples suggest, some of the formal and informal coalitions that emerged during welfare reform united groups that were similar with respect

---

[12] *Contract with America – Welfare Reform: Hearing before the Subcommittee on Human Resources of the Committee on Ways and Means, United States House of Representatives,* 104th Cong. (1995), 735.

[13] *Contract with America – Welfare Reform,* 1027.

[14] *Welfare Reform – Views of Interested Organizations: Hearing before the Committee on Finance, United States Senate,* 104th Cong. (1995), 128.

to their professional identity, policy domain, or ideological orientation. The list of cosignatories to the United Way's testimony provides evidence of collaboration across charitable service providers. Such coalitions did not necessary bring diverse informational resources to their lobbying efforts. The cosigned statement from the United Way provided evidence that a large number of charitable providers engaged in service delivery across the country agreed that charities lacked the capacity to care for the millions of Americans who would lose welfare benefits if conservative welfare reforms were enacted. This information was important because it could help legislators evaluate the potential consequences of curtailing federal assistance to needy families. Yet because the coalition consisted of similar types of organizations, the informal coalition was only able to offer a single reason for opposing conservative welfare reform proposals.

That many instances of collaboration occurred between similar groups is consistent with existing research that finds that coalitions most often form between groups that are similar with respect to their area of interest or orientation toward policy (e.g., Hula 1999). Many coalitions during welfare reform fulfilled this expectation, joining together groups that were similar with respect to their interest in social welfare policy or orientation toward liberal causes. To be clear, the theory presented in this book does not claim that coalitions that unite a single type of resource are unimportant. Rather, the theory posits that coalitions that unite a single type of resource do not necessarily provide an opportunity for member organizations to extend the range of information or tactics available to the coalition. However, because many legislators are involved on any given policy decision, and because legislators are accountable to different interests and constituents, there are strong reasons to suspect that broadening a coalition's access to information plays an important role in helping coalitions gain influence in the policy process.

CONCLUSION

This chapter illustrates the types of groups that were active during welfare reform and introduces three salient types of diversity across groups: professional diversity, domain diversity, and ideological diversity. Though the groups that testified in the initial welfare reform hearings were largely unrepresentative of the Washington lobbying community as a whole, such groups represented a range of professional identities, were engaged in different policy domains, and some were affiliated with distinct partisan or ideological interests.

The chapter also provides evidence of collaboration among organized interests during welfare reform and offers several examples of coalitions that varied in their degree of formality. Some partnerships, such as the Coalition on Human Needs and the Child Welfare League of America, were distinct organizational entities. Yet other partnerships remained informal in nature. In congressional hearings, groups communicated their informal collaborative efforts by including lists of cosignatories in written statements, submitting joint press releases, and cosigning letters to members of Congress, to name just a few examples.

While many of the coalitions described in this chapter united groups that were similar, others drew together groups that differed with respect to the professional, domain, or ideological identity. The next chapter explores such diverse coalitions in greater depth and, in doing so, analyzes the empirical support for the *resource mobilization mechanism* of the theory of diverse coalitions. Specifically, the chapter examines the extent to which coalitions that contained professional diversity, domain diversity, or ideological diversity increased access to information and lobbying tactics.

6

Collaboration and the Mobilization of Diverse Resources

INTRODUCTION

Interest groups collaborate, in part, to mobilize the resources necessary for reaching the many legislators involved in any given policy decision. By working in partnership, a set of organizations is able to devote more hours and dedicate more organizational resources to a given lobbying effort. The theory developed in Chapter 2, however, posits that it is not simply the number of resources that helps a coalition gain legislative influence. Rather, it is diversity of coalitional resources that matters for coalition influence. According to the *resource mobilization mechanism* of the theory of diverse coalitions, coalitional diversity is important because it draws together varying forms of information and enables a wide array of tactics for communicating information. Informational and tactical heterogeneity in turn allows a set of organizations to reach the multiple legislators involved in policymaking and, in doing so, helps a coalition gain influence in the policy process.

In this chapter, I provide empirical support for the resource mobilization mechanism of the theory of diverse coalitions. Specifically, I demonstrate that during welfare reform, coalitions that contained diverse partners united different types of informational resources and allowed coalition partners to incorporate information pertaining to constituents, policies, and politics into their advocacy activities. In addition, I show that coalitional diversity enabled partners to engage in a broad range of lobbying tactics that drew on the unique resources and capabilities of different member organizations.

As in the previous chapter, I focus on professional, domain, and ideological diversity. To review, professional diversity refers to heterogeneity with respect to the vocational or non-vocational interests represented by a group (e.g., a service provider and research organization, or a women's group and social welfare group); domain diversity refers to heterogeneity with respect to the policy domain in which a group is active (e.g., a health policy group and

76

union of educational professionals); and ideological diversity refers to heterogeneity with respect to partisan or ideological interest (e.g., a conservative group and a liberal group).

In the first section of the chapter, I describe how professional, domain, and ideological diversity within coalitions allowed groups to draw different types of electoral and policy information to their lobbying efforts. The second section shows how such diversity permitted coalition partners to engage in a wider array of lobbying activities than would have been possible individually. Throughout each section, I discuss how informational and tactical heterogeneity allowed access to the many legislators involved in welfare reform policymaking. The final section of the chapter discusses the key findings and implications of the analysis and concludes.

DIVERSE COALITIONS UNITE DIFFERENT TYPES OF INFORMATION

The previous chapter demonstrated that both formal and informal coalitions were active in the welfare reform debates of the 104th Congress. While many of these coalitions united similar types of groups, others brought together diverse actors. This chapter focuses on those coalitions that were diverse with respect to the professional identity, policy domain, and ideological or partisan affiliations of member organizations. In this section, I demonstrate how coalitions that were diverse along these lines expanded the informational resources available to coalition members, in three ways. First, I show that diversity within coalitions brought together electoral information, or information about constituents, with policy information, or technical information about policy proposals and their likely effects. Second, I demonstrate that diversity drew together different types of policy information and expertise. Third, I show that coalitions containing diverse partners united different types of electoral information.

Diversity within Coalitions Unites Electoral and Policy Information

The first way that diversity within coalitions expanded informational lobbying capabilities was by bringing together groups that possessed information about constituents with groups that possessed information about policy. Typically, this took the form of coalitions that united groups with different professional classifications or from different policy domains.

Among advocates for low-income children and families, professional and domain diversity within coalitions united the expertise of research groups and service providers with crucial constituent information from citizen groups and unions. By the early 1990s, the policy expertise of liberal advocates was strong. State-level experimentation over the previous three decades had been accompanied by several rigorous, large-scale evaluations of state welfare programs (Cammisa 1995; Rich 2004). Over the same period, academic scholarship had emphasized the use of applied social sciences to support and evaluate government efforts to improve the well-being of low-income populations (Danziger 2001; Nathan 2000). A large body of research existed on the needs of low-income Americans and the effects of government programs, and advocates were experienced in using this research to support their lobbying efforts. Indeed, prominent advocates such as the Center on Budget and Policy Priorities (CBPP) produced their own research, synthesis, and analysis and were regularly called on to present this expertise in congressional hearings.

What leading advocates such as the CBPP lacked was a politically active membership base to mobilize after the Republicans gained majority control of Congress. Because the Democrats had held the majority in Congress in at least one chamber (and typically, both chambers) for nearly 40 years, advocates had long enjoyed access to legislators in leadership positions. Once Republicans won majority control of the House and Senate in 1994, advocates found their access curtailed, as long-standing groups such as the Children's Defense Fund were perceived by newly empowered Republican legislators as politically and ideologically aligned with Democratic interests (Weaver 2000).

Compounding their limited access was the fact that many advocates were social welfare organizations and service providers that had few resources in the form of politically engaged membership bases. The lack of electoral resources was problematic for advocates because electoral resources enhance the ability of interest groups to gain access to legislators unresponsive or hostile to their concerns (Hojnacki and Kimball 1998). Liberal advocates therefore worked collaboratively with groups that possessed large membership bases, including citizen groups with broad interests in child well-being, women's interests, and civil rights, and to a lesser extent unions.

A prominent example of a coalition that united policy and electoral information is the Coalition on Human Needs (CHN). Formed in the early 1980s in response to President Reagan's proposed cuts to social welfare spending, the CHN is a partnership of more than 100 organizations concerned with issues involving low-income Americans. Its membership includes research organizations and service providers that specialize in policy information as well as citizen groups mobilized around issues related to women, civil rights, and the disabled (Coalition on Human Needs 2010). Both primary and secondary sources reveal that the CHN was active on the issue of welfare reform in the 104th Congress, both publicly and behind the scenes.[1]

Early in the welfare reform debate, the CHN formed a Welfare Reform Task Force in response to President Clinton's proposals to reform the welfare

---

[1] See, for instance, Child Exclusion Task Force Meeting Minutes of June 6, 1995, and CETF Alert of May 31, 1995, Box 33, folder #10 and 11, Legal Momentum Records, 1968–2008, Schlesinger Library, Radcliffe Institute, Harvard University, Cambridge, Massachusetts; various documents, folder "Advocacy Groups." Bruce Reed Welfare Reform Collection: William J. Clinton Presidential Library; Weaver 2000; Winston 2002; also see Weaver 2000 and Winston 2002 for discussion and indicators of CHN activities.

program. Among other activities, the task force released a statement of principles on welfare reform, coordinated meetings with key representatives, and set up briefing and strategy discussions for interested senators.[2] Members of the Welfare Reform Task Force included social welfare advocacy groups such as the Center on Budget and Policy Priorities; service providers such as the United Way of America; mainstream religious organizations such as the National Council of Churches; public sector unions such as the American Federation of State, County, and Municipal Employees; civil rights organizations such as the National Urban League; women's groups such as the National Organization for Women; and professional organizations such as the National Association of Social Workers.[3] In drawing together groups with varying types of professional engagement in the social policy domain (e.g., advocates and service providers), as well as citizen groups and unions that were mobilized around other types of issues and policy domains (e.g., women's issues and civil rights), the coalition thus brought together groups with research and service-based expertise and groups with membership-based resources.[4]

[2] "Welfare Reform Task Force Principles," Coalition on Human Needs, 22 November 1993, Box 1, Folder "Advocacy Groups." Bruce Reed Welfare Reform Collection: William J. Clinton Presidential Library; CETF Alert of May 31, 1995, Box 33, folder #10 and 11, Legal Momentum Records, 1968–2008, Schlesinger Library, Radcliffe Institute, Harvard University, Cambridge, Massachusetts.

[3] The full list of Welfare Reform Task Members includes American Federation of State, County & Municipal Employees; American Friends Service Committee; American Jewish Congress; Bread for the World; Catholic Charities USA; Center for Community Change; Center on Budget and Policy Priorities; Center for Law and Education; Center for Law and Social Policy; Center for Social Policy Studies; Center on Social Welfare Policy & Law; Center for Women Policy Studies; Child Welfare League of America; Children's Defense Fund; Church Women United; Community Family Life Services; Community Service Society of New York; Council of Jewish Federations; Economic Policy Institute; Family Service America; Food Research and Action Center; Human Services Forum; Institute for Women's Policy Research; Joint Center for Political and Economic Studies; Lutheran Office of Governmental Affairs (ELCA); National Alliance to End Homelessness; National Association of Child Advocates; National Association of Homes and Services for Children; National Association of Social Workers; National Board, YWCA of the USA; National Coalition for the Homeless; National Community Action Foundation; National Congress for Community Economic Development; National Council of Churches; National Council of Jewish Women; National Council of La Raza; National Displaced Homemakers Network; National Legal Aid and Defenders Association; National Neighborhood Coalition; National Organization for Women; National Puerto Rican Coalition; National Urban League; National Women's Law Center; NETWORK: A National Catholic Social Justice Lobby; National Organization for Women Legal Defense Fund; OMB Watch; Presbyterian Church of the USA; RESULTS; Save Our Security Education Fund; Service Employees International Union; Southport Institute; Union of American Hebrew Congregations; Unitarian Universalist Service Committee; United Cerebral Palsy Associations; United Church of Christ; US Catholic Conference; United Methodist Church, GBCS; United Way of America; Wider Opportunities for Women; Women and Poverty Project; and the Youth Policy Institute.

[4] "Welfare Reform Task Force Principles," Coalition on Human Needs, November 22, 1993, Box 1, Folder "Advocacy Groups." Bruce Reed Welfare Reform Collection: William J. Clinton Presidential Library.

A second example of a liberal coalition that united groups with varying electoral and policy information is the Child Exclusion Task Force (CETF), an ad hoc policy coalition aimed to prevent the adoption of policies that denied welfare benefits to a child if the mother was younger than age 18 or gave birth while receiving welfare for a different child. Collectively, these policies were referred to as "child exclusion policies." The coalition was founded by the NOW Legal Defense and Education Fund (NOW-LDEF), a nonmembership group organized to provide legal advocacy on women's issues, and the American Civil Liberties Union (ACLU), a membership-based public interest law firm that engages in legal advocacy on issues related to civil rights.[5] While some of the nearly 100 partner organizations of the CETF were nonmembership organizations engaged in social policy advocacy, research, or service delivery, others were membership-based groups representing different issues and policy domains, such as the NARAL (the National Abortion and Reproductive Rights Action League), the National Consumers League, and the Service Employees International Union.[6] In addition to being diverse with respect to profession and

---

[5] Box 33, folders 4 and 5, Legal Momentum Records, 1968–2008, Schlesinger Library, Radcliffe Institute, Harvard University, Cambridge, Massachusetts.

[6] Submitted testimony of the Child Exclusion Task Force, December 1994. "Contract with America – Welfare Reform." U.S. House of Representatives Committee on ways and Means, Subcommittee on Human Resources, 1625–1626. The full list of members (as of December 1994) is Advocates for Youth; American Association of University Women; Americans for Democratic Action; American Friends Service Committee; Association for Children for Enforcement of Support, Inc.; BPW (USA); Boston Women's Health Book Collective; Bread for the World; California Homeless and Housing Coalition; California Women's Law Center; Catholics for a Free Choice; Center for Advancement of Public Policy; Center for Community Change; Center for Constitutional Rights; Center for Law and Social Policy (CLASP); Center for Women Policy Studies; Center on Social Welfare Policy and Law; Child Care Law Center; Church Women United; Coalition of Labor Union Women; Coalition on Human Needs; Connecticut Alliance for Basic Human Needs; D.C. Rape Crisis Center; Eight Day Center for Justice, Chicago; Feminist Majority; Feminists for Life; Food Research and Action Center; Institute of Sisters of Mercy of the Americas, Leadership Team; Interfaith Impact; Jesuit Social Ministries National Office; Justice, Economic Dignity, and Independence for Women (Utah); Labor Project for Working Families; Legal Assistance Resource Center of Connecticut; Los Angeles Coalition to End Homelessness; Lutheran Office for Governmental Affairs, ELCA; Maryland Food Committee; Mennonite Central Committee, WDC; Mississippi Human Services Coalition; 9 to 5: National Association of Working Women; NARAL; NOW; National Abortion Federation; National Association for the Education of Young Children; National Association of Child Advocates; National Association of Social Workers; National Black Women's Health Project; National Coalition for the Homeless; National Consumers League; National Council of Churches; National Council of Jewish Women; National Council on Family Relations; National Jewish Community Relationship Advisory Council; National Low Income Housing Coalition; National Welfare Rights and Reform Union; National Welfare Rights Union; National Women's Conference Committee; National Women's Law Center; Ohio Association of Child Caring Agencies; Planned Parenthood Federation of America; Pratt Institution Center for Community and Environmental Development (Brooklyn); Religions Coalition for Reproductive Choice; Seamless Garment Network, Inc.; Service Employees International Union; Sigma Gamma Rho; Unitarian Universalist Association; Unitarian Universalist Service Committee; United Church of

policy domain, the CETF also included ideological diversity, as some partners, such as NARAL, were ardent supporters of reproductive rights, while others, such as Catholic Charities USA and Feminists for Life, were staunch opponents of abortion.

Among conservative organizations, informal partnerships between research organizations and citizen groups representing "family values" similarly united the expertise of policy intellectuals with the electoral resources of membership-based groups. As was the case for liberal advocates, conservative policy intellectuals had amassed considerable expertise on the topic of social welfare policy by the early 1990s. Charles Murray's influential *Losing Ground*, published in 1984, argued that social welfare programs such as AFDC were a primary cause of the problems that the programs sought to remedy. Lawrence Mead's 1986 book *Beyond Entitlement* argued that the welfare program contributed to a lack of work effort and growing dependence on government benefits. Other scholars, including Robert Rector of the Heritage Foundation, connected the welfare program to rising rates of out-of-wedlock pregnancy, viewed by prominent conservative membership groups as one of the most pressing social problems of the era (Haskins 2006; Mead 1986; Murray 1984; Toner 1994).

The work of scholars such as Charles Murray and Lawrence Mead offered reasoned arguments for opposing generous welfare programs. In particular, this work provided an explanation as to how and why the welfare program had devastating consequences for children and families, effectively countering the claim that efforts to scale back social welfare programs reflected hostility or apathy toward the poor. The "compassionate" approach to the problem of poverty, such scholars argued, lay not in expanding social welfare programs; rather, "true compassion lay in saving people from a demoralizing and dysfunctional federal program of welfare dependency" (Heclo 2001: 182). In addition to providing an intellectual rationale for opposing generous welfare programs, Robert Rector of the Heritage Foundation offered technical support for conservative proposals to reform the welfare program, routinely providing members of Congress with substantive information, key arguments, and legislative language for policy proposals (Haskins 2006; Stout 1995).

Rector in particular worked to build informal coalitions with citizen groups mobilized around "family values" issues (Weaver 2000; Winston 2002). Membership-based organizations such as the Christian Coalition, the Family Research Council, the Eagle Forum, and the Traditional Values Coalition shared with conservative intellectuals a concern with the moral

Christ; United Auto Workers, the International Union; US Steel Workers; Women Activist Fund; Women of Reform Judaism, the Federation of Temple Sisterhoods; Women Lawyers Association of Los Angeles; Women Work! The National Network for Women's Employment; Women's Economic Agenda Project; Women's International League for Peace and Freedom; Women's Law Center, Inc.; Women's Legal Defense Fund; YWCA of the USA.

decay of America, including the decline of two-parent families. These organizations possessed extensive membership bases and had been instrumental in helping the Republican Party ascend to power in 1994 (Heclo 2001; Toner 1994; Witham 1994). The Christian Coalition, which claimed a base of more than 1.5 million people in 1995, distributed more than 40 million voter guides and became involved in more than 100 House races during the 1994 elections. Yet although such groups supported the Republicans' campaign platform, the Contract with America, the Contract itself addressed few of their primary concerns. As a result, welfare reform became a particularly important vehicle through which the Republicans could reward such groups for their past support and maintain that support into the future (Balz and Brownstein 1996; Haskins 2006).

Thus the informal coalition united behind conservative proposals to reform the welfare state drew together the electoral resources of groups such as the Christian Coalition with the policy expertise of groups such as the Heritage Foundation. Groups including the Christian Coalition were able to provide an electoral base that could be mobilized to pressure legislators to maintain a focus on out-of-wedlock pregnancy in welfare reform efforts. This electoral pressure was particularly important given that provisions involving family formation were generally unsupported by moderate Republicans and the nation's governors (Haskins 2006). Yet because such organizations focused on a large number of issues and had limited staff in Washington, their own policy expertise on the issue of welfare was relatively narrow (Weaver 2000). Research organizations and policy intellectuals therefore provided the substantive arguments to support conservative policy positions. Informal alliances between conservative groups that differed with respect to their professional identity thereby united two types of information for use in lobbying efforts: information about constituents and information about policy.

Diversity within Coalitions Unites Different Types of Policy Expertise

The second way that diversity drew varied types of information to a collaborative lobbying effort was by uniting groups with different types of policy expertise. Specifically, partnerships that were diverse with respect to the profession of coalition members united expertise that arose from different perspectives, specialization, and engagement with antipoverty programs. Such coalitions united groups that were similar in that they were concerned with social welfare policy, but different with respect to their professional roles or area of specialization within that domain.

One example of this type of coalition is the informal collaboration that occurred between liberal advocates with expertise in different program areas within the social welfare policy domain. In his study of the 1996 welfare reform law, Weaver (2000) describes how informal collaboration between liberal advocacy organizations including the CBPP, CLASP, and the Children's

Defense Fund (CDF) made use of the technical expertise of each group, which in turn allowed the groups to respond to legislators' informational needs in multiple program areas. A CBPP staff member interviewed in Weaver's study described how the three organizations provided information on different aspects of reform based on their specific area of expertise:

[The Children's Defense Fund] clearly has an expertise on child care and child support which we don't have. It would be the same thing with CLASP: they have child support. We have an expertise with food programs that they don't have. With the [Earned Income Tax Credit] we obviously are the lead group in town on the lobbying end, on the advocacy end, and on the policy and research end. (CBPP staff member, as quoted in Weaver 2000: 203)

Because they each possessed specialized information about different program areas, the CDF, CLASP, and CBPP were able to provide legislators with expertise on different parts of the welfare reform legislation. During the 104th Congress, this range of expertise was important given the breadth of the proposed changes to the social welfare system.

A second example of a diverse coalition uniting varying policy expertise emerged in the form of long-standing and formal partnerships that united different professional groups within a single policy domain or area of specialization.[7] For example, the Child Welfare League of America (CWLA) is a formal coalition of groups that serves vulnerable children and families. The CWLA was an active participant in welfare reform, testifying five times at hearings during the 104th Congress (Winston 2002). Still in existence, the organization consists of public and private organizations that operate in a wide range of areas related to child welfare, including adolescent pregnancy and adoption, child protection, juvenile justice, and positive youth development (Child Welfare League of America 2012). Members of the CWLA are similar in that they provide services in the area of child welfare, but different in that they administer different services and thus have knowledge regarding different types of child welfare programs.[8]

---

[7] Coalitions uniting varying professional groups within a single policy domain closely resemble trade associations, which are organizations that unite groups within a single industry.

[8] An additional example in the area of disability includes the Consortium for Citizens with Disabilities (CCD). The CCD, an organization that testified during congressional hearings in opposition to changes to the child disability program (U.S. House Congress. House of Representatives. Committee on Ways and Means. *Contract with America Hearings on Welfare Reform* 1995: 1059), is a coalition consisting of groups of professionals and providers that serve disabled populations, as well as groups that represent disabled populations and advocate on their behalf. Partner organizations include professionals involved with mental and physical disability issues such as the National Association of State Directors of Development Disabilities Services, service providers, and national membership-based advocacy organizations such as the American Council for the Blind and the Autism National Committee (U.S. House, 1059; 1468). The CCD therefore unites organizations that administer policies or provide services to various groups of disabled individuals, as well as those that represent the targets of disability policies.

The National Child Support Enforcement Association (NCSEA) also provides an example of a coalition uniting groups with different professional specializations within a given domain. The NCSEA is an association of organizations that represents different types of child support professionals, including public agencies, caseworkers, and judges, as well as advocates and parents. The organization's members engage in unique ways with the child support system, thereby allowing it to offer a set of unique perspectives about the system. When the organization offered a series of concrete policy recommendations in its testimony before the Subcommittee on Human Resources in the House Ways and Means Committee, this suggested that a wide range of professional groups agreed on a set of proposals to strengthen child support collection among poor families.

Moreover, the NCSEA bolstered the argument that different types of professional groups supported its policy recommendations by citing its work with the U.S. Commission on Interstate Child Support in developing the recommendations. The commission also united a wide array of professionals engaged in this policy area, including child support administrators, lawyers, advocates, and public officials.[9] That both the NSCEA and the U.S. Commission on Interstate Child Support included a diverse array of professionals with different forms of professional engagement with the child support system thus communicated to legislators that support existed for a concrete set of proposals from groups with different forms of policy expertise arising from their varying involvement with the system.[10]

From the perspective of "good policymaking," diversity with respect to professional involvement within a single industry or domain is important. Policies that are supported by different organizations within a single policy domain may be more likely to have their intended impacts, relative to policies that are supported by only a subset of interested actors. For example, a policy that has the support of disability advocates, professionals who administer care to disabled individuals, hospitals and facilities that provide services to disabled populations, and researchers who study disability policy may be more likely to achieve its desired outcomes, relative to a policy that only has the support of a subset of professionals within that domain.

Though few observers would argue that good policymaking was the driving force behind welfare reform in the 104th Congress, the varied expertise of different professional organizations did appear to be an important aspect of the partnerships that were active on child support enforcement – one of the rare

---

[9] U.S. Congress, House of Representatives, Committee on Ways and Means, *Child Support Enforcement Provisions Included in Personal Responsibility Act as Part of the CWA: Hearing before the Subcommittee on Human Resources of the Committee on Ways and Means.* 104th Congress, 1st sess., February 6, 1995.

[10] Many of the recommendations offered by the NCSEA were actually mirrored in a report issued in 1992 by the bipartisan U.S. Commission on Interstate Child Support.

issues with bipartisan agreement. Indeed, participants cited the diverse perspectives of members of the U.S. Commission on Interstate Child Support as evidence that interested actors agreed about the appropriate steps forward in child support enforcement. Haskins (2006) notes:

> Members of the commission represented a wide array of interests and views. When the commission reached near agreement on a set of serious recommendations ... it was a clear sign to policymakers that there was a great deal of consensus about the next steps in child support enforcement. (154)

Consensus across diverse actors helped prompt legislators to include the commission's recommendation in the welfare reform legislation (Haskins 2006). Thus in this instance, professional diversity that drew together multiple forms of expertise provided strong evidence in support of a single set of policy recommendations.

Diversity within Coalitions Unites Different Types of Electoral Information

The previous sections show how coalitions that were diverse drew together different types of information, thereby enhancing the informational lobbying capabilities of coalition members. Specifically, coalitions that were diverse with respect to the professional identity and policy domain of member organizations brought together electoral and policy information, as well as different types of policy information. The third way that diversity within coalitions expanded access to information was by uniting groups with different types of electoral information. Specifically, collaboration between membership-based groups that were mobilized around different professions and policy domains allowed groups to unite information about different groups of constituents in their lobbying efforts.

Perhaps the most prominent examples involve the informal collaborative efforts that occurred between children's groups mobilized in different policy domains. Such collaboration is evident in advertisements, press conferences, and protests, to name just a few examples.[11] The Coalition for America's Children (CAC) was active during the 104th Congress in attempting to focus public attention on the children affected by conservative proposals to scale back social welfare programs. The CAC was founded in 1990 with the aim of educating state and local children's groups for political advocacy. The membership of the CAC consisted of organizations mobilized around the needs of children, in a variety of policy domains. Coalition members included regional and national organizations mobilized around general children's interests, such as the National Association of Child Advocates; children's organizations within the health policy domain, including the American

---

[11] See, for instance, discussion of the Stand for Children March later in this chapter and discussions of press conferences and advertisements sponsored by child advocates in Chapter 7.

Academy of Pediatrics and the National Association of Children's Hospitals; education associations such as the American Federation for Teachers, the American Association of Colleges for Teachers' Education, and the National PTA; and mainstream organizations representing different populations, such as the American Association of Retired Persons (Coalition for America's Children 1995; Szerlag 1996).

For the CAC, as well as other informal and formal coalitions of child advocates, collaboration across organizations from varying policy domains drew different sets of constituents – and thus, electoral information – to the welfare reform debate. Mainstream educational and health organizations represented thousands of teachers, school administrators, and health professionals. One source estimated that the CAC could reach up to 40 million people through its membership organizations, though it could not necessarily induce these people to engage in political activity on behalf of children (Szerlag 1996). Nevertheless, electoral information was critical for advocates for poor children, who faced the difficult task of lobbying for government benefits on behalf of a population that did not vote. As a result, child advocates did not simply aim to ally with welfare advocates facing similar resource constraints but rather sought partnerships with a wide range of children's organizations engaged in numerous issue areas. Diversifying the set of children's groups opposing conservative reform provided child advocates with electoral information that, at least in some instances, could be marshaled to exert pressure on legislative actors.[12]

Coalitions that united different types of electoral information are also evident in partnerships of women's membership-based organizations mobilized around different professional interests. For instance, the Council of Presidents of National Women's Organizations, which included 90 women's groups representing 6 million women, created a "National Women's Pledge on Welfare Reform" to communicate opposition from a range of feminist professional groups (Abramovitz 2000). The council consisted of the leadership of organizations such as the Business and Professional Women/ USA, the Coalition of Labor Union Women, and Church Women United.[13]

---

[12] Indeed, collaboration by children's groups during welfare reform reflected a larger effort by child advocates to increase their legislative influence by partnering with groups engaged in different aspects of child well-being. Fragmentation among children's groups was noted as hindering the effectiveness of child advocates in Congress (State Legislative Leaders Foundation 1995; Vobejda 1996). The director of governmental relations at the National Parent Teaching Association, for instance, argued that child advocates historically found their influence limited because each advocate lobbied exclusively for a "narrow piece of the child" – for example, advocates interested in education lobbied only on education bills, while child health advocates participated only in health-related legislation. To augment their influence, child advocacy organizations attempted to engage other organizations in a "whole-child approach" to lobbying by collaborating with groups interested in a range of issues related to children (Stepp 1995).

[13] "National Women's Pledge on Welfare Reform," Council of Presidents of National Women's Organizations, undated, Folder "Women." Bruce Reed Welfare Reform Collection: William J. Clinton Presidential Library.

Similarly, the Women's Network for Change, founded by the American Association of University Women, consisted of more than 40 organizations that were similarly mobilized around a broad range of issues concerning professional women. During the 104th Congress, the coalition released biweekly "Get the Facts" bulletins to inform women of the status of welfare reform legislation and to urge members to contact their representatives regarding the legislation.[14] By uniting membership-based organizations mobilized around different professional interests, such coalitions drew different types of electoral information to their collaborative efforts.

Together, the examples presented illustrate how diversity within coalitions allowed groups to draw many types of information to their lobbying efforts. Partnerships united the membership-based resources, and thus the electoral information, of citizen groups with the expertise of researchers and service providers. Coalitions also united diverse types of policy expertise from professionals engaged in different aspects of a single policy domain as well as electoral information from groups representing different professions and policy domains. Bringing different types of information to a coalition gave coalition members access to information about constituent support or opposition as well as expertise and analysis. This in turn gave them greater ability to address legislators' need for technical information on the broad welfare reform legislation and signal constituency interest in welfare reform. While there are more instances of diverse collaboration among liberals, both liberal and conservative groups utilized partnerships between groups with varying information in their attempts to influence welfare reform.

DIVERSITY ALLOWS GROUPS TO ENGAGE IN MULTIPLE LOBBYING TACTICS

The resource mobilization mechanism posits that in addition to diversifying the type of information that a coalition can offer, partnerships that contain diverse partners broaden the lobbying tactics available to coalition members. Interest group scholars typically divide lobbying tactics into two general types: outside lobbying and inside lobbying. Outside lobbying aims to influence a policymaker indirectly through the mobilization of constituents. This type of lobbying includes press conferences, media advertisements, protests, and mobilizing constituents to communicate with their representatives through letters, phone calls, or emails. Inside lobbying refers to any effort to influence a policymaker

[14] "Get the Facts: Welfare Reform Leaves Women without Job Training or Child Care" Women's Network for Change, October 19, 1995, Folder "Women." Bruce Reed Welfare Reform Collection: William J. Clinton Presidential Library.

through direct contact and includes meeting with legislators or their staff, testifying at congressional hearings, and drafting legislation (Baumgartner et al. 2009).[15]

In this section, I show how coalitions that brought together groups representing varying professional, domain, and ideological interests allowed coalition members to exploit a wide range of lobbying tactics. The first part of this section demonstrates how diversity allowed coalition members to employ outside lobbying tactics such as the mobilization of constituents, protests, and letter-writing campaigns in their lobbying efforts. The second part of this section shows how coalitional diversity also allowed coalitions to engage in a wider range of inside lobbying tactics than would have been possible if group members had acted on their own.

Diversity Allows Coalition Members to Engage in Outside Lobbying Activities

During welfare reform, professional and domain diversity within policy coalitions allowed coalition partners to engage in a wider range of outside lobbying activities than would have been possible on their own. This was particularly true for organizational advocates for low-income populations, many of which were nonmembership organizations that lacked the resources deriving from a politically active constituent base.

First, professional and domain diversity within coalitions allowed groups with limited electoral resources to engage in rallies to communicate opposition to Republican-backed reform efforts. One example is the Stand for Children March, which was a rally organized by the Children's Defense Fund (CDF) to focus public attention on the needs of America's children. Held in Washington D.C., the Stand for Children March was attended by more than 200,000 people and endorsed by more than 3,000 organizations, including parents' organizations and child advocates, educators, unions, religious organizations, and service providers (Weiner 1996; Wetzstein 1996; Vobejda 1996). Endorsements came from a wide range of organizations including some less immediately concerned with children's issues, including the U.S. Conference of Mayors, the American Association of Retired Persons, and the AFL-CIO (Superville 1996). Child advocates, religious organizations, and interested individuals travelled to Washington from states as far away as Georgia, Florida, and Minnesota (Lanpher 1996). Because the CDF lacked an active membership base, it would have been unable to undertake such a protest on its own. The informal coalition consisting of children's groups mobilized in a broad range of policy areas

---

[15] This definition of "outside lobbying" merges the categories of "outside advocacy" and "grass-roots advocacy" presented in Baumgartner et al. (2009).

allowed the CDF to capitalize on the membership-based resources of organizations mobilized in other domains.

Second, coalitions that were diverse with respect to the professions of member organizations allowed national advocacy groups to expand outside lobbying efforts through the mobilization of local- and state-level organizations. Specifically, collaboration between advocates in Washington and state and local service providers permitted protests and demonstrations to take place in cities across the country.[16] Groups engaged in advocacy and service at the state and local levels possessed resources that were particularly important for Washington-based advocates with few individual members and a limited presence at the state level.

For instance, the National Association of Child Advocates (NACA) drew on its organizational members at the state and local levels to mobilize grassroots opposition to Republican-led welfare reform efforts, as well as to pressure state lawmakers on the issue of welfare reform. The NACA, an association of state and local child advocacy organizations, mobilized a "National Day of Action" Speak-Out in February 1995. Alongside Representatives Patsy Mink and Eleanor Holmes Norton and Senator Paul Wellstone, the NACA held a press conference in Washington to publicize the needs of children on welfare. Leveraging its network of state and local affiliates, the organization coordinated simultaneous events in 70 cities and 40 states across the country and collected more than 60,000 postcards from different districts to send to members of Congress (De Vita, Mosher-Williams, and Stengel 2001).[17] In this instance, groups engaged in children's advocacy at the national level drew on the resources of groups engaged in advocacy and service provision at the state and local levels in order to engage in a broad set of outside lobbying activities.

The Women's Committee of One Hundred (WCOH), a membership organization of prominent female leaders, also collaborated informally with groups with a state and local presence to mobilize grassroots opposition to conservative welfare reform efforts. On August 8, 1995, the WCOH sponsored an advertisement in the *New York Times* entitled "Why Every Woman in America Should Beware of Welfare Cuts" (*New York Times* 1995b). This advertisement drew attention to the multiple benefits of the welfare program for poor women. In a press release dated August 29, 1995, the WCOH encouraged its organizational contacts with a state and local presence to "paper the country" with the advertisement in anticipation of Senate activity

---

[16] In this and the following examples, I am categorizing state and local advocacy and service organizations as distinct, professionally, from national advocacy and service organizations. Thus a coalition that unites national groups with state and local groups is categorized as professionally diverse.

[17] Memo to Child Exclusion Task Force Members: Minutes of February 21st Meeting, March 7, 1995. MC 727, Box 33, folder #11, Legal Momentum Records, 1968–2008, Schlesinger Library, Radcliffe Institute, Harvard University, Cambridge, Massachusetts.

on the House-passed welfare reform.[18] This activity aimed to engage organizations across the country to exert electoral pressure on Senators. In other words, collaboration between the nationally based citizen group and an array of subnational organizations allowed the WCOH to engage in tactics that would have been difficult to do independently given its lack of a state and local presence. Together, these examples provide evidence of Washington-based advocates relying on organizations with a presence at the state and local levels to mobilize and exert grassroots pressure on elected leaders.

Third, advocates with limited electoral resources relied on partners with membership bases to engage in other types of outside lobbying tactics. Meeting minutes from the CETF illustrate that coalition members routinely attempted to leverage the electoral resources of groups with membership bases. Recall from the previous section that the CETF was a coalition organized to lobby against the adoption of policies that would deny welfare benefits to certain individuals, such as the children of teen mothers. In preparation for Senate activity on welfare reform, the task force created a grassroots subcommittee to facilitate and coordinate constituent pressure on senators. A memo describing the formation of the subcommittee noted the importance of mobilizing constituent opposition to the House-passed welfare reform legislation: "We must step up our grassroots efforts in anticipation of a Senate debate and heated conference committee meeting around the welfare reform bill. Come to the grass roots meeting ... especially if you represent a membership organization."[19] By developing a grassroots subcommittee, the CETF aimed to exert pressure on members of Congress by mobilizing the electoral resources of its partners with membership bases. The fact that the CETF contained groups with electoral resources, which were often mobilized around different professionals or in different domains, meant that advocates could engage in outside lobbying activities that would have been difficult for groups without membership bases, such as coalition co-founder NOW-LDEF, to conduct on their own.

Among conservative groups, informal partnerships between conservative intellectuals such as Robert Rector of the Heritage Foundation and pro-family membership groups such as the Christian Coalition and Concerned Women for America allowed the set of actors to mobilize electoral pressure on legislators in the form of letters and calls at key legislative moments. For example, on June 21, 1995, six conservative pro-family groups sent a letter to Senator Lauch Faircloth, a strong supporter of provisions aimed at combatting out-of-wedlock childbirth, decrying the lack of illegitimacy provisions in the Senate Finance Committee

---

[18] Press Release from the Women's Committee of One Hundred, August 29, 1995, MC 727, Box 33, folder #11, Legal Momentum Records, 1968–2008, Schlesinger Library, Radcliffe Institute, Harvard University, Cambridge, Massachusetts.

[19] Grassroots and Tops Meeting Alert, July 26, 1995, MC 727, Box 33, folder #11, Legal Momentum Records, 1968–2008, Schlesinger Library, Radcliffe Institute, Harvard University, Cambridge, Massachusetts.

bill.[20] The activities of such membership groups typically occurred in conjunction with inside lobbying by Rector (Stout 1995). As Winston (2002: 91) argues, conservative membership groups possessed "the ability to make their displeasure felt in congressional offices through phone calls and letters if Rector's demands were ignored." By working collaboratively with membership-based groups, organizations such as the Heritage Foundation were able to communicate grassroots support for conservative policy recommendations – an activity that would have been difficult if not impossible if acting alone. Put another way, the inclusion of membership-based citizen groups in the partnership meant that the informal coalition was able to utilize outside tactics when lobbying for conservative policy reforms.

Diversity Allows Coalition Members to Engage in Inside Lobbying Activities

Coalitional diversity also permitted a broad range of inside lobbying tactics. The first way that diversity facilitated inside lobbying efforts was by giving coalition partners access to a wide range of legislators. Specifically, coalitions that were diverse with respect to the ideological and partisan leanings of member organizations were able to utilize the contacts of member organizations to communicate with the large set of legislators involved in welfare policymaking.

The CETF leveraged the differential contacts of its pro-life members to reach conservative Republican legislators. Though the CETF often divided up phone campaigns and congressional office visits in arbitrary ways – for instance, by dividing up a phone list alphabetically – the coalition recognized that different partners had contacts with different legislators. In June 1995, the members of the CETF coordinated a phone campaign to notify senators of the negative consequences of child exclusion policies.[21] Members of the task force distributed the names of senators in alphabetical order, but meeting notes indicate that Feminists for Life, a nonpartisan, pro-life feminist organization, "agreed to assist any of the above organizations by calling pro-life Senators," and that Senator Pete Domenici, a Republican from New Mexico, was to be targeted by a pro-life group, rather than NOW-LDEF.[22]

---

[20] Letter from leaders of six pro-family organizations to Senator Lauch Faircloth, June 21, 1995. Box 31, Folder "Republican Statements." Bruce Reed Welfare Reform Collection: William J. Clinton Presidential Library.

[21] Members engaged in the phone lobbying effort included the American Association of University Women (AAUW), American Civil Liberties Union (ACLU), National Organization for Women Legal Defense and Education Fund (NOW-LDEF), National Organization for Women (NOW), Feminist Majority, AGI, National Council on Jewish Women, Planned Parenthood Federation of America, NFRA, and the People for the American Way.

[22] Child Exclusion Task Force Lobby Corps Meeting Minutes, June 6, 1995; and Notes on Senate Welfare Staff, undated; MC 727, Box 33, folder #10, Legal Momentum Records, 1968–2008, Schlesinger Library, Radcliffe Institute, Harvard University, Cambridge, Massachusetts.

Reflecting coalition members' recognition of the differential contacts of partner organizations, CETF relied heavily on its Catholic and pro-life member organizations, including Catholic Charities, the U.S. Conference of Bishops, and Feminists for Life. Pro-life members, whether formal members or informal collaborators, assisted in the inside lobbying efforts of the CETF by holding briefings for Republican and pro-life legislators and meetings with key congressional decision makers (Rosenfeld 1995; Weaver 2000). In February 1995, for example, Catholic Charities held a meeting on child exclusion policies for pro-life legislators in which representatives from the U.S. Conference of Catholic Bishops, not formally a member of the CETF, issued a statement opposing child exclusion policies.[23]

Representatives for Catholic Charities and Feminists for Life also held meetings with Republican senators such as Lauch Faircloth, John Ashcroft, Chuck Grassley, and Rick Santorum to assess the senators' policy preferences and report on the likely actions of the senators.[24] The lobbying activities of such groups allowed the CETF to communicate with, gather information from, and maintain pressure on legislators with whom antipoverty advocates had few connections. In other words, the differential contacts of coalition partners that were ideologically diverse – at least with respect to the issue of abortion – allowed the set of organizations to reach legislators responsive to different interests and constituents.

Second, coalitions that were diverse with respect to the professional identity of partner organizations used the expertise of partners with different types of engagement in the social welfare arena to inform their own lobbying activities. A July 1995 memo from the NOW-LDEF to CLASP, both members of the Child Exclusion Task Force, offers an example of an organization drawing on the distinct resources of a partner organization to inform its own advocacy efforts. In the memo, a representative for the NOW-LDEF asked the president of CLASP, a social policy research and advocacy organization, to review draft legislative language for a proposed amendment,[25] thereby drawing on CLASP's substantive policy expertise to assist in developing draft legislation.[26] In this

<hr/>

[23] Child Exclusion Task Force Lobby Corps: February 21, 1995 Meeting Minutes, March 7, 1995, MC 727, Box 33, folder #10, Legal Momentum Records, 1968–2008, Schlesinger Library, Radcliffe Institute, Harvard University, Cambridge, Massachusetts.
[24] Child Exclusion Task Force: July 13, 1995 Meeting Minutes, undated, MC 727, Box 33, folder #10, Legal Momentum Records, 1968–2008, Schlesinger Library, Radcliffe Institute, Harvard University, Cambridge, Massachusetts.
[25] The proposed legislative language would replace the family cap policy with a voucher policy. A family cap policy would deny additional welfare benefits to women who had additional children while currently receiving welfare. A voucher policy would provide women who had additional children with a voucher for goods and services, rather than a benefit increase.
[26] Memo from Martha Davis of NOW to Mark Greenberg of CLASP, July 18, 1995, MC 727, Box 105, Legal Momentum Records, 1968–2008, Schlesinger Library, Radcliffe Institute, Harvard University, Cambridge, Massachusetts.

example, the expertise of CLASP allowed NOW-LDEF to draft an amendment that could be offered as an alternative to the family cap policy.

In another example, organizations engaged in service delivery made use of research and analysis conducted by partner organizations in their independent lobbying efforts. The chief lobbyist for Catholic Charities USA readily employed research conducted by the CBPP, one of its partners in the CETF, during congressional visits to lobby against the family cap policy (Rosenfeld 1995). Hearings testimony also provides numerous examples of organized interests using the expertise of their partners to provide support for policy recommendations in areas in which the organizations had limited knowledge. For example, the CWLA cited research findings from the Center on Social Welfare Policy and the National Women's Law Center in its written testimony during House subcommittee hearings to provide information on state-level welfare-to-work and child support policies (U.S. Congress. House of Representatives. Committee on Ways and Means. *Contract with America Hearings on Welfare Reform* 1995, 842–51). All three organizations worked collaboratively through the Coalition on Human Needs Welfare Reform Task Force. In this instance, professional diversity within the coalition allowed the CWLA, an association of service providers, to draw on the policy expertise of members that engaged primarily in research and legal advocacy.

Such patterns are also evident for proponents of conservative reform, as membership-based conservative groups employed the analyses and reports from the Heritage Foundation and Robert Rector in their own lobbying efforts (see Weaver 2000). Rector was cited as "the think-tanker for a large network of people," many of whom supported efforts to use the welfare program to deter teen and out-of-wedlock pregnancy but lacked substantive knowledge of welfare policy (Stout 1995). During welfare reform, conservative, pro-family organizations relied extensively on Rector's expertise and analysis. As the director of legislative affairs at the Christian Coalition noted: "I just know that I can always pick up the phone and call Robert. It's like calling your mechanic or doctor . . . You can get a diagnosis over the phone" (quoted in Stout 1995). Organizations such as the Christian Coalition and the Family Research Council largely followed the welfare reform plan offered by Rector and the Heritage Foundation, readily employing the organization's analyses in their hearings testimony and policy briefs (Rosenfeld 1995; Stout 1995; Weaver 2000). Thus the informal partnership between Rector at the Heritage Foundation and the set of conservative pro-family groups allowed the latter to utilize the findings from the former in their own lobbying efforts, thereby permitting a broader range of lobbying tactics than either could have employed on its own.

On both sides of the political aisle, partnerships between groups that were diverse with respect to profession, policy domain, and ideology permitted organizations with similar policy preferences to pursue many types of lobbying tactics. For example, domain diversity within coalitions of children's advocates allowed nonmembership groups to engage in protests and demonstrations. For Washington-based antipoverty advocates with few members and limited presence at the state level, partnerships with membership-based citizen groups and organizations with a state or local presence allowed the different coalitions to engage in grassroots mobilization against conservative reform efforts. On the issue of child exclusion policies, coalitions that united welfare advocates with pro-life organizations gave opponents of such policies an audience with conservative Republican legislators. For organizations that supported child exclusion policies, diversity within coalitions allowed groups to communicate the policy expertise of researchers as well as the electoral strength of pro-family membership groups. Put another way, diversity within coalitions strengthened groups' lobbying efforts by permitting coalition members to engage in a wider range of outside and inside lobbying tactics than would have been possible on their own.

DISCUSSION AND CONCLUSION

The coalitions and activities described in this chapter demonstrate how organizations working collaboratively drew on the diverse informational resources of member organizations to enhance their lobbying activities during welfare reform. Coalitions that united groups from varying professions and policy domains allowed partners to draw information about constituents and policy to their lobbying effort, as well as diverse forms of electoral information and substantive expertise. At the same time, diversity expanded the range of tactics available to coalition partners. Coalitional diversity allowed coalition partners with few electoral resources to participate in protests and coalitions partners with limited expertise to use research and analysis in support of their policy recommendation.

Thus coalitional diversity was associated with informational and tactical diversity, which allowed coalition members to mobilize a broader range of arguments and activities in support of their policy positions. The value of such diversity was clearly recognized by participants in welfare reform. As one organizational actor stated: "We get different types of information. We all [have] different contacts. We have different constituents with different connections to different members [of Congress]. So we all use those, obviously, to maximize our coverage" (Intergovernmental staff member involved in welfare reform, as quoted in Weaver 2000: 208). By working alongside groups representing varying professional, domain, and ideological interests, organized interests on both sides of the policy debate were able to enhance their lobbying capabilities, providing strong support for the resource mobilization mechanism.

It is important to note that during welfare reform, there is limited evidence that coalitions had the effect of dramatically expanding the financial resources available to coalition partners. Indeed, advocates routinely drew attention to the lack of financial resources in both newspaper articles and archival documents.[27] The lack of attention to expanding material resources likely reflects that few social policy organizations have the large budgets or organizational staffs that characterize the business and professional interests that dominate Washington politics. Perhaps as a result, lobbying in this policy domain tends not to involve activities requiring considerable material resources, such as television commercials or ad campaigns. The limited attention to monetary resources is likely to distinguish collaborative lobbying in the social policy domain from other policy domains, in which lobbying campaigns may be characterized by greater spending and higher cost activities. In such instances, there may be more attention within collaborative efforts to expanding or diversifying material resources.

Yet the analysis suggests that information can act as an equally important resource in the policymaking process, particularly on social welfare policy issues. On both sides of the policy debate, coalitions united varying form of policy expertise with information about different groups of constituents. Diverse informational resources allowed coalition partners to access different legislators and aspects of the welfare reform legislation. Though monetary resources dominate theoretical and empirical explanations for interest group influence within the political science literature, the welfare reform case suggests that an exclusive focus on monetary resources as a mechanism of influence is limited. Information may function as a powerful instrument of influence, particularly in those policy domains characterized by groups with limited financial resources.

---

[27] For example, see Toner (1995) for references to the limited financial resources of advocacy groups. Also, welfare reform meeting minutes between the National Organization for Women, NAACP, ACLU, Puerto Rican Legal Defense Fund, Center on Social Welfare Policy and Law, Federation of Protestant Welfare Agencies, and several prominent feminist leaders explicitly draw attention to the limited financial resources available for welfare reform (Welfare Reform Meeting Minutes, December 15, 1993, Box 105, Legal Momentum Records, 1968–2008, Schlesinger Library, Radcliffe Institute, Harvard University, Cambridge, Massachusetts).

7

Diverse Coalitions and Political Signaling

INTRODUCTION

Interest group coalitions play an important signaling role in the policymaking process. By communicating information to legislators about the underlying support for policy change, coalitions address legislators' uncertainty regarding the consequences of their policy decisions. Yet not all coalitions are equally effective in reducing legislative uncertainty. The theory of diverse coalitions posits that it is the *diversity* of partners that allows a coalition to reduce legislative uncertainty and gain influence. When different types of groups lobby collaboratively, I argue, their diversity enhances the credibility of the information that the set of groups provides. I propose two general mechanisms through which diversity promotes credibility, which I refer to as the *political signaling mechanisms*. First, diversity enhances credibility by providing evidence that groups with varying preferences, specialties, or sources of expertise either support or oppose a policy (the *heterogeneous signaling mechanism*). Second, diversity enhances credibility by providing evidence that groups are willing to pay a cost to lobby (the *costly lobbying mechanism*).

The previous chapter introduced the many types of diverse coalitions active during welfare reform. This chapter provides empirical support for the political signaling mechanisms of the theory of diverse coalitions by analyzing the signals sent and the costs incurred by the coalitions introduced in the previous chapter.

In the first section of the chapter, I analyze the empirical support for the heterogeneous signaling mechanism. Specifically, I examine the content of coalition statements to determine whether the signals sent by diverse coalitions contained information about the heterogeneity of coalition partners. The section shows that coalitions that were diverse with respect to policy domain and ideology routinely communicated their diversity to legislators, in both direct and indirect ways.

In the second section, I analyze numerous costs that organizations incurred to collaborate with diverse partners. While my empirical focus on coalitions makes group-level costs somewhat difficult to detect, the section provides evidence that diverse coalitions experienced resource and policy costs to collaborate with diverse partners. There is also evidence that groups that participated in diverse coalitions lobbied independently and drew attention to their distinctiveness, perhaps in an effort to protect against opportunity and reputational costs.

In the chapter's final section, I review the key findings and argue that the case of welfare reform provides support for the political signaling mechanisms and demonstrates how these mechanisms operate in practice.

DIVERSE COALITIONS AND HETEROGENEOUS SIGNALING

The first mechanism through which diversity enhances credibility is called the *heterogeneous signaling mechanism*. This mechanism posits that when a coalition provides information to a legislator, the diversity of the coalition's membership enhances the credibility of that information by providing heterogeneous signals about the consequences of legislative action or inaction. A diverse coalition might contain signals from groups engaged in different aspects of policy implementation and analysis (such as charitable service providers, government administrators, and policy analysts), groups drawn from different policy domains (such as education, health, and civil rights), or groups with ties to different ideological or partisan communities (such as conservative and liberal organizations), to name a few examples. These heterogeneous signals provide enhanced support for a coalition's policy position, thereby reducing legislators' uncertainty about the consequences of their policy choices.

The previous chapter presented evidence that coalitions active during welfare reform drew together partners with varying types of information. Diversity was important, I argued, because it gave coalition partners access to different types of information. This chapter makes a slightly different claim. Namely, diversity is important because it enhances the credibility of information – in effect, making a legislator more likely to believe a coalition's claims. In this sense, diversity matters not just because of what it brings to partners in terms of information and resources but also because of what diversity conveys to legislators.

If the diversity of coalition partners matters to legislators, then coalition partners should emphasize this aspect of their partnership when communicating with legislators. If coalitional diversity matters only with respect to resource mobilization, then there is no reason for groups to draw attention to their diversity when communicating with legislators.

In this section, I examine the signals sent by diverse coalitions, including statements in hearings, press conferences, and media communications, to determine whether coalitions highlighted their diversity when engaging in lobbying members of Congress. As the section makes clear, coalitions that were diverse with respect to policy domain and ideology actively communicated this diversity to legislators. The fact that coalitions prioritized their diversity when communicating with legislators provides evidence that the heterogeneity of group partnerships, and by extension the heterogeneity of perspectives and interests represented within a coalition, was considered by coalition members to be a salient characteristic of the partnership.

Heterogeneous Signaling from Diverse Coalitions

Welfare reform witnessed numerous instances of collaboration that united groups from different professions, policy domains, and to a lesser extent ideologies. For example, advocates for low-income children collaborated with groups engaged in different aspects of child well-being, while women's organizations collaborated with civil rights groups and welfare rights organizations. Hearings testimony, statements to the press, and press releases suggest that when coalitions contained diverse partners – especially partners that were diverse with respect to policy domain and ideology – coalition members communicated the heterogeneity of their partnerships in various ways.

One way that coalitions conveyed their diversity was by presenting multiple arguments for a unified policy position. An October 1995 news conference attended by prominent women's groups and civil rights and social welfare organizations shows how partners utilized the diverse informational resources of organizations to broaden the range of arguments against Republican-led efforts to reform the welfare program. In this news conference, the National Association for the Advancement of Colored People (NAACP) was joined by the Children's Defense Fund (CDF), the National Organization for Women (NOW), the Consortium for Citizens with Disabilities, and Bread for the World. The news conference was organized to provide an opportunity for organizations to communicate their opposition to the welfare reform bill that had passed by the House of Representatives and the Senate.[1]

During the news conference, each organization offered a distinct reason for opposing congressional welfare reform efforts. CDF President Marian Wright Edelman declared the bills "morally wrong," "unjust," and "un-American." The president of Bread for the World, a Christian anti-hunger organization, expressed his organization's opposition with reference to religious authority, while offering technical policy information about the inability of charitable organizations to care for the poor under congressional welfare reform

[1] "Children's Advocacy Groups Hold News Conference on Congressional Welfare Reform Proposals" October 5, 1995. Text from: *Federal Document Clearing House (FDCH) Political Transcripts.* Available from LexisNexis Academic; accessed February 1, 2009.

proposals. The chair of the Consortium for Citizens with Disabilities discussed the damaging effects of the House and Senate welfare reform bills for disabled children, and the representative for NOW argued that women, regardless of their economic position, would notice and punish (electorally) those supporting conservative welfare reform.

In this instance, organizations that possessed different information were able to articulate a range of reasons for opposing conservative policy proposals. It was not simply that the House and Senate bills were unethical, but they also placed an unrealistic burden on charities, would have damaging impacts for disabled children, and could lead to negative electoral consequences for legislators. The signal sent by the set of actors – that legislators should oppose the welfare reform bills – thus contained heterogeneous cues that drew on the unique perspectives of each member organization.

Organizations also communicated their diversity by explicitly naming coalition members. Figure 7.1, which shows a newspaper advertisement run in the *New York Times* as welfare reform moved through the Senate in late 1995, provides evidence of informal collaborative activities between organizations representing different interests and policy domains. Titled "The Contract with America: How Much Will All This Cost Our Kids?" the advertisement describes the potential impact of changes included in the Republican's Contract with America, focusing on structural changes to child welfare, child care, cash welfare, and food and nutrition programs. A text box displayed prominently on the right side of the advertisement contains a list of organizations supporting the views contained in the advertisement. This list includes several leading organizations from a variety of policy domains, including social welfare advocacy groups such as the Center for Law and Social Policy, child welfare service organizations such as the Child Welfare League of America (CWLA), and membership-based education organizations such as the National Education Association, a labor union of educational professionals including teachers, administrators, and students (*New York Times*, 1995a).[2]

Hearings testimony provides evidence of groups communicating their diversity by explicitly referencing differences across coalition partners. For instance, in her testimony to members of the Subcommittee on Human Resources of the House Ways and Means Committee, the executive director of the Coalition on Human Needs (CHN), a prominent formal coalition of advocates from multiple policy domains, introduced her organization as "an

---

[2] The full list includes the National Education Association, the Coalition for America's Children, the Children's Defense Fund, the National Association of Child Advocates, the Child Welfare League of America, the National Parenting Association, Children Now, the National Black Child Development Institute, the Center for Law and Social Policy, the Child Care Action Campaign, the Food Research and Action Center, the Children's Partnership, Statewide Youth Advocacy, and the Citizens' Committee for Children in New York.

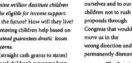

FIGURE 7.1 *New York Times* Advertisement, August 8, 1995
Source: Image reprinted with the permission of the California Wellness Foundation.

alliance of over 100 national organizations working together to promote public policies which address the needs of low-income Americans. The coalition's members include civil rights, religious, labor and professional organizations and those concerned with the well-being of children, women, the elderly and people with disabilities."[3] In this statement, the speaker emphasizes the diversity within the group alongside its size. Although the speaker notes that the group contains more than 100 organizations, members of Congress have no way of knowing how many constituents these organizations represent. Indeed, many of the organizational members of the CHN are institutional actors, meaning that they have no membership base.[4]

Children's advocates, who were active in building coalitions with organizations outside the social welfare policy domain, also routinely drew attention to the heterogeneity of coalition partners in their lobbying activities. The "Contract with America's Children," developed by the Coalition for America's Children and the policy research organization Children Now, provides one such example. A play on the Republican's Contract with America, the Contract with America's Children listed a set of 10 principles that members of Congress were asked to honor when legislating on issues such as welfare reform. On December 15, 1994, Children Now, the National Parent Teacher Association, and the Child Welfare League of America held a joint press conference on the Capitol steps to publicize the contract, which was endorsed by more than 100 members of the Coalition for America's Children and distributed to all congressional offices (Stepp 1995). In this instance, mainstream children's organizations including Children Now and the Coalition for America's Children were joined by social welfare organizations such as the Child Welfare League of America and educational organizations such as the National Parent Teacher Association.

This informal coalition also prioritized the diversity of its membership in its communications. In the press conference describing the coalition of organizations supporting the Contract with America's Children, the executive director of Children Now drew attention to the heterogeneity of member interests by stating the following:

---

[3] *Contract with America – Welfare Reform: Hearing before the Subcommittee on Human Resources of the Committee on Ways and Means, United States House of Representatives*, 104th Cong. (1995), 1065.

[4] In another example, when introducing his partner organizations at the news conference described earlier, the director of the NAACP Washington Bureau announced that his organization was "joined today by leaders of a uniquely broad and diverse coalition of civil rights and women's rights organizations; children's rights groups; those providing direct service to poor families with children; religious organizations; and those who assist persons with disabilities" ("Children's Advocacy Groups Hold News Conference on Congressional Welfare Reform Proposals" October 5, 1995), thereby highlighting policy domain diversity across groups focused on issues related to civil rights, women, children, low-income families, and disability.

We are indeed a very diverse coalition. We not only include Children Now, the National [Parent Teacher Association], and the Child Welfare League, but we include Big Brothers and Big Sisters, the United Way, children's hospitals from cities all over the country, the American Academy of Pediatrics for Dentistry, the National Association of Secondary School Principals, the National Head First, the Coalition of Community Foundations, the Institute for Black Child Development. We come from all quarters of America to say to the kids "We promise to do right by your future." (Statement of Lois Salisbury, "Contract with America's Children," 1995)

In this statement, the executive director highlights the multiple policy domains from which coalition members are drawn, including social welfare, health, and education. The statement suggests that although coalition members represent a variety of interests and are engaged in different issue areas, they are united behind policies that support children. Thus the statement includes information about the heterogeneity of interests supporting a single policy choice.

The Stand for Children March, organized by the CDF, similarly prioritized the range of interests represented by partner organizations. As discussed in the previous chapter, the Stand for Children March was a rally held in Washington, D.C., in the summer of 1996. The rally was trumpeted by organizers as a nonpartisan and nonpolitical event, and a wide variety of individuals and groups were encouraged to attend (Children's Defense Fund 1996). Reflecting the varied interests of attendees and the policy domains from which they were drawn, the rally was endorsed by groups including Catholic Charities USA, the American Association of Retired Persons, the American Academy of Pediatrics, the U.S. Conference of Mayors, and the children's cable network Nickelodeon (Jones 1996; Lanpher 1996; Pear 1996).

CDF President Marian Wright Edelman drew attention to the diversity of participants in her statements to the media, noting on the eve of the event that participants were "coming to stand together across race and class and age and region and faith" (Wetzstein 1996). Such statements highlight diversity across groups active in the rally, as well as diversity among individual participants. In highlighting the diversity of its partners, Edelman communicated that the informal coalition united behind the Stand for Children March reflected a wide range of interests. The message to legislators – from both the informal coalition united behind the Contract with America's Children and the coalition supporting the Stand for Children March – was that many types of interest groups and constituents opposed the welfare reform provisions being put forth by congressional Republicans.

Much like the coalitions that united groups from different policy domains, partnerships that drew together groups that differed with respect to their ideological orientation or partisan affiliation similarly highlighted the diverse viewpoints of coalition partners. Recall from the previous chapter that the Child Exclusion Task Force (CETF) was an ad hoc policy coalition aimed at preventing the adoption of the policies that would restrict welfare benefits to young, unwed mothers and those having children out of wedlock. The CETF was active in lobbying legislators directly and indirectly, submitting testimony during House and Senate hearings on welfare reform, sponsoring media events, issuing press releases, and coauthoring editorials with prominent antiabortion organizations including the National Right to Life Council (Daly and Lewis 1994; Weaver 2000).[5]

In statements to legislators and the media, the CETF regularly drew attention to diversity among coalition partners, particularly with respect to the issue of abortion. Figure 7.2 shows the testimony submitted by the CETF during House subcommittee hearings in early 1995. In its first line of written testimony to members of the Subcommittee on Human Resources in the House Committee on Ways and Means, the CETF stated: "As national, state and local organizations with a diversity of views on many issues, we are united in our efforts to promote the health and welfare of America's children" (U.S. Congress. House of Representatives. Committee on Ways and Means. *Contract with America Hearings on Welfare Reform* 1995: 1625–26). This statement is noteworthy because the task force says nothing about the size of the coalition, or the size of its extended membership base, but rather focuses exclusively on the diversity of viewpoints united behind a particular set of reforms. In addition, the second page of testimony (not shown in Figure 7.2) prominently displays the testimony's cosigners, which include civil rights organizations, women's groups, antipoverty advocacy organizations, and one pro-life organization.[6]

Similarly, on June 14, 1995, the CETF's media advisory announcing a joint press briefing with the American Civil Liberties Union, NOW, Feminists for Life, and Catholic Charities highlighted the diversity among participants by stating, "Despite intense disagreement over reproductive rights issues, both pro-choice and pro-life groups are united in opposition to child exclusion proposals" ("Pro-Life and Pro-Choice Groups Schedule Joint Press Briefing Wednesday on Child Exclusion Policies," 1995). Thus in communicating their joint opposition to child exclusion programs, the organizations also communicated differences across the partners in terms of their positions on other policies. This provides evidence that such groups perceived such ideological differences to matter to legislators engaged in policymaking on welfare reform.

A second instance of ideological and partisan diversity occurred among the nation's governors. Although governors were largely united in their support of welfare policies that would transfer more authority to the state level, the

---

[5] *Contract with America – Welfare Reform: Hearing before the Subcommittee on Human Resources of the Committee on Ways and Means, United States House of Representatives,* 104th Cong. (1995), 1625–26; "Pro-Life and Pro-Choice Groups Schedule Joint Press Briefing Wednesday on Child Exclusion Policies," 1995, Box 4, folder "Catholic Church." Bruce Reed Welfare Reform Collection: William J. Clinton Presidential Library.

[6] A full list of cosignatories to the testimony is included in note 46 in Chapter 6.

CHILD EXCLUSION TASK FORCE

December, 1994

Dear Members of Congress,

As national state and local organizations with a diversity of views on many issues, we are united in our efforts to **promote the health and welfare of America's children.** We came together this past year in opposition to welfare reform proposals that would allow states to deny benefits to innocent babies simply because they were born into families receiving AFDC. As the 104th Congress debates welfare reform, more punitive child exclusion proposals have appeared which could endanger the health and welfare of America's children. The following provisions would severely harm the children of already impoverished families.

- **WE OPPOSE PROVISIONS THAT WOULD DENY BENFITS TO CHILDREN SIMPLY FOR BEING BORN INTO FAMILIES RECEIVING WELFARE.**

- **WE OPPOSE PROPOSALS THAT WOULD DENY BENEFITS FOR CHILDREN WHOSE PATERNITY HAS NOT BEEN OFFICIALLY ESTABLISHED BY THE STATE.**

- **WE OPPOSE ANY PROVISION THAT WOULD DENY BENEFITS TO THE CHILDREN OF UNMARRIED TEENAGERS.**

Our principal concern with excluding children from subsistence welfare benefits is that, if enacted, each of these provisions will hurt the children of already impoverished families. Years of social science scholarship makes it clear that people make childbearing decisions for complex and varied reasons. The promise of a tiny incremental gain in welfare benefits is not an inducement to have additional children. Family values will not be advanced by making it more difficult for poor mothers to provide for their children and escape from poverty. Any short-term fiscal savings gained by excluding children from receiving subsistence benefits will be outweighed by the long-term social costs of their impoverishment and the further deterioration of families already in distress.

We urge you to oppose the anti-child, anti-family provisions.

Please contact Martha Davis of NOW Legal Defense and Education Fund at (212) *925–6635, Debarah Lewis, ACLU at* (202) *675–2312 if you have questions or need more information.*

Figure 7.2 Submitted Testimony of the Child Exclusion Task Force

National Governors Association (NGA) was unable to reach a bipartisan consensus regarding the transition of welfare from an entitlement to a block grant program in early 1995.[7] After President Clinton twice vetoed the Republican-backed welfare reform in 1996, the NGA negotiated an agreement among its members in February 1996 in an attempt to restart welfare reform policymaking. Agreed to by all 50 governors, the NGA's proposal transformed welfare into a block grant but relaxed some of the work requirements and illegitimacy provisions, while adding more federal dollars for child care (Haskins 2006; Rubin 1996). The NGA, in reaching an agreement between the interests represented by the Republican Governors Association and Democratic Governors Association, therefore represented a coalition that was diverse with respect to the partisan orientation of its members.

Much like the CETF, representatives of the NGA drew attention to partisan diversity. During House subcommittee hearings on the NGA proposal in early 1996, for example, Governor Tommy Thompson of Wisconsin highlighted differences across the actors united behind the proposal:

We would like to present to you the NGA ... policy on welfare reform, which was adopted with unanimous – and I want to underscore that – unanimous partisan support ... We also came together, equally divided, with very strong, different philosophies, different positions. We were able to meld those together and come to a bipartisan conclusion.[8]

The bipartisan nature of the coalition was similarly referenced by Governor Tom Carper of Delaware in his statement to subcommittee members.[9] The governors therefore sought to emphasize that partners with ideological and partisan divisions were united in their support of the NGA welfare reform bill – in effect, drawing attention to the diverse actors were united behind the agreement.

Such statements provide evidence that groups that collaborated with diverse partners viewed their diversity as an important characteristic of their partnership. This argument finds further support from the fact that organizations *opposing* diverse coalitions publicly disputed the diversity of interests represented within those coalitions. For example, while the CDF highlighted the range of actors involved in the Stand for Children March, conservative groups highlighted the *lack* of diversity among supporters,

---

[7] While the 30 Republican governors were largely united in their support of block grants, the NGA was unable to muster enough support from the Democratic governors to obtain the three-fourths vote necessary to adopt an organizational policy position (Pear 1995). The Republican Governors Association (RGA) therefore assumed a more prominent role in welfare policy-making in early 1995, while the Democratic Governors Association (DGA) was largely side-lined (Winston 2002).

[8] *The National Governors' Association Welfare Reform Proposal: Hearing before the Subcommittee on Human Resources of the House Ways and Means Committee*, 104th Cong. (1996), 13.

[9] *The National Governors' Association Welfare Reform Proposal* (1996), 16.

categorizing participants as liberal organizations seeking only a government handout.

In a statement to the media, a representative of the conservative Cato Institute noted, "the 'Stand for Children' this weekend in Washington is organized by the Children's Defense Fund and is co-sponsored by the usual suspects among liberal interest groups." (Tanner 1996). The director of government affairs for the conservative membership-based Traditional Values Coalition stated, "These groups are liberal ... [Edelman] did not want to bring in everybody" (CNN 1996). At a press conference hosted by the Family Research Council and attended by several conservative organizations including the Christian Coalition and Concerned Women for America, a Heritage Foundation spokesperson similarly noted, "I really think that this march should actually be called the March of the Social Service Administrators,"[10] thereby emphasizing similarities between organizations in their receipt of government funding or administration of government programs. While children's advocates sought to portray the Stand for Children March as engaging a diverse range of participants from multiple policy domains, conservative opponents disputed the diversity of participants by drawing attention to the dimensions along which participants were similar.

These examples provide evidence that during welfare reform, coalitions that united groups from varying policy domains and with different partisan identities actively communicated the heterogeneity of their partnerships to legislators. Consistent with the expectations of the theory, the heterogeneity of coalition partners was prioritized in the signals that were sent by coalitions engaged in collaborative efforts, providing evidence that diversity was viewed as an important characteristic of the partnership. The activities of groups during welfare reform thus provide support for the heterogeneous signaling mechanism of the theory of diverse coalitions, which holds that diversity within coalitions provides additional information to legislators about the information being communicated by a coalition – namely, that the information is credible.

DIVERSE COALITIONS AND COSTLY LOBBYING

The second mechanism through which diversity enhances credibility is called the *costly lobbying mechanism*. The theory suggests that organizations incur several types of costs through their collaborative efforts. Groups pay a resource cost to coordinate activity, negotiate policy agreement, or host coalitional activities, and incur a policy cost if collaboration requires partners to deviate from their preferred policy position. Organizations pay an opportunity cost by collaborating because they lose the opportunity to build a group's reputation

[10] Kenneth Weinstein, Director of Government Programs at the Heritage Foundation. *Who Stands for Children?* C-SPAN video, May 31, 1996, www.c-span.org/video/?72623–1/stands-children.

and define its unique area of expertise. Particularly in the case of rival organizations, groups may also face a reputational cost to collaborate. This section examines the opportunity, resource, policy, and reputational costs that organizations incur when collaborating with diverse partners.

It is important to note that the data collection strategy adopted in this project emphasizes coalitions rather than individual groups and thus has implications for the extent to which group costs are observable in the data. Specifically, because my empirical design focused on gathering information on informal and formal coalitions, the resource costs of individual actors are difficult to observe in my data. Some costs, apparent from media reports and secondary sources, are analyzed in this section. The analysis also relies heavily on the organizational records the NOW Legal Defense and Education Fund (NOW-LDEF), which co-founded the CETF. These records provide a window into the costs incurred by individual participants of the task force as well as the founding organization itself.

Resource Costs

Resource costs include the material and personnel costs associated with collaborating, such as staff time to organize coalition members and activities, space to host coalition meetings, and monetary costs associated with publishing coalition materials or funding advertisements. The records of the NOW-LDEF provide considerable evidence of the resource costs incurred by coalition partners of the CETF. The task force had at least three subcommittees staffed by slightly different organizational actors: a legislative subcommittee, a "lobby corps," and a subcommittee focused on grassroots efforts. The subcommittee on legislation had more than 10 organizational members, while the lobby corps included more than 25 organizational members.[11]

Members of the subcommittees met monthly through 1995, and organizations devoted staff time to meeting with legislators, phone campaigns, press briefings, and protests, particularly as welfare reform legislation moved into the Senate in the fall of 1995. The task force submitted testimony during House and Senate hearings, drafted letters to senators and President Clinton, created reports detailing the potential consequences of child exclusion provisions, and dropped packets of information about child exclusion policies to all Senate offices (Legal Momentum Records, Box 33).[12] Such activities reflect a cost to the NOW-LDEF and partner organizations,

[11] Miscellaneous documents from the Child Exclusion Task Force, Box 33, Folder 4, Legal Momentum Records, 1968–2008, Schlesinger Library, Radcliffe Institute, Harvard University, Cambridge, Massachusetts.
[12] Miscellaneous documents from the Child Exclusion Task Force, Box 33. Legal Momentum Records, 1968–2008, Schlesinger Library, Radcliffe Institute, Harvard University, Cambridge, Massachusetts.

particularly with respect to staff time and material resources (such as meeting space and photocopies).

Though the resource costs of other organizations engaged in formal and informal collaborative activities are not observable in my data, it is likely that at least some of the organizations incurred considerable resource costs in their efforts to work collaboratively with diverse partners on welfare reform. The CHN is cited by secondary sources as one of the more prominent advocates for low-income populations during welfare reform (see Weaver 2000; Winston 2002). The coalition's activities, including forming a welfare reform task force, holding meetings with key senators and briefings held on the Senate floor, and engaging in other direct lobbying activities on issues such as child welfare are also routinely referenced in the records of the CETF.[13] It is also likely that organizations such as the Children's Defense Fund, also cited by secondary sources as a prominent advocate as well as the lead organization behind the Stand for Children March, incurred significant resource costs to bring diverse children's groups together for the march (see Weaver 2000; Winston 2002).

Policy Costs

A policy cost is present when an organization deviates from its preferred position to collaborate with other organizations. During welfare reform, the policy costs of diverse collaboration are perhaps most apparent for coalitions that united children's organizations from different policy domains. To mobilize a wider array of organizations concerned with the well-being of children, child advocates moved away from direct criticism of specific provisions of the Republican's welfare reform proposal and toward a broader criticism of policies that were "bad for kids." The Contract with America's Children was intentionally worded to attract support from a range of organizations (Stepp 1995). For example, signatories pledged to "ensure that all children get the basics they need to grow up healthy" and "help working families stay out of poverty" rather than to oppose specific programs or policies.

The Stand for Children March similarly diluted its policy recommendations in an effort to engage more participants (Weaver 2000). The event was advertised as a nonpartisan and nonpolitical event, and no politicians were invited to speak. In her 30-minute statement before attendees of the Stand for Children March, Edelman expressed the movement's goals in general terms: "We stand today ... to commit ourselves to putting our children first. We commit ourselves to building a just America that leaves no child behind and we commit ourselves to insuring all our children a healthy and safe passage to

---

[13] Child Exclusion Task Force Meeting Minutes, February 21, 1995; May 31, 1995; June 6, 1995. MC 727, Box 33, folder #10, Legal Momentum Records, 1968–2008, Schlesinger Library, Radcliffe Institute, Harvard University, Cambridge, Massachusetts.

adulthood."[14] For the CDF, the nonpartisan and nonpolitical nature of the event was in stark contrast to the organization's stated policy preferences as well as its reputation. The organization was unequivocal in its opposition to Republican welfare reform proposals in subcommittee hearings as well as statements to the media and to the administration (Haskins 2006; Weaver 2000).[15] CDF President Marian Wright Edelman, for example, urged the president to "fight unwaveringly to maintain the entitlement status of key child survival programs including AFDC, food stamps … and child support enforcement."[16] Thus the organization articulated its substantive opposition to government actions differently when lobbying on its own in congressional hearings and when engaging in collaborative outside lobbying efforts with diverse actors.

Policy costs are also evident for Republican and Democratic governors who deviated from their preferred policy positions to reach a welfare reform compromise. Specifically, the National Governors Association compromise negotiated in February 1996 transformed the structure of the welfare program from an entitlement program to a block grant program and imposed strict work requirements on welfare recipients. The transformation to a block grant represented a compromise for Democratic governors, who had previously expressed reservations about ending the entitlement status of welfare. Republican governors, for their part, added an additional $4 billion in child care support to facilitate the transition from welfare to work, and an additional $1 billion to a fund for states during times of hardship (Havemann 1995). The additional funding represented a compromise for Republican governors, as it reduced the expected savings from welfare reform by $16 billion over a seven-year period and thus contributed less money toward balancing the budget ($44 billion rather than $60 billion) (Havemann 1995). Thus for both child advocates and governors, diverse collaboration required organizations to deviate from their preferred policy position.

Not all coalitions experienced policy costs. In particular, there is limited evidence that policy costs were experienced by the coalition of groups that opposed child exclusion provisions. Both liberal groups and abortion opponents within the coalition opposed legislation that mandated the family cap, teen mother exclusion, and paternity establishment, though for different

---

[14] Marian Wright Edelman. *Stand for Children Rally.* C-SPAN video, June 1, 1996, www.c-span .org/video/?72650–1/stand-children-rally.

[15] See, for example, *Contract with America – Welfare Reform: Hearing before the Subcommittee on Human Resources of the Committee on Ways and Means, United States House of Representatives*, 104th Cong. (1995), 830; miscellaneous formal correspondence from Marian Wright Edelman to President William J. Clinton, Folder "Children's Defense Fund (1)." Bruce Reed Welfare Reform Collection: William J. Clinton Presidential Library.

[16] Formal correspondent from Marian Wright Edelman to President William J. Clinton, January 30, 1995, Folder "Children's Defense Fund (1)." Bruce Reed Welfare Reform Collection: William J. Clinton Presidential Library.

reasons. The NOW-LDEF articulated its opposition in terms of the unconstitutionality of the provisions, the lack of support from social science research, and the potential harm to children.[17] Catholic Charities and Feminists for Life, in contrast, emphasized the potential impact on the abortion practices of teen and unwed mothers (Goldstein 1999). Though the arguments were different, the policy preferences of partner organizations on this particular set of issues were largely aligned. Moreover, meeting minutes of the CETF provide limited evidence that groups disputed or negotiated over the policy position of the coalition. Rather, meeting minutes focused on strategies for ensuring the defeat of child exclusion provisions.[18] While the resources costs were great, the policy costs for the coalition opposing child exclusion provisions were minimal, particularly relative to the policy costs incurred by children's advocates and governors.

Opportunity Costs

With respect to opportunity costs, any collaborative effort represents the redirection of organizational resources away from independent activity and toward collaborative activity. Thus by definition, all organizations paid an opportunity cost to collaborate. Yet it is not the case that organizations engaged in collaborative activity during welfare reform lost all opportunity to distinguish themselves as independent actors. Many of the organizations that participated in alliances also engaged in independent lobbying activities. Leading advocates who participated in the Coalition on Human Needs and the Child Exclusion Task Force also testified or submitted testimony on behalf of their individual organization during congressional hearings on welfare reform, including the CWLA, the Center for Law and Social Policy (CLASP), the Center on Budget and Policy Priorities, and NOW. The CDF, which organized the Stand for Children March and was a member of the Coalition for America's Children and the CETF, similarly released editorials, testified in congressional hearings, and offered statements to the media, thereby allowing the organization to distinguish itself from other groups.

Organizational records of the CETF provide further evidence that groups sought to distinguish themselves even when acting collaboratively. During a Senate lobbying campaign, members of the task force were instructed to introduce themselves as both a representative for the task force and a

---

[17] *Contract with America – Welfare Reform: Hearing before the Subcommittee on Human Resources of the Committee on Ways and Means, United States House of Representatives,* 104th Cong. (1995), 1622.

[18] Miscellaneous meeting minutes from the Child Exclusion Task Force, Box 33. Legal Momentum Records, 1968–2008, Schlesinger Library, Radcliffe Institute, Harvard University, Cambridge, Massachusetts.

representative for their individual organization.[19] Members were also asked to draft letters from their organization to President Clinton urging him to halt the approval of welfare waivers that included child exclusion provisions, and to write or call senators from their home states.[20] Thus while collaboration technically represented a lost opportunity for groups to distinguish themselves from one another, some participants, especially those with a long-standing interest in welfare policy, pursued independent activities that provided an opportunity to reaffirm a distinct organizational identity.

Reputational Costs

A reputational cost occurs if collaboration with diverse partners dilutes or otherwise contaminates an organization's identity – whether to policymakers, members, or funders. For example, coalition participation may lead to a drop in membership if a group's members view an issue lobbied on in coalition as irrelevant to their interests or view a coalition partner as a policy opponent rather than an ally.

Reputational costs are particularly hard to observe in my analysis, as I do not have data on group decisions to collaborate or on the future consequences of collaborating with diverse partners. The data do, however, provide evidence of activities that may have protected against reputational costs. Members of the ideologically diverse CETF were careful to delineate the lines of policy agreement and disagreement between groups within the coalition. For example, in June 1995, the American Civil Liberties Union (ACLU), one of the co-founders of the CETF, released a statement entitled "Apart on Abortion, Together on Benefits for Children: Congress Must Not Overhaul Welfare by Gutting Civil Liberties." The statement notes that while the ACLU "unequivocally supports a woman's right to reproductive freedom," the organization "today joins with our opponents on the abortion issue in opposing welfare measures that would harm children."[21] This statement is noteworthy because it draws attention to a shared policy position while affirming that lines of disagreement persist between coalition partners.

Similarly, a coauthored editorial in the *Chicago Tribune* by representatives from the Catholic Charities and the ACLU in 1994

---

[19] Child Exclusion Task Force Meeting Minutes, June 6, 1995 MC 727, Box 33, folder #10, Legal Momentum Records, 1968–2008, Schlesinger Library, Radcliffe Institute, Harvard University, Cambridge, Massachusetts.

[20] Child Exclusion Task Force Meeting Minutes, July 13, 1995 MC 727, Box 33, folder #10, Legal Momentum Records, 1968–2008, Schlesinger Library, Radcliffe Institute, Harvard University, Cambridge, Massachusetts.

[21] ACLU News: "Apart on Abortion, Together on Benefits for Children: Congress Must Not Overhaul Welfare by Gutting Civil Liberties," ACLU, June 14, 1995, Box 4, folder "Catholic Church." Bruce Reed Welfare Reform Collection: William J. Clinton Presidential Library.

identifies the partners' differences and similarities: "It is no surprise that the Catholic Church and the American Civil Liberties Union do not agree on abortion. Many people are surprised, then that Catholic Charities USA and the ACLU are allies" (Daly and Lewis 1994). This statement similarly highlights that while organizations were united in their opposition to child exclusion provisions, they maintained their disagreements regarding abortion and reproductive rights. By highlighting their disagreement on abortion policy, partners may have protected against the potential reputational costs of allying with partners with fundamentally opposing positions in other issue areas.

The examples discussed in this section provide evidence that organizations engaged in collaborative lobbying efforts with diverse partners experienced costs to collaborate. The CETF experienced considerable resource costs in its efforts to oppose child exclusion policies. There is evidence that policy costs were experienced by the National Governors Association and by the informal coalitions united behind the Contract with America's Children and the Stand for Children March. At the same time, evidence indicates that during welfare reform, groups engaged in activities that may have protected against opportunity and reputational costs, such as lobbying independently as well as collaboratively and drawing attention to the terms of agreement and disagreement across coalition partners.

It is important to note that costs associated with collaboration are likely distributed unevenly between coalition partners and across different partnerships, with core coalition organizers such as the CDF and NOW-LDEF assuming a disproportionate share of the costs. Many of the collaborative efforts identified earlier represented relatively low-cost activities for at least a subset of coalition partners. For instance, organizations that cosigned the Contract with America's Children simply had to communicate the organization's support for the contract via fax (Stepp 1995). In addition, not all organizations that signed onto the CETF were active in the legislative, lobbying, or grassroots subcommittees.[22] This is particularly true of unions such as the American Federation of State, County, and Municipal Employees (AFSCME), Service Employees International Union (SEIU), and the United Auto Workers (UAW). Such organizations signed onto various coalitions, including the Child Exclusion Task Force (SEIU and UAW) and the Coalition on Human Needs Welfare Reform Task Force (AFSCME and SEIU), but they do not appear to be prominent collaborators behind the scenes.[23]

[22] Memo to Child Exclusion Task Force Members, July 7, 1995, MC 727, Box 33, folder #10, Legal Momentum Records, 1968–2008, Schlesinger Library, Radcliffe Institute, Harvard University, Cambridge, Massachusetts.

[23] See Weaver 2000 for a discussion of the limited activity of labor unions during welfare reform.

DISCUSSION AND CONCLUSION

The evidence presented in this chapter provides support for the political signaling predictions of the theory of diverse coalitions. During welfare reform, coalitions that were diverse with respect to policy domain and ideology actively communicated their diversity to legislators and experienced several types of costs to collaborate, thereby providing support for the theory's posited mechanisms of influence. The evidence shows that coalitions communicated their diversity to members of Congress both by offering different arguments for a given policy position and by explicitly referencing the diversity of coalition partners. Moreover, the fact that diversity was both communicated by coalition members and opposed by challengers indicates that groups perceived diversity to be an important characteristic of their coalitions. This in turn provides support for the argument that diversity functions as an important mechanism of political influence for coalitions.

The case of welfare reform also provides evidence of resource and policy costs among diverse partners, as well as activities that may have protected against opportunity and reputational costs. With respect to resource costs, the records of the NOW-LDEF indicate that the CETF spent considerable staff time coordinating coalition activities and contacting and meeting with members of Congress and incurred material costs associated with distributing information to legislators.

Policy costs appeared in various ways. Democratic and Republican governors deviated from their preferred positions by engaging in a trade: Democratic governors agreed to transform welfare into a block grant while Republican governors agreed to add funding for child care support. Child advocates, in contrast, did not engage in a trade but rather diluted their overall policy message to collaborate with diverse partners. In addition, groups engaged in activities that mitigated the opportunity and reputational costs of diverse collaboration. Groups testified on their own while also cosigning statements with other organizations. Perhaps in an effort to guard against reputational costs, groups that collaborated with "strange bedfellows" carefully specified the terms of collaboration.

Though not directly observable in my data, it seems probable that groups experienced differential costs to collaborate with diverse partners, an idea that finds support in other work. Hula (1999) distinguishes between core members of a coalition, consisting of coalition founders and groups that devote resources to coalitional activity; players, consisting of specialists that join a coalition for specific policy reasons; and tag-alongs, consisting of peripheral groups that participate for non-policy benefits (such as information) (Hula 1999: 39–50). During welfare reform, groups such as the NOW-LDEF and the CDF likely functioned as core members of advocacy coalitions, while labor unions likely acted as tag-alongs.

It is important to note that with the exception of the National Governors Association, nearly all the coalitions described in this chapter united advocates for poor children and families, rather than proponents of conservative reform. While the previous chapter describes how conservative membership groups collaborated informally with research organizations behind the scenes, advocates for low-income populations were much more likely to engage in public displays of collaboration, whether in the form of a press conference, rally, newspaper advertisement, or congressional hearings. Because the Republican Party controlled the House and the Senate, conservative organizations had greater access to legislators in key positions of power. Indeed, political leaders met frequently with leaders of conservative membership-based groups as well as leading research organizations (Haskins 2006). As the following chapter will make clear, this access meant that there were fewer incentives for conservative groups to mobilize efforts outside Congress and as a result, fewer instances of public signaling to legislators.

Yet an analysis of the instances of public signaling that *did* occur among conservative groups indicates that conservative groups rarely provided information about the diversity of their partnerships. Rather, they drew attention to their size. A letter submitted to Senator Lauch Faircloth by six leading conservative organizations begins by stating: "On behalf of the millions of members of our collective organizations, we believe that the welfare bill must include the family cap."[24] This is consistent with an argument that it is particular *types* of diversity – namely, diversity with respect to policy domain and ideology – that may be important to legislators in a signaling sense. Coalitions of conservatives were not diverse along these dimensions but rather were professionally diverse, allowing them to unite electoral and policy information in their lobbying efforts.

The activities of organized interests during welfare reform lend support to the argument that diversity within coalitions functions as an important mechanism of influence in the legislative process. The analysis shows that diversity is not simply valuable to coalition members but also relevant to legislators. In the next chapter, I turn to an analysis of diverse collaboration across four issues in welfare reform to examine the relationship between diverse collaboration and issue context.

---

[24] Letter from conservative organizations to Lauch Faircloth, June 21, 1995. Bruce Reed Welfare Reform Collection: William J. Clinton Presidential Library.

8

The Conditions of Diverse Coalition Formation

INTRODUCTION

The Personal Responsibility and Work Opportunity Reconciliation Act of 1996 (PRWORA) is often described as a unitary policy change. Yet the law reforming the nation's welfare program actually involved multiple changes to the American social safety net. These changes affected a range of programs that provided benefits to distinct target populations, involved different governmental actors, and engaged varying sets of organized interests. In this chapter, I exploit variation across issues to examine the empirical support for the political context predictions of the theory of diverse coalitions. Specifically, I examine how collaborative activity between diverse partners differed across a subset of issues that varied with respect to the salience and uncertainty surrounding each issue, as well as the nature of the opposition between policy sides.

The chapter focuses on four of the most prominent issues within welfare reform: welfare-to-work, program structure, child exclusion, and child disability issues. Welfare-to-work issues aimed to increase work activity among recipients of cash assistance by conditioning benefit receipt on work activity. Program structure issues involved the proposed conversion of Aid to Families with Dependent Children (AFDC) into a program that allocated federal funding to states in the form of a capped block grant, thereby eliminating the federally guaranteed individual entitlement to assistance. Child exclusion policies prohibited the payment of additional welfare benefits to children born to mothers currently receiving AFDC and denied assistance to children born to unmarried mothers under the age of 18. Finally, child disability policies sought to narrow the eligibility criteria for disabled children for the Supplemental Security Income (SSI) program.

These four issues differed with respect to the level of salience and uncertainty in the policy environment, as well as the nature of the conflict between opposing policy sides. The issues therefore provide an ideal opportunity to examine the empirical support for the political signaling predictions of the theory of diverse coalitions, which posit that diverse coalitions will be more likely to form when issues are salient and uncertain, and when opponents are perceived as strong. I begin the chapter by reviewing the political signaling predictions. This section also explains how I define and measure features of the issue context. In the second section, I provide an overview of the four issues and describe the nature of salience, uncertainty, and opposition on each issue.

The third part of the chapter analyzes the extent of diverse collaboration across the four issues. This section reveals that among advocates, the most prominent collaborative activity across diverse partners emerged on child exclusion issues and to a lesser extent on program structure issues, which were characterized by high levels of uncertainty and salience to outside actors and on which opponents were perceived as strong. Diverse coalitions were relatively less active on welfare-to-work issues, on which uncertainty was low, and child disability issues, which lacked salience to a broad range of actors. Moreover, the vast majority of collaborative efforts emerged among advocates for low-income populations, with few coalitions forming among proponents of conservative reform.

In the final part of the chapter, I argue that the analysis offers evidence consistent with the political signaling predictions of the theory of diverse coalitions. During welfare reform, organized interests exhibited different patterns of collaborative behavior in different issue contexts. Rather than pursue the same lobbying strategies across issues, groups lobbied independently on some issues and collaborated with diverse partners on others, with diverse coalitions most likely to emerge on uncertain issues that were salient to a range of interested actors and on which opponents were perceived as strong. The analysis thus provides support for the theory's central predictions and suggests the importance of salience, uncertainty, and opposition strength as issue-level factors shaping coalitional activity across diverse partners.

THE POLITICAL SIGNALING PREDICTIONS OF THE THEORY OF DIVERSE COALITIONS

The final predictions of the theory of diverse coalitions are called the *political signaling predictions*. These predictions hold that coalitions uniting diverse actors will emerge when an issue is salient to different types of actors, when uncertainty is high, and when opponents are perceived as strong. This section reviews the political signaling predictions and explains how I define and measure the level of salience, nature of uncertainty, and strength of opposing policy sides across four issues in welfare reform.

With respect to salience, the theory predicts that issue salience creates *opportunities* for diverse collaboration because salience increases the range of organizations with an interest in an issue, thereby creating more potential partners with which to collaborate. Formally, I define *salience* as the "importance of an issue to constituents, organized interests, and governmental actors." I measure salience in two ways: the number of mentions of a policy problem or solution in the *New York Times* in the two years preceding PRWORA's passage[1] and the number of panels devoted to the topic in the first set of hearings on welfare reform in the House Ways and Means Committee and the Senate Finance Committee.[2] While the first measure attests to salience to actors outside government, the second measure provides evidence of salience to congressional policymakers. An issue that has a large number of media mentions and significant congressional attention is considered to be a highly salient issue. I provide additional support for measures of salience by analyzing the oral and written statements of organized interests during the first set of congressional hearings.

While salience creates opportunities for diverse collaboration, uncertainty creates *incentives* for interest groups to lobby collaboratively. When a legislator does not know whether a policy change has broad support (or in the language of a standard signaling game, does not know whether a group is a low or high type), groups have incentives to collaborate with diverse partners to communicate information about the level of underlying support. I define *uncertainty* as "ambiguity regarding the electoral or policy consequences of a legislative policy choice."[3] An issue is uncertain when the impact of a policy

---

[1] This time period spans November 8, 1994 (the date of the midterm elections) to August 22, 1996 (the date that President Clinton signed the PRWORA).

[2] The first set of congressional hearings included six days of hearings held before the House Subcommittee of Human Resources of the Ways and Means Committee between January 13 and February 2, 1995, and nine days of hearings held before the Senate Finance Committee between March 8 and April 27, 1995. This set of hearings is the same set analyzed in the Chapter 5.

[3] The theory uses the framework of a standard signaling game to identify the conditions under which a group will collaborate with diverse partners. In this framework, uncertainty exists when a legislator does not know if the advocate exists in an environment where outside groups support the advocate's proposal (a high-type advocate), or if the advocate exists in an environment where no outside groups support the proposal (a low-type advocate). In this chapter, I operationalize uncertainty in terms of the policy and electoral consequences of a policy choice. When the consequences of a policy choice are known, a legislator is better able to infer the policy position of interested actors and thus determine the type of environment in which she is operating. In contrast, when the consequences of a policy choice are unclear, it is more difficult for a legislator to determine which type of environment she is operating within. For example, if it is clear that a policy will leave millions of children without government assistance while imposing financial burdens on charities and state and local actors, then it is likely that the legislator is dealing with a group whose opposition to a policy is shared by numerous types of outside actors – or a high-type group. In contrast, if the effects of a policy are uncertain, it is more difficult for

choice on constituents, organized interests, and substantive policy outcomes is unknown.

To assess uncertainty empirically, I examine whether the policy change proposed in the initial House welfare reform legislation had been previously enacted. For example, I investigate whether the proposed policy or programmatic change had been adopted at the state level through the welfare waiver program, which allowed states to implement programmatic changes to AFDC. A policy change that was previously enacted provides legislators with opportunities to observe the substantive and electoral consequences of that policy, thereby reducing uncertainty. I also consider the state of technical research on the topic as well as public opinion polls. Uncertainty is high when the proposed policy change had not been previously enacted, when the technical research on the topic is either absent or inconclusive, and when public support for the proposed changes is ambiguous.

Like uncertainty, strong opponents create *incentives* for interest groups to collaborate because the varied resources of diverse groups are necessary to defeat the powerful set of organizational and governmental actors pushing forth a particular policy proposal.[4] I define *opposition strength* in terms of the relative strength of a policy *side*, rather than the strength of a particular group. This approach recognizes that the overall set of actors supporting or opposing a policy choice is more likely to shape the actions of organized interests and governmental actors in the policymaking process, relative to a single actor (see Baumgartner et al. 2009; Heaney and Lorenz 2013; Mahoney and Baumgartner 2015). I define strength in terms of the support of important policymakers and outside interests. A strong policy side enjoys the support of relevant actors inside the government, such as the congressional majority party or the administration, and important actors outside the government, such as an interest group with an engaged membership base or with ties to legislators in leadership positions.

I assess opposition strength qualitatively. I rely on the set of historical sources (including hearings, media reports, and case studies) to evaluate the policy positions of important actors outside the government. I also examine the support for a particular policy side among legislative and administrative policymakers. A side is strong when its non-governmental proponents enjoy access to policymakers and when the side has considerable support among congressional legislators as well as the support of the administration. During welfare reform, proponents of conservative policy choices generally enjoyed access to congressional policymakers in leadership positions, whereas

---

a legislator to determine the policy preferences of other interested actors and thus more difficult to determine when a group is a low or high type.

[4] It is important to note that the presence of opponents presumes that there is conflict on an issue. When all interested actors agree on the appropriate policy change, then there are no opposing sides to an issue and no opponents to fight against.

advocates for liberal policy choices lacked such access. The support for conservative policy change within the Clinton administration varied across issues. Yet in general, the side supporting Republicans' proposed policy changes was strong, while the side opposing such changes was weak.

As the previous discussion suggests, the measures of salience, uncertainty, and opposition strength are matters of degree rather than absolutes. It is not the case, for example, that a policy choice is either completely certain or completely uncertain in its implications. Rather, some issues encounter higher levels of certainty than other issues. Yet while the characteristics are generally matters of degree, the indicators do allow me to distinguish between "high" and "low" levels of salience, uncertainty, and opposition strength across the four issues.

In addition, it is important to note that diverse coalitions are only likely to emerge when the legislative outcome is unknown. Recall from Chapter 2 that the signaling model presumes that the legislator will make one of two policy choices – accepting policy p when it enjoys strong support from a diverse set of actors and rejecting policy p when support from organized actors is low. In other words, the legislator's choice to accept or reject policy p is not already determined at the start of the signaling game.

In this analysis, the legislative outcome was unknown for all four issues. All four policies involved relatively large changes to the safety net; while support for change among policymakers was strong, it was not clear at the onset of welfare reform policymaking whether such policies would ultimately be enacted into law. This particular feature of the issue context is therefore held constant across issues, allowing me to focus on the relationship between diverse collaboration and salience, uncertainty, and opposition strength. The next section turns to an analysis of these issue characteristics across four prominent issues within welfare reform.

THE VARYING ISSUE CONTEXTS OF WELFARE REFORM

In this section, I analyze the nature of salience, uncertainty, and opposition strength across program structure, welfare-to-work, child disability, and child exclusion issues. For each issue, I begin by identifying the goals of each policy or set of policies and the problems the policy aimed to address. Next, I describe the policy proposal that was contained in the welfare reform legislation introduced in the House of Representatives in early 1995. This legislation, which was given the designation H.R. 4, represented the legislative proposals deriving from the Republican's Contract with America.[5] Finally, I examine the level of salience, uncertainty, and nature of conflict on each issue.

---

[5] *Personal Responsibility Act of 1995*, HR 4, 104th Cong., 1st sess., *Congressional Record* 141:1 (January 4, 1995): H122–123.

Program Structure Issues

The first issue involved the proposed transformation of the AFDC program. Program structure issues involved restructuring AFDC by transforming it from a categorical grant into a block grant, which would end the entitlement of needy families to cash assistance. This structural change aimed to address two of the most important goals in welfare reform: curtailing the growth in federal spending on social programs, which by 1994 exceeded $60 billion,[6] and enhancing state discretion over AFDC.[7]

Under existing law, AFDC funding arrived to states in the form of a categorical grant, in which the federal government retained considerable programmatic discretion and set rules regarding work incentives, eligibility, and activities requirements. Beyond setting benefit levels, states were limited in their ability to change program requirements without approval at the national level. AFDC also represented an entitlement to states and indirectly to individuals, and all individuals who met eligibility criteria were legally entitled to receive cash assistance. The entitlement structure meant that federal welfare expenditures were provided automatically to states and fluctuated annually based on need: if the number of families eligible for cash assistance increased, so did federal expenditures for the welfare program.

To control federal welfare spending and enhance state discretion, H.R. 4 proposed to end the individual entitlement to welfare assistance and cap federal spending on the AFDC program. States were given the option of opting out of the AFDC program in favor of receiving funds in the form of a block grant, in which a state would receive a set amount of federal funds to use for the welfare

---

[6] All figures are in 1994 dollars. The figure for cash aid includes 11 programs including SSI, AFDC, the earned income tax credit, and foster care. The figure for food aid includes Food Stamps, school lunch programs, Special Supplemental Nutrition Program for Women, Infants, and Children (WIC), the school breakfast program, child and adult care food program, nutrition programs for the elderly, among other smaller programs. Source: U.S. House of Representatives, Committee on Ways and Means, *Background Material and Data on Programs within the Jurisdiction of the Committee on Ways and Means (Green Book)*, 105th Cong., 2nd sess., 1998, Committee Print 105-7.

[7] By the time welfare reform emerged on the political agenda in the early 1990s, federal spending on social welfare programs had been trending upward for several decades. The federal government spent just over $20 billion on cash aid in 1968, but by 1994 the figure had grown to $60 billion (U.S. House of Representatives, Committee on Ways and Means, 1998). Despite the fact that only a small portion of the overall growth was due to increased spending on AFDC, controlling welfare costs became a central focus of reform efforts. Rising costs were a particularly prominent concern among conservatives, who argued that federal spending had increased dramatically since the War on Poverty with limited impact on poverty (Weaver 2000: 102-6). Alongside concerns over federal welfare spending were complaints about the lack of discretion afforded to state governments. Although states were granted some discretion through the welfare waiver program, which allowed a state to apply to the Department of Health and Human Services for a waiver to experiment with alternate program designs, the process of applying for waivers was perceived by state actors as onerous and overly complicated.

program.[8] Spending on welfare would be subject to the annual congressional appropriations process and would not increase automatically alongside need. This created the possibility that individuals who became eligible for cash assistance during economic downturns would be unable to receive assistance if funds were depleted. Block grants would also shift considerable programmatic discretion over welfare programs from the federal to the state level.

1 *Salience*

The issue of transforming the structure of AFDC was one of the most salient issues in welfare reform. Between November 1994 and August 1996, the *New York Times* published 327 articles on the topic of welfare and block grants. Structural changes to the welfare program were also prioritized in congressional hearings on welfare reform. In both the House and the Senate, the first half-day panels on welfare reform in early 1995 focused on the topics of controlling costs and enhancing state discretion by shifting away from federal entitlements and toward block grants. Though the Republican legislation proposed block grants in several different program areas (including food and nutrition programs), structural changes to the AFDC program received considerable attention in the hearings. A total of 9 witnesses were invited to testify over the course of 4 panels in subcommittee hearings in the House Ways and Means Committee and committee hearings in the Senate Finance Committee, and included 4 governors, 1 member of the Clinton administration, and 4 policy experts.[9]

Throughout congressional hearings, the issue of structural changes to the AFDC program received attention from a wide range of organized interests. Perhaps the most ardent supporters of structural changes were Republican governors, for whom block grants would afford unprecedented discretion (Haskins 2006; Pear 1995). Other intergovernmental groups also prioritized the issue in hearings testimony, though not all supported block grants. Local governmental actors, for instance, were wary of block grants because of the

---

[8] *Personal Responsibility Act of 1995*, HR 4, Sec. 301, 302, and 601.

[9] The hearings include *Costs of Welfare, Role of Entitlements, and Block Grants*, held on January 13, 1995, before the Subcommittee on Human Resources in the House Ways and Means Committee (part of the larger *Contract with America – Welfare Reform* hearings), and *States' Perspectives on Welfare Reform*, held on March 8, 1995, before the Senate Finance Committee (see the Appendix for full citation). Invited witnesses included Governor John Engler of Michigan; Governor Thomas Carper of Delaware; Mary Jo Bane, assistant secretary for children and families of the U.S. Department of Health and Human Services; Robert Rector, senior policy analyst at the Heritage Foundation; Michael Horowitz, senior fellow at the Hudson Institute; Martin Olasky, professor at the University of Texas at Austin; Robert Greenstein, executive director of the Center on Budget and Policy Priorities; Governor Howard Dean of Vermont; and Governor Tommy Thompson of Wisconsin.

possibility that local governments would be required to bear the cost of increased need for cash assistance.[10]

Structural changes were extremely salient to advocates for low-income families, who strongly opposed ending the 60-year guarantee of cash assistance to needy families. The importance of this issue is evident in the priority given to it by a range of organizational actors in congressional testimony. Leading advocates including the Coalition for Human Needs (CHN) and the Children's Defense Fund (CDF) testified against ending the entitlement to a range of programs during House subcommittee hearings on welfare reform.[11] Prominent groups involved in the provision of child welfare services, such as the Child Welfare League of America (CWLA) and the United Way, similarly discussed block grants in their hearings testimony.[12] Charitable organizations were also active on this issue, both inside and outside Congress. Prior to the Senate floor debate on welfare reform, the president of Catholic Charities wrote to President Clinton: "It has become clear that the *single most important* issue will be continuation of a federal guarantee, an entitlement, for children in poor families" (emphasis in original).[13]

In addition to advocates and service providers, prominent women's organizations and unions communicated their opposition to block grants, including the National Council of Presidents of National Women's Organizations; the AFL-CIO; the American Federation of State, County, and Municipal Employees; and the United Auto Workers.[14] Health professionals including the American Pediatrics Association cautioned that eliminating entitlements for welfare would put vulnerable children at risk.[15] On the opposing policy side, conservative groups including the Concerned Women for America expressed support for transforming AFDC into a capped block grant to states.[16]

---

[10] See, for example, "Recommendations for Welfare Reform Legislation," Local Government Coalition on Welfare Reform," folder "NACO [National Association of Counties]," Welfare Reform Series, Bruce Reed Collection, William J. Clinton Presidential Library.

[11] *Contract with America – Welfare Reform: Hearing before the Subcommittee on Human Resources of the Committee on Ways and Means, United States House of Representatives,* 104th Cong. (1995), 830–41.

[12] *Contract with America – Welfare Reform,* (1995), 842–51, 1021–34.

[13] Letter from Fred Kammer, president of Catholic Charities USA, to President William Clinton, 1 June 1995, Box 4, folder "Catholic Church," Welfare Reform Series, Bruce Reed Collection, William J. Clinton Presidential Library.

[14] See *Contract with America – Welfare Reform* (1995), 1119–28; *Broad Policy Goals of Welfare Reform: Hearing before the Committee on Finance, United States Senate,* 104th Cong. (1995), 107–9; *Welfare to Work: Hearing before the Committee on Finance, United States Senate,* 104th Cong. (1995), 88–93; "National Women's Pledge on Welfare Reform: Principles for Eliminating Poverty," Council of Presidents, undated, Box 47, folder "Women." Bruce Reed Welfare Reform Collection: William J. Clinton Presidential Library.

[15] *Welfare Reform – Views of Interested Organizations: Hearing before the Committee on Finance, United States Senate,* 104th Cong. (1995), 20.

[16] *Contract with America – Welfare Reform* (1995), 823–28.

That many types of organized interests communicated their preferences on structural changes to the AFDC program provides additional evidence that the issue was salient to a wide range of organizations, including intergovernmental groups, researchers, advocates, service providers, as well as groups representing women, organized labor, and conservative interests.

2 Uncertainty

Program structure issues were also highly uncertain, in part because the proposed transformation of AFDC represented such a dramatic departure from the status quo. As Secretary of Health and Human Services Donna Shalala noted in a January 1995 memo to President Clinton: "It is hard to overestimate how radical a change this would be. Since the establishment of the AFC program in 1935 ... every needy family or individual ... has been entitled to get help" (Donna Shalala, Memorandum to the President, January 19, 1995). As the secretary's statement indicates, the proposal to end a policy that had been in place for 60 years was a striking shift from the past. Although states were permitted to enact changes to their welfare programs through the waiver program, it was not possible for states to apply for a waiver to receive welfare funds as a block grant. As a result, no states had experimented with a block grant approach, and it was uncertain how either states or poor families would fare if the entitlement was terminated, federal funds were capped, or welfare was transformed into a block grant.

Thus the policy consequences of such structural changes were unclear. Opponents of structural changes were concerned that block grants would not provide sufficient funding during times of state economic hardship (Blank 1997). Although proponents argued that increasing state discretion had potential benefits, state-level innovation carried with it inherent risks. Because block grants represented a new approach, technical research did not reveal whether enhanced discretion would curtail the growth of the welfare program and increase work activity among welfare recipients, or whether such changes would lead to the under-provision of benefits across states, particularly during times of increased need. As a result, consensus was limited regarding the likely impact of structural changes to the AFDC program, with conservative scholars drawing attention to the potential for improved outcomes and liberal scholars highlighting the potential for negative outcomes.

The uncertainty of policy consequences meant that electoral consequences were also uncertain, as negative policy outcomes had the potential to affect constituent opinion. Public opinion polls consistently revealed that Americans held a fundamental ambivalence toward the poor (Hochschild 1986; Weaver, Shapiro, and Jacobs 1995). While a majority of Americans disliked the welfare program, a majority also supported government assistance to "the poor" and especially to sympathetic groups such as poor children. For instance, polls conducted in 1994 revealed that while 44 percent of Americans believed that the government ought to reduce spending on welfare, 47 percent reported that the government was spending too little on poor children (Weaver et al. 1995: 619). Entitlement programs guaranteed access to at least some assistance, but block grants offered no such assurances. Eliminating the entitlement to cash assistance created the possibility that poor children would be denied welfare assistance because of a lack of funding. If poor children were denied access to cash assistance under block grants, such an outcome would be in contrast to stated preferences of most Americans, thereby creating the potential for a negative electoral backlash against legislators who supported ending the welfare entitlement.

3 Opposition Strength

The policy sides in the debate over the structure of the AFDC program maintained a fundamental difference of opinion regarding the appropriate role of the federal government in providing for the poor, as well as practical considerations pertaining to effective policymaking and state budgetary capacity. Proponents of the proposed changes in H.R. 4 rejected the current structure of the welfare program as ineffective and overly burdensome for state governments and viewed state experimentation as more effective than a uniform approach from the federal government. Groups supporting structural changes prioritized the issue of controlling federal welfare spending and were relatively less concerned about the ability of states to provide for the poor during times of increased need.

The forces propelling these structural changes forward were strong. Transferring power out of Washington and curtailing federal spending had long been important goals of the Republican Party. Because structural changes to the welfare program would further both goals, strong support for such changes existed among the congressional leadership. Though the transformation of AFDC into a block grant had been a virtual impossibility when Democrats controlled Congress during President Clinton's first term, the Republicans' victory in the 1994 elections opened the door to significant structural changes that would both enhance state discretion and cut federal expenditures on welfare programs.

Considerable support for structural changes – especially block grants – also existed among Republican governors, many of whom had been at the forefront of state welfare experimentation under the waiver program (Weaver 2000; Winston 2002). Republican governors represented both an important source of policy expertise and a critical political ally for Republicans in Congress. As such, they were granted considerable access to legislators during the initial stages of welfare reform. House Majority Leader Newt Gingrich and Senate Majority Leader Bob Dole, for instance, attended meetings of the Republican Governors Association (RGA) and developed task forces with the governors to write portions of the welfare legislation. The RGA and a select group of governors, including John Engler of Michigan and Tommy Thompson of Wisconsin, were actively involved in shaping the early contours of welfare reform (Gray 1995; Haskins 2006; Vobejda 1995; Katz 1995c).

In contrast, opponents of the program structure proposals contained in H.R. 4 were weak. Groups opposing such provisions advocated maintaining the existing entitlement of needy families to cash assistance. For such actors, shifting to a block grant structure represented, in part, an abdication of federal responsibility for the poor.[17] Opposition to block grants also reflected the very real possibility that welfare funds would dry up mid-year, leaving states unable to provide for families in need during times of economic downturns.[18] Unfortunately, groups that opposed structural changes, including many social welfare advocacy groups, service providers, and women's organizations, were at a distinct disadvantage in Congress, as the Republican Party's victory in the midterm elections had sharply reduced the access of such groups to legislators in leadership positions.

In addition, the Clinton administration was reluctant to oppose the proposed conversion of the AFDC program or issue a veto threat on the issue of block grants, meaning that such groups could not count President Clinton as an ally on this issue (see Weaver 2000: 252–93). Although a large and diverse set of groups vigorously objected to ending the entitlement to cash assistance, opponents lacked the support of the congressional leadership or the administration on this issue. Thus proponents of block grants held a privileged position in Congress, while opponents were comparatively weak.

Welfare-to-Work Issues

The second issue concerned low levels of work activity among welfare recipients. In the early 1990s, the work participation rate of recipients of cash assistance – the majority of whom were single mothers – was far below that of women nationally. Although past reforms had attempted to address low levels

---

[17] This rationale is evident in the statements of groups opposing structural changes. The National Women's Pledge on Welfare Reform stated: "We cannot allow the federal government to abandon its commitment to a basic safety net for poor mothers and their children" ("National Women's Pledge on Welfare Reform: Principles for Eliminating Poverty," Council of Presidents, undated, Box 47, folder "Women." Bruce Reed Welfare Reform Collection: William J. Clinton Presidential Library). Similarly, the executive director of the CWLA spoke of a "sacred trust" between the government and the poor and cautioned "to break that sacred trust now for our poorest children would be an absolute disaster" (*Contract with America – Welfare Reform* [1995], 842).

[18] See, for instance, the testimony of Robert Greenstein of the Center on Budget and Policy Priorities before the Senate Finance Committee (*Broad Policy Goals of Welfare Reform: Hearing before the Committee on Finance, United States Senate*, 104th Cong. [1995]).

of work activity among recipients of cash assistance, the work requirements within existing law were relatively modest and work-oriented programs had been slow to emerge across states.[19] By 1994, 72 percent of welfare recipients were neither working nor actively seeking work.[20] In contrast, the labor market participation rate for women was more than 65 percent nationwide (Blank and Schmidt 2001).

The legislation introduced in the House of Representatives included a set of requirements aimed to move recipients off welfare and into jobs. The emphasis was on discouraging long-term welfare receipt and encouraging employment. Indeed, H.R. 4 stated that the aim of welfare-to-work provisions was to "provide States with the resources and authority necessary to help, cajole, lure, or force adults off welfare and into paid employment as quickly as possible."

To this end, H.R. 4 proposed a combination of individual- and state-level work participation requirements. The legislation required single parents who had received welfare for at least two years to work a minimum of 35 hours per week, and it required states to move 50 percent of the welfare caseload into work activities by 2003. States were permitted to impose sanctions, such as reducing cash payments, to individuals who failed to meet the work activity requirement. Lifetime limits on welfare receipts were imposed, with no guarantee of publicly supported employment if private sector jobs were unavailable.[21]

1 *Salience*

The welfare-to-work issue was perhaps the most salient in the popular media. From November 1994 to August 1996, the *New York Times* published 691 articles addressing the topic of welfare and employment. Elected officials also prioritized welfare-to-work issues. The transition into work had been the primary focus of the Clinton administration's Work and Responsibility Act of 1994.[22]

---

[19] For instance, the Work Incentives Program of 1967 required all states to establish a work program that included financial incentives to encourage work activity and child care assistance. The Reagan administration encouraged states to experiment with their welfare programs, with the majority of early state reforms focused on helping recipients transition into labor market activities (Danziger 2001; Teles 1998 [1996]). In addition, the Family Support Act of 1988 (FSA) required states to develop work-oriented welfare programs and move modest, though increasing, percentages of the welfare caseload into employment. However, work-oriented programs under the FSA emerged slowly in the late 1980s and early 1990s as a result in part to the limited economic capacity of states following the 1990–1991 recession (Focus 1988; Patterson 2000 [1981]; Weaver 2000).

[20] U.S. House of Representatives, Committee on Ways and Means, *Background Material and Data on Programs within the Jurisdiction of the Committee on Ways and Means (Green Book)*, 104th Cong., 2nd sess., 1996, Committee Print 104–14.

[21] *Personal Responsibility Act of 1995*, HR 4, Sec. 202.

[22] See *Work and Responsibility Act of 1994*, HR 4605, 103rd Cong., 2nd sess., *Congressional Record* 140 (June 21, 1994): H4779.

In Congress, the Human Resources Subcommittee of the House Ways and Means Committee and the Senate Finance Committee devoted a half day of hearings to the topic of employment, with 13 individuals testifying over five panels of witnesses. Attesting to the breadth of organizational interest in the issue, witnesses represented varying types of interest groups, including think tanks, intergovernmental actors, nonprofit service providers, and one union.[23]

In congressional testimony, a wide range of organizations discussed welfare-to-work issues, providing further evidence that the issue was salient to many types of organized interests. Advocates for the poor, public interest groups, private and nonprofit organizations that provided employment-related services to welfare recipients, intergovernmental actors, research organizations, and women's organizations testified on issues related to the welfare-to-work transition. Groups representing the interests of poor families, such as the Pennsylvania Welfare Rights Union, the Poor People's Coalition, and the Public Welfare Coalition, prioritized topics related to employment by drawing attention to the lack of available jobs for low-income mothers, and the fact that work requirements in the absence of supportive services had limited potential for adults with few skills and multiple barriers to employment.[24] Such statements were echoed by nonprofit service providers, including the United Way, the Chicago-based Project Match, and the CWLA, organizations that had long integrated employment and training programs into their services for poor individuals.[25]

Work requirements were also a prominent topic among intergovernmental actors, such as state administrative agencies and associations of state and county welfare administrators, as many states had previously experimented with work-oriented welfare reforms through demonstration projects and welfare waivers (Teles 1998). A small number of professional and business organizations also testified on welfare-to-work issues, including the U.S.

---

[23] The welfare-to-work hearings include *Welfare Dependency and Welfare to work Programs*, held January 23, 1995, before the Subcommittee on Human Resources of the House Ways and Means Committee (part of the larger *Contract with America – Welfare Reform* hearings) and *Welfare to Work*, held March 20, 1995, before the Senate Finance Committee (see the Appendix for full citations). Witnesses testifying on welfare-to-work issues included Judith M. Gueron, president of the Manpower Demonstration Research Corp; Lawrence Mead, professor at Princeton University; Toby Herr, founder and director of Project Match; Lawrence Townsend, director of Riverside County (CA) Department of Public Social Services; Gary Stangler on behalf of the American Public Welfare Association; J. Jean Rogers, administrator at the Madison (WI) Department of Health and Social Services; Charles Hobbs, senior fellow at the American Institute for Full Employment; Stephen Martin on behalf of the American Legislative Exchange Council; Stephen Minnich, administrator in the Oregon Department of Human Resources; Robert Friedman, director of the Corporation for Enterprise Development; Joseph Jeffrey, vice president for Domestic Policy at the U.S. Chamber of Commerce; William Marshall, president of the Progressive Policy Institute; and Gerald Shea on behalf of the AFL-CIO.

[24] *Contract with America – Welfare Reform* (1995), 1108–9; 1042–43; 1638–40.

[25] *Contract with America – Welfare Reform* (1995), 1021–22; 844–51.

Chamber of Commerce, a federation of business associations;[26] the American Rehabilitation Association, a trade association of rehabilitation facilities;[27] and Cleveland WORKS, a private employment organization for low-income individuals.[28]

As individual work requirements would primarily affect the single mothers who made up the majority of the welfare caseload, women's organizations also took an active interest in the issue. Women's groups often drew attention to the supportive services that would be necessary for mothers to successfully transition from welfare into work. The importance of welfare-to-work issues to women's groups is evident in hearings testimony, as well as the activity of such organizations outside Congress. In a 1996 meeting with President Clinton's chief of staff, a group of national leaders of women's organizations argued that adequate and affordable child care and training and transportation services for working mothers, as well as adequate wages, were among the most prominent concerns of leaders from women's organizations.[29]

Numerous sources, including newspaper articles, congressional hearings, and archival documents, therefore suggest that welfare-to-work issues were salient to a wide range of organized interests, including advocates for the poor, social service providers, intergovernmental groups, women's organizations, and professional organizations.

2   Uncertainty

Unlike other issues, a relatively high level of certainty regarding the consequences of policy adoption characterized welfare-to-work issues. Most of the early policies adopted through the welfare waiver program had focused on helping women transition from welfare and into employment (Teles 1998). State experimentation with welfare-to-work programs had been accompanied by large-scale national evaluations of state welfare-to-work programs. By the late 1980s, evaluations had produced evidence to suggest that work and training programs had positive, though modest, impacts on work effort and activity (Blank 1997; Cammisa 1995; Danziger 2001; Patterson 2000; Teles 1998). In hearings testimony, research organizations, state elected officials, and state and local administrators reported confidence in the positive impacts of welfare-to-work requirements on work activity and welfare caseloads.[30]

---

[26] *Welfare to Work: Hearing before the Committee on Finance, United States Senate*, 104th Cong. (1995), 26–27.

[27] *Welfare to Work: Hearing before the Committee on Finance, United States Senate*, 104th Cong. (1995), 94.

[28] *Contract with America – Welfare Reform* (1995), 1074.

[29] Memorandum to Leon Panetta 1996. Box 47, folder "Women." Bruce Reed Welfare Reform Collection: William J. Clinton Presidential Library.

[30] Hearings before the House Subcommittee on Human Resources of the Ways and Means Committee illustrate consensus over the general goal of increasing work activity among welfare recipients. In two panels held on January 23, 1995, representatives from organizations engaged

Moreover, the public overwhelmingly supported efforts to enhance work activity. Public opinion polls revealed that 73 percent of Americans believed that the current public assistance system discouraged people from working (Weaver et al. 1995). Another poll found that 95 percent of those surveyed favored requiring welfare recipients to work in exchange for their benefits (Weaver 2000: 182).[31] Thus it was clear that a majority of Americans perceived the welfare system as discouraging recipients from working and that proposals to require work enjoyed a high level of popular support.

Of course, like any policy proposal, the impact of the proposed welfare-to-work policies was not entirely certain. For instance, it was not clear how welfare recipients would fare if private sectors jobs were unavailable, nor was there any guarantee that the jobs that low-income women would be able to find would be stable or high quality (Blank 1997). But because such policies had been enacted at the state level, the policy impacts of such proposals had been studied, and the public consensus on the policy approach was generally supportive, uncertainty over the substantive and electoral impacts of welfare-to-work policies was relatively low.

3   Opposition Strength

The policy sides on welfare-to-work issues reflected varying approaches to helping poor mothers transition off welfare and into employment. Unlike program structure issues, there was general consensus over the goal of encouraging work. However, disagreement existed over the best way to support this transition. The policy side supporting the welfare-to-work provisions contained in H.R. 4 supported relatively strict work requirements, a limited role for education and training, and time limits on welfare. The opposing policy side recognized the importance of work but argued that efforts to promote work must occur alongside broader antipoverty efforts that prioritized education and training; allowed parents to obtain affordable child care, health care, and transportation; recognized the problems of instability and low wages in the labor market; and allowed appropriate work exemptions for certain groups of women, including those caring for young children, disabled children, and victims of domestic violence.

in different aspects of research, implementation, and service provision and from different ideological perspectives communicated support for welfare-to-work efforts and work participation requirements specifically (U.S. House of Representatives January 23, 1995: 249–357). This agreement was noted by Representative Levin, who challenged the witnesses to identify their sources of disagreement: "I think we need to probe your differences, and I don't know that they are as deep as they are made out to be" (297). The witnesses affirmed their support for the goal of increasing work activity and the effectiveness of work-oriented approaches, although they differed in their recommendations regarding education and training programs and the ability of the job market to absorb large numbers of low-skilled workers.

[31] The public's support for requiring mothers with young children to work was less pronounced but still ranged from around 40–64 percent with the percentage of the public in support increasing over time (Weaver 2000: 182).

As with program structure issues, the set of actors supporting strict welfare-to-work policies in the absence of additional supports was strong, while the set of actors opposing such policies was relatively weak. In Congress, members of both parties supported strengthening work requirements, with both Republicans and Democrats accusing the opposing side as "weak on work" at various points in the policymaking process (Haskins 2006). Moreover, support was limited among the majority party to develop programs supporting the welfare-to-work transition because of their cost: programs that provided education and training or government support for child care, health care, and transportation were expensive. Work requirements were already costly to implement – the Congressional Budget Office estimated that the costs for administration and child care would increase by $28 million a year for each additional percentage point increase in the work participation rate (Haskins 2006: 144). Support was limited among congressional Republicans for programs that would add to federal spending.

The administration also supported strict work requirements and modified time limits, which had been central components of President Clinton's pledge to transform the welfare system. The administration's welfare reform plan sought to ease the transition into work by allowing welfare recipients to take community service jobs if private sector jobs were unavailable; exempting certain recipients, such as those with very young children, from work requirements; and permitting education and training to count as work activities (Weaver 2000: 242–44). However, once Republicans took the lead in welfare policymaking, Clinton's blunt campaign rhetoric – especially his promise of "two years and you're off" – created pressure for the president to support strict welfare-to-work provisions even in the absence of additional supports (Weaver 2000). Thus those groups that opposed strict welfare-to-work policies found their interests pitted against the Republicans' support for such policies and promise to cut federal expenditures, as well as President Clinton's promise to eliminate welfare dependency, even in the absence of stable and high-quality employment.

Child Disability Issues

While many issues within welfare reform involved changes to the AFDC program, reform efforts extended to a range of assistance programs targeting low-income individuals and families. One of the programs targeted by welfare reform efforts was the Supplemental Security Income Program (SSI), a means-tested program providing assistance to low-income individuals who are aged, blind, or disabled.[32] During welfare reform, congressional Republicans

---

[32] Reform efforts also targeted the eligibility of immigrants and disabled individuals whose primarily disability involved alcohol or drug dependency. In this chapter, I focus exclusively on changes in children's eligibility for the SSI program for the following reasons. First, the issue of

proposed to reform the SSI program by replacing the existing eligibility criteria for child disability and transforming some child disability funds into a block grant. Such changes to the SSI program would have the effect of limiting the number of children eligible to receive any SSI benefits while limiting the number of eligible children entitled to cash assistance through the program.[33]

Changes to the child disability program were intended to address two problems. The first involved high levels of spending: in 1994, the SSI program served approximately 6.5 million individuals and federal expenditures exceeded $30 billion.[34] Moreover, the child disability component of the program had experienced dramatic growth in recent years as a result of a 1990 Supreme Court decision that had effectively expanded the eligibility criteria for children (Daly and Burkhauser 2003).[35] The second problem involved perceived program abuse, in which children with relatively mild disabilities were able to qualify for SSI benefits.[36]

H.R. 4 proposed to replace the existing definition of disability with a stricter, child-specific definition that required that a physical or mental impairment be included on an established list of impairments created by the Social Security Administration (SSA). In addition, the legislation sought to eliminate part of the disability determination process known as the individual functional assessment

immigrant eligibility extended beyond just SSI, as congressional Republicans proposed limiting the eligibility of immigrants for a range of public assistance programs. Moreover, the issue of immigrant eligibility was highly salient in both the media and congressional hearings. Second, the eligibility of individuals whose disability was based on drug addiction or alcoholism was not ultimately addressed in the PRWORA. Rather, such changes were addressed in the Contract with America Advancement Act of 1996 (Public Law 104–21).

[33] Although changes related to children's eligibility for SSI were not addressed in the bill that was first introduced in Congress, such changes were addressed in the legislation that passed the House on March 24, 1995.

[34] U.S. House of Representatives, Committee on Ways and Means, *Background Material and Data on Programs within the Jurisdiction of the Committee on Ways and Means (Green Book)*, 104th Cong., 2nd sess., 1996, Committee Print 104–14.

[35] The child caseload grew from 185,000 in 1990 to 955,000 in 1996 (Daly and Burkhauser 2003). During the same period, the process for determining mental impairments in children was expanded to reflect medical advances. Such changes in the disability determination process contributed to an increase in the child SSI caseload, particularly among children with mental impairments (including ADHD) that were relatively less severe than those necessary to qualify for benefits in earlier years.

[36] In late 1994 and early 1995, the national news media, including the ABC television program *Prime Time Live* and the *Baltimore Sun*, reported on cases of children being coached to act out to qualify for the SSI program (*Prime Time Live*, 13 October 1994; John B. O'Donnell and Jim Haner, "America's Most Wanted Welfare Plan." January 22, 1995, Baltimore Sun. See also Christopher Georges, "A Media Crusade Gone Haywire," *Forbes Media Critic*, September 1995 and U.S. Department of Health and Human Services, Office of Inspector General, "Concerns about the Participation of Children with Disabilities in the Supplemental Security Program," A-03-94-02602 [October 1994]). Though the extent of program abuse was unknown, critics challenged the eligibility determination process as overly permissive even for those families not engaged in fraudulent behavior.

(IFA).[37] Through the IFA, a child was able to qualify for SSI if her impairments limited her ability to engage in age-appropriate activities but were not otherwise listed on the SSA's list of impairments (Daly and Burkhauser 2003; U.S. General Accounting Office 1994). Such changes would essentially make it harder for poor children with relatively less severe limitations, especially those that were behavior related, to qualify for SSI benefits.

In addition, under H.R. 4, cash benefits would only be available to children who met the new criteria for disability and required institutionalized care or the full-time support of a parent or caregiver. Block grants totaling $5.4 billion over five years would be available to states to provide services (rather than cash assistance) to children who qualified for SSI but possessed physical or mental impairments that were relatively less severe (Haskins 2006; Katz 1995a).

1 *Salience*

Of the four policy changes examined in this chapter, changes to children's eligibility for the SSI program were the least salient to the public, congressional policymakers, and organized interests. Between November 1994 and August 1996, there were 62 articles addressing welfare, SSI, and disability in the *New York Times*, attesting to the relatively low level of public salience on the issue. In the first series of welfare reform hearings, the Subcommittee on Human Resources in the House Ways and Means Committee devoted one full day of hearings and the Senate Finance Committee devoted one morning to proposed changes in SSI.[38] However, because the proposed changes to the SSI program also included changes in eligibility for immigrants and adults whose disability was in part related to an alcohol or drug problem, attention during these hearings was divided between proposed changes for children, immigrants, and adults with substance abuse problems. Of the 11 witnesses who testified during the SSI hearings, 6 discussed issues related to child disability while the remaining 5 focused on the eligibility of immigrants and substance abusers.

Moreover, testimony from the wider set of congressional hearings reveals that across a range of organizations, issues related to child disability were *not* a central focus. During House subcommittee hearings, leading advocates did

---

[37] *Personal Responsibility Act of 1995*, HR 4 (Engrossed in House), Title VI, Sec. 602, Sec. 1641–46.

[38] The Congressional hearings include *Changing Eligibility for Supplemental Security Income*, held on January 27, 1995, before the Human Resources Subcommittee of the House Ways and Means Committee (part of the *Contract with America – Welfare Reform* hearings) and *Growth of the Supplemental Security Income Program*, held before the Senate Finance Committee on March 27, 1995 (see Appendix for full citations). Witnesses testifying on child disability issues included Jane Ross, director of income security for the U.S. General Accounting Office; Jerry Mashaw, chair of the Disability Policy Panel of the National Academy of Social Insurance; Carolyn Weaver, resident scholar at the American Enterprise Institute; Wayne Parker, area manager of the Disability Determinations Service in Shreveport, Louisiana; James Gardner, past president of the ARC; and Karen Higginbotham, private citizen and parent of a disabled child.

not mention changes in child eligibility for the SSI program. Representatives from the CHN, CDF, and CWLA discussed welfare-to-work issues and communicated their opposition to block grants and child exclusion provisions but did not discuss changes to SSI.[39]

Issues related to child disability were not included in the testimony of prominent women's and civil rights groups, including the NOW Legal Defense and Education Fund and the ACLU.[40] And although the Supplemental Security Income program was mentioned by the policy experts in the context of structural changes to federal welfare programs, the majority of experts' testimony was dedicated to issues related to the block granting of welfare.[41] Thus, across many different types of organized interests, child disability issues received considerably less attention than issues related to program structure, work provisions, and child exclusion policies, providing further support for the argument that salience on child disability issues was low.

2 Uncertainty

The consequences of changing children's eligibility for SSI were uncertain, even though H.R. 4 included provisions that were similar to those of the SSI program that had been in place prior to 1990. For instance, the House-passed legislation included a restrictive definition of disability that was comparable to a definition used prior to 1990. In addition, the legislation sought to eliminate the IFA in the disability determinations process, which had not been in place before 1990.[42] However, the precise definition of disability proposed in H.R. 4 had not been previously enacted in policy. The legislation did not revert to the pre-1990 definition, under which children were considered to be disabled if they possessed an impairment of "comparable severity" to a disabling impairment in an adult (Social Security Administration 1997). Rather, the legislation imposed a new definition of disability that was specific to children. In addition, the proposal to restrict cash assistance to children with severe disabilities requiring institutionalization was entirely new.

Together, the political and policy implications of such changes, including the new definition of disability, elimination of the IFA, restriction on cash assistance, and provision of assistance for services through a block grant, raised significant policy questions (Erkulwater 2006). It was unclear whether

---

[39] *Contract with America – Welfare Reform* (1995), 1065, 830–41, 842–51.
[40] *Contract with America – Welfare Reform* (1995), 1622–37; 1369–77.
[41] *Contract with America – Welfare Reform* (1995), 63–131.
[42] In its *Sullivan v. Zebley* decision (1990), the Supreme Court found that the process for determining child eligibility for SSI did not mirror the process for determining adult eligibility for the program. While both children and adults were eligible for SSI if they had an impairment that was on a list of impairments established by the SSA, only adults could become eligible through an IFA. Following the *Zebley* decision, the SSA revised its eligibility determination process to allow children to become eligible for disability benefits through an IFA (U.S. General Accounting Office 1994).

the new definition of disability, which was considerably more restrictive, would preserve benefits for children who were truly needy. With respect to the provision of services (as opposed to cash assistance) to children with less-severe impairments, guidance was limited as to how administrators would determine which services a family needed and how much those services cost, particularly given the heterogeneity of disabilities among children. Finally, the introduction of a block grant raised questions as to whether such a program would provide sufficient funding to states to care for disabled children and their families.

Indeed, the high level of uncertainty surrounding the consequences of changing child disability eligibility criteria had prompted Congress to appoint a commission to study the issue in 1994. The National Commission on Childhood Disability (NCCD), chaired by Democratic Senator Jim Slattery of Kansas, consisted of leading experts in the areas of medicine, law, education, psychology, social insurance, and program administration. The NCCD was charged with reviewing the existing definition of child disability and offering recommendations for reform, but it was not scheduled to release its findings until late in 1995 (National Commission on Childhood Disability 1995). In both House and Senate hearings on SSI, witnesses advocated delaying the changes proposed under H.R. 4 until the commission had completed its work, thereby allowing legislators to make a more informed decision on child eligibility changes.

The statements of witnesses in congressional hearings testimony also reveal considerable uncertainty regarding how a block grant for services would operate in practice. In testimony before the Senate Finance Committee, several witnesses drew attention to the heterogeneity among disabled children and the difficulty of providing services for children with different needs. The director of income security from the GAO noted: "I do not think we really know enough at this point about the variety of expenditures, or costs to various disabled children to know how to cash out that program and provide services. I think that is worrisome."[43] Without access to cash assistance, it was unclear whether the needs of children with severe disabilities that did not necessitate full-time care could be met through a program providing assistance for services.

The possibility that disabled children and their families would be left without assistance created the potential for a negative constituent response, as disabled children represented a particularly sympathetic population. Because disabled individuals (especially children) were perceived to be poor through no fault of their own, a majority of Americans viewed this group as especially "deserving" of government assistance (Appelbaum 2001; Weaver et al. 1995). If the policy changes passed by the House led to higher levels of poverty and homelessness

---

[43] *Growth of the Supplemental Security Income Program: Hearing before the Committee on Finance, United States Senate*, 104th Cong. (1995), 16.

for disabled children and their families – as one advocate suggested – constituents were unlikely to respond favorably.[44] Such ambiguous policy and electoral impacts meant that the level of uncertainty on child disability issues was high.

3 Opposition Strength

On the issue of child disability, the forces propelling conservative change forward were strong. The child disability provisions within the House-passed legislation reflected the Republican's broader policy agenda for SSI, which included reducing fraud and abuse, controlling federal spending by capping funding or converting SSI into a block grant, and preserving SSI benefits only for those with severe disabilities. Fraud and abuse were frequently the topic of discussion in congressional hearings, yet it was the budgetary impact of such provisions that was perhaps the more relevant focus.[45] By capping the amount of federal funding available and reducing the number of eligible beneficiaries, the legislation would decrease current and future spending on SSI.

The savings generated from SSI were intended to help Republicans meet their goals of financing a middle-class tax cut and balancing the budget. Though the vast majority of the savings would come from eliminating the eligibility of noncitizens for the SSI program, the proposed changes in child eligibility would eliminate more than 250,000 children from the SSI rolls, and cash benefits would be preserved for only one-third of future applicants. Such changes were projected to produce a savings of $12 billion over a five-year period. Because changes to the SSI program would produce considerable savings, support for such policy changes was strong, particularly in the House (Haskins 2006).

As with the previous issues, the policy side opposing the child disability provisions in H.R. 4 was not particularly strong. Opponents found little support in the House among the majority party but did find some support in the Senate, especially from Republican Senator John Chafee of Rhode Island, who was a veteran member of the Finance Committee and had long supported children's health issues (Erkulwater 2006). Disability advocates, working through Senator Kent Conrad of North Dakota and Senator Tom Daschle of South Dakota, also attempted to mobilize support behind an alternative bill that would not directly remove any children from SSI eligibility.[46] With respect to the administration, the Clinton welfare reform bill did not address changes in child eligibility for the SSI program (Work and Responsibility Act of 1994 [H.R. 4605]

---

[44] See *Contract with America – Welfare Reform* (1995), 384–90.

[45] See *Contract with America – Welfare Reform* (1995), 359–503; *Growth of the Supplemental Security Income Program* (1995), 1–89.

[46] Memo to Bruce N. Reed from Diana M. Fortuna. "SSI Kids: Conrad vs. Slattery." April 26, 1995; Memo for Leon Panetta from Diana Fortuna, "Children's SSI Program." April 27, 1995. Domestic Policy Council, Bruce Reed, and Welfare Reform Series, "SSI [Supplemental Security Income]," *Clinton Digital Library*.

1994).[47] Thus although opponents of conservative policy changes found some support among Democrats and moderate Republicans in the Senate, the strength of this policy side during welfare reform debates was not particularly high.[48]

Child Exclusion Issues

A final goal of welfare reform was to reduce the incidence of out-of-wedlock childbirth, especially among teenagers. Between 1960 and 1990, the country witnessed a sharp increase in the share of births to unmarried women and the number of births to teens.[49] Upward trends in non-marital childbirth and teen pregnancy were considered problematic for several reasons. First, single adults with children were more likely than other adults to be poor. In 1993, 40 percent of white, single-mother families were poor, and more than 50 percent of African American, single-mother families were poor. In contrast, approximately 10 percent of white families and just under 30 percent of African American families were poor (Blank 1997). Second, children born to teen mothers were more likely than other children to experience educational and behavioral problems throughout their childhood (Brooks-Gunn and Furstenberg 1986). Relative to other young adults, teenagers who gave birth to children out of marriage also experienced lower rates of high school graduation and higher rates of poverty (Furstenberg et al. 1989).

   Child exclusions provisions aimed to arrest the rate of increase in teen and out-of-wedlock pregnancy by eliminating welfare benefits to children of single, teen mothers or current welfare recipients. Specifically, H.R. 4 mandated that welfare benefits be denied to the children of unmarried teen mothers under the age of 18 with the option for states to extend the exclusion to mothers under the age of 21 (the "teen mother exclusion") and children born to mothers currently receiving welfare (the "family cap").[50] The provisions were termed "child exclusion provisions" because they eliminated the child's eligibility to receive welfare benefits, sometimes for the child's life. Child exclusion policies reflected the belief, popularized by conservative policy intellectuals such as Charles Murray, that public assistance contributed to the rise in teen and out-of-

---

[47] See *Work and Responsibility Act of 1994*, HR 4605, 103rd Cong., 2nd sess., *Congressional Record* 140 (June 21, 1994).

[48] After the passage of the PRWORA, the Clinton administration did pressure Congress to alleviate some of the hardships resulting from the policy. For instance, the 1997 Balanced Budget Act allowed children who had been cut from SSI to retain their Medicaid benefits until age 18 and established the State Children's Health Insurance Program, which devoted federal funding to encourage states to provide health insurance for low-income families (Erkulwater 2006).

[49] In 1960, 5 percent of all births to women between the ages of 15 and 44 were to single women. Thirty years later, that figure had grown to 28 percent. The issue of childbirth outside marriage intersected with the problem of teen pregnancy, as teen mothers were more likely than other mothers to have children outside marriage. In 1990, 56 percent of all births to white teenagers and 92 percent of all births to black teenagers occurred outside marriage (Blank 1997).

[50] *Personal Responsibility Act of 1995*, HR 4, Sec. 105–7.

wedlock pregnancy by providing the means for women to support their children at a young age and outside marriage (Murray 1984). Eliminating access to public assistance, child exclusion proponents argued, would deter teens and current welfare recipients from having children out of wedlock.

1 *Salience*

Though less salient in the popular media than either welfare-to-work or program structure issues, child exclusion issues nevertheless received notable media attention. Between November 1994 and August 1996, the *New York Times* published 114 articles on welfare and child exclusion provisions. Congressional policymakers also devoted considerable attention to the topics of teen pregnancy and out-of-wedlock childbirth. Half-day hearings were held before the House Ways and Means Committee's Subcommittee on Human Resources and the Senate Finance Committee in early 1995.[51] During these hearings, legislators received testimony from 12 witnesses in the course of four panels, which was roughly comparable to the attention paid to program structure and welfare-to-work issues in congressional hearings.

While the breadth of organizational involvement across the four panels was somewhat low – most witnesses were policy intellectuals or represented research organizations – an analysis of interest group testimony across the wider set of subcommittee hearings in the House of Representatives reveals the importance of the issues of teen pregnancy, family formation, and child exclusion provisions to a varied set of organized interests. Many types of organizations discussed such issues in their oral and written statements. Among conservative groups, fathers' rights organizations such as the Texas Father's Alliance highlighted the dual problems of teen pregnancy and out-of-wedlock childbirth in hearings testimony.[52] Reflecting the priority placed on child exclusion issues by traditional values groups, the Concerned Women for

---

[51] The hearings include *Illegitimacy and Welfare*, held before the Subcommittee on Human Resources in the House Ways and Means Committee on January 20, 1995 (part of the larger *Contract with America – Welfare Reform* hearings), and *Teen Parents and Welfare Reform*, held before the Senate Committee on Finance on March 14, 1995 (see Appendix for full citations). The witnesses before the House subcommittee include Glenn Loury, professor at Boston University; James Q. Wilson, professor at the University of California Los Angeles; William Bennett, co-director of Empower America; Pam Harris White, private citizen; Amy Hendricks, private citizen; Rebecca Blank, professor at Northwestern University; Reverend Robert A. Sirico, president of the Acton Institute for the Study of Religion and Liberty; and Ruth Ethen Wasem of the Congressional Research Service. The witnesses before the Senate committee include Douglas Besharov of the American Enterprise Institute for Public Policy Research; Robert Granger, senior vice president of the Manpower Demonstration Research Corporation; Rebecca Maynard, professor at the University of Pennsylvania; and Kristin Moore, executive director and director of research at Child Trends.

[52] *Contract with America – Welfare Reform* (1995), 1245–63.

America also expressed strong support for child exclusion provisions to combat such problems in oral and written testimony.[53]

Many other groups testified in opposition to child exclusion policies, including antipoverty advocates, charitable service providers, women's organizations, and civil rights groups. Because child exclusion policies would leave certain groups of children without access to welfare benefits, advocates for poor families and children, including the Coalition on Human Needs, opposed the policies. Groups including the NOW Legal Defense and Education Fund and the ACLU objected to child exclusion policies on constitutional grounds.[54] Reproductive rights groups including the National Abortion and Reproductive Rights Action League (NARAL) were also opposed, arguing that child exclusion policies represented an infringement on women's liberties.[55] Intergovernmental actors such as governors objected to child exclusion policies because they limited state discretion by imposing mandates on states.[56] Finally, religious and antiabortion groups such as Catholic Charities opposed such policies in part because they could potentially lead more poor women to seek abortions.[57] Thus although witnesses invited to testify on child exclusion issues consisted primarily of policy experts, such issues were clearly salient to a wide and varied set of organized interests.

2 Uncertainty

There was a great deal of uncertainty regarding the potential of child exclusion policies to curb birthrates and encourage marriage, even though the family cap had recently been enacted in a handful of states through the welfare waiver program. Evaluation research focused on the policy's impact in New Jersey, which had been the first state to enact a statewide family cap in 1992. Unfortunately, this research yielded mixed results, with early studies showing a significant decline in out-of-wedlock births and later studies showing no effect. In addition, one study appeared to show an increase in abortions following the enactment of the family cap (Preston 1998; Rector 1995; Weaver 2000). The policy impacts of the family cap were therefore unclear. By 1995, no state had yet adopted the more punitive teen mother exclusion; as a result, the impacts of the exclusion were unknown.

Such uncertainty regarding the likely impact of child exclusion policies is evident in the testimony and question-and-answer sessions of congressional hearings. Numerous policy intellectuals challenged the underlying logic of child exclusion policies, drawing into question the potential of the family cap and teen mother exclusion to alter patterns of childbirth and family formation

---

[53] *Contract with America – Welfare Reform* (1995), 823–28.
[54] *Contract with America – Welfare Reform* (1995), 1622–37; 1369–77.
[55] *Contract with America – Welfare Reform* (1995), 829–30.
[56] *Contract with America – Welfare Reform* (1995), 11–35; see also Haskins 2006.
[57] *Contract with America – Welfare Reform* (1995), 715.

in low-income communities. Indeed, policy intellectuals on both the left and the right highlighted the uncertain impacts of child exclusion policies. Even a panel of experts invited by Republican leaders to make a "coherent case" for child exclusion policies expressed uncertainty regarding the impacts of the family cap and teen mother exclusion, surprising Republican leaders. Though the experts supported the emphasis on teen pregnancy and out-of-wedlock childbirth, two of the panelists expressed skepticism regarding the ability of the family cap and teen mother exclusion to address such complex problems (Haskins 2006).[58]

With respect to popular support for child exclusion provisions, public opinion polls also yielded mixed results. Although a poll commissioned by the conservative Family Research Commission found overwhelming support for the family cap, other polls revealed that the percentage of individuals supporting family cap policy ranged from 36 to 68 percent. Public support for the teen mother exclusion was decidedly lower, ranging from 20 to 44 percent across a set of six national polls. Moreover, the public did not appear to prioritize the problems motivating child exclusion policies, with less than 20 percent of individuals surveyed stating that reducing out-of-wedlock births was the most important goal of welfare reform (Weaver 2000: 169–95). Tepid public support for child exclusion policies, alongside ambiguous research findings, raised the possibility that the family cap and teen mother exclusion would fail to work as intended, thereby leading to negative policy and electoral consequences. Thus the level of uncertainty surrounding such policies was high.

3 Opposition Strength

For child exclusion issues, the policy sides reflected different perspectives regarding the focus of welfare reform efforts and the likely impact of child exclusion policies. The side supporting the child exclusion mandates in H.R. 4 prioritized the issue of family formation as a central component of welfare reform. For organizations and individuals supporting the teen mother exclusion and family cap, efforts to increase work activity among welfare recipients were less important than efforts to combat the problems of teen pregnancy and out-of-wedlock childbirth (Haskins 2006). The policy side opposing the child exclusion policies in H.R. 4 did not place the same priority on such problems, questioned the causal link between the welfare program and patterns of family formation, and rejected the mandate to enact uniform policies across states.

The set of actors supporting the family cap and teen mother exclusion was extremely strong. Conservative groups such as the Christian Coalition, Heritage Foundation, and Empower America had the ear of the newly empowered Republican leadership as well as conservative Republican legislators in the House and Senate. Such membership groups had been

---

[58] *Contract with America – Welfare Reform* (1995), 149–78.

TABLE 8.1 *The Varying Issue Contexts of Welfare Reform*

	Program Structure	Welfare to Work	Child Disability	Child Exclusion
Salience	High	High	Low	High
Uncertainty	High	Low	High	High
Strength: Side supporting H.R. 4	High	High	High	High
Strength: Side opposing H.R. 4	Low	Low	Low	High

instrumental in helping Republicans gain majority power in the midterm elections, and the party leadership was committed to addressing their concerns in welfare reform (Balz and Brownstein 1996). Such groups had lobbied aggressively to shape the welfare reform bill included in the Contract with America and were granted considerable access to congressional leaders as welfare reform moved through the legislative process (Bennett 1994; Brownstein 1994; DeParle 1994; Haskins 2006; Pear 1995).

Child exclusion policies, however, differ from the previous policies in that the side opposing family caps and teen mother exclusions was also relatively strong. While opposition to the family cap and teen mother exclusion from traditional liberal advocates was considerable, opposition also came from right-to-life groups as well as intergovernmental groups. Groups including the National Right to Life Committee and the U.S. Catholic Conference had ties to conservative legislators, which meant that the policy side opposing child exclusion provisions had access to members of Congress with conservative views on abortion. In addition, both the Clinton administration and most governors rejected a uniform child exclusion policy mandate across states. In the Clinton administration's plan, family caps were allowed as state options but not mandated (Weaver 2000). Relative to other issues, the policy side that opposed the conservative change in H.R. 4 had broader legislative access and at least some support from governors and the administration, making it relatively strong on this particular issue.

Table 8.1 summarizes the salience, uncertainty, and nature of opposition across the four policy issues. This table shows that for program structure, welfare-to-work, and child disability issues, the side supporting the policies in H.R. 4 was strong while the side opposing such policies was weak. For child exclusion issues, both policy sides were relatively strong. Whereas both program structure and child exclusion issues were salient and uncertain, welfare-to-work issues were highly salient but not uncertain and child disability issues were uncertain but lacked salience.

The political context predictions hold that diverse coalitions will emerge on issues that involve high levels of salience and uncertainty and on which opponents are perceived as strong. Thus the theory predicts that diverse coalitions will form on the liberal policy side for program structure issues and on both the conservative and liberal policy sides for child exclusion issues. Diverse coalitions are not expected to form on welfare-to-work or child disability issues. In the following section, I examine whether the empirical evidence bears out these predictions across the four issues.

COLLABORATION

The data reveal that different patterns of diverse collaboration emerged across the four issues. Consistent with the expectations of the theory, coalitional activity across diverse actors on welfare-to-work or child disability issues was limited. The House and Senate hearings focused on work-oriented reform efforts overwhelmingly involved researchers, intergovernmental actors, and service providers testifying as independent actors. Some coalitions did testify against the punitive welfare to work proposals contained within H.R. 4, including coalitions of organizations representing different groups of women. Coalitions of women's organizations also maintained a presence outside Congress by lobbying administration officials, releasing advertisements, and holding protests.[59] Yet while these coalitions included women's groups that were aligned with different professions or interests, they did not tend to draw together groups operating in distinctly different policy domains or with heterogeneous partisan or ideological leanings.

Organizational involvement on child disability issues beyond disability advocates, program administrators, and policy experts was limited, reflecting the low level of salience beyond the disability community. Similar to welfare-to-work issues, many of the groups that attempted to influence policymaking on child disability issues did so as independent actors. Although disability advocates are described as active in fighting against the SSI provisions contained within the House-passed legislation, hearings testimony, media reports, and archival sources provide limited evidence of diverse collaboration. One formal coalition, the Consortium for Citizens with Disability, testified against policies that would change the SSI program. While this coalition united groups engaged in varying aspects of advocacy and service

---

[59] See, for example, the statement from the Council of Presidents of National Women's Organizations, a coalition consisting of the leaders of prominent women's organizations, articulating a set of principles on welfare reform that included access to supportive services and investment in training and education. ("National Women's Pledge on Welfare Reform: Principles for Eliminating Poverty," Council of Presidents, undated, Box 47, folder "Women." Bruce Reed Welfare Reform Collection: William J. Clinton Presidential Library). See also the Women's Committee of One Hundred advertisement discussed in Chapter 6 (Press Release from the Women's Committee of One Hundred, August 29, 1995, MC 727, Box 33, folder #11, Legal Momentum Records, 1968–2008, Schlesinger Library, Radcliffe Institute, Harvard University, Cambridge, Massachusetts.)

delivery for disabled individuals and thus contained professional diversity, its membership did not unite groups from varying policy domains nor did the coalition draw attention to any ideological or partisan diversity among its members. With the exception of this coalition, independent rather than collaboratively lobbying characterized advocacy on child disability issues.

Both formal and informal coalitions containing actors that were diverse with respect to policy domain and ideology lobbied against the child exclusion policies, both inside and outside Congress. The Coalition on Human Needs, which was diverse with respect to policy domain, stated unequivocally during House subcommittee hearings its opposition to proposals that would deny assistance to children of teen mothers.[60] In addition, child exclusion policies led to the formation of the Child Exclusion Task Force, an ad hoc and formal partnership consisting of groups from different policy domains and with different ideological perspectives. The coalition was active in lobbying against the child exclusion proposals contained within H.R. 4, establishing subunits within the coalition to monitor policy developments, engaging in lobbying of members of Congress, and mobilizing grassroots support.

Child exclusion issues were also unique in that opponents of conservative policy change were relatively strong. Thus the theory predicts that diverse coalitions should form among groups supporting child exclusion policies. Indeed, as discussed in the Chapter 6, child exclusion issues were the only issues to witness informal collaboration between social conservative membership groups, including the Christian Coalition and the Concerned Women for America, and conservative research organizations, such as the Heritage Foundation. Such collaboration contained professional diversity and united the constituent resources of the former with the policy expertise of the latter. Yet the collaboration was distinctly different from that of advocates, as it did not unite groups from various domains or with different partisan leaning but rather united groups with varying types of engagement in the social policy domain.

Program structure issues were also characterized by uncertainty over potential policy and electoral outcomes, salience to interested actors, and a strong set of actors supporting structural changes to the welfare program. Thus the theory predicts that diverse coalitions should emerge among those groups opposing such changes, but not among those groups supporting such changes. With respect to the activities of advocates, there are several instances of diverse collaborative activity on program structure issues. As noted previously, formal and diverse coalitions including the Coalition on Human Needs expressed opposition to block granting the AFDC programs. The *New York Times* advertisement presented in Chapter 7 articulated the shared opposition of antipoverty advocates, children's groups, and an education group to block grants. The news conference held by the CDF,

[60] *Contract with America – Welfare Reform* (1995), 1065.

National Organization for Women, NAACP, Consortium for Citizens with Disabilities, and Bread for the World focused heavily on opposition to block grants. Thus groups representing different domains and with different sources of expertise jointly communicated their opposition to structural changes through hearings, advertisements, and press conferences.

Despite high levels of conflict, uncertainty, and salience, ad hoc diverse coalitions did not emerge among advocates on program structure issues. The evidence suggests that collaboration may have been limited by a shift in the political environment over the course of the welfare reform debate. Specifically, once the Clinton administration communicated that it would accept the transformation of AFDC into a block grant, such structural changes became likely to pass. Block grant opponents therefore shifted away from lobbying against the transformation itself and toward protections that would discourage states from under-providing funding (Weaver 2000). The shift in position created an environment in which a particular policy side was almost certain to prevail, creating limited incentives for actors to build costly coalitions across diverse partners on the issue.

DISCUSSION AND CONCLUSION

Consistent with the expectations of the theory, organized interests exhibited different collaborative behavior across welfare-to-work, program structure, child disability, and child exclusion issues. For both conservative and liberal groups, collaboration between diverse partners is least evident on child disability issues, which were salient to a small range of organized interests, and welfare-to-work issues, which were characterized by low levels of uncertainty. To the extent that diverse collaboration occurred, it was between groups that differed with respect to their professional engagement in a given policy domain rather than their policy domain or ideology. The previous chapter suggested that the latter are particularly salient types of diversity, as these were the types of diversity that were communicated to legislators by groups acting in partnership.

Among opponents of conservative change, diverse collaboration was considerably more pronounced on program structure and child exclusion issues. Yet while coalitions that were diverse with respect to domain and ideology communicated opposition to program structure and child exclusion issues, ad hoc and diverse collaborative efforts – arguably the most costly type of collaboration – only emerged among advocates on child exclusion issues, which were both salient and uncertain and on which opponents were strong. While program structure issues also involved strong opponents, uncertainty, and salience to many actors, the analysis suggests that advocates faced decreased incentives to collaborate because of a shift in the political environment over the course of the policymaking process.

A striking finding is the extent to which diverse collaboration among advocates is not mirrored by diverse collaboration among proponents of conservative policy change. Indeed, child exclusion issues were the only issue to witness informal collaboration between conservative groups with varying types of engagement in the social policy domain. Child exclusion issues were also the issue on which advocates were relatively strong. Because conservative groups had strong access to members of Congress during welfare reform, and because their opponents were relatively less powerful, incentives for such groups to undertake the costs of diverse collaboration on other issues were limited. Thus the analysis provides evidence consistent with the argument that collaboration across diverse partners is more likely when opponents are perceived as strong.

Also important are the qualitative differences in the types of diverse coalitions that emerged across issues and in the larger policy debate. On child exclusion issues, opponents of conservative change formed informal and formal coalitions that included members from diverse policy domains and with diverse ideological leanings. These actors brought a range of electoral and policy information to their lobbying efforts. The Child Exclusion Task Force and its broader network of partners had a specific goal: to oppose the family cap and teen mother exclusion. On program structure issues, formal and informal coalitions active early in the process similarly united groups from a range of policy domains but notably did not unite groups with distinct partisan or ideological differences.

It is important to note that many of the coalitions that were discussed in previous chapters were organized around a much broader goal: to oppose policies that were "bad for kids." Both the Contract with America's Children and the Stand for Children rally explicitly downplayed specific policy recommendations in an attempt to engage a broader range of participants. The Contract with America's Children promised to "consider children's needs and well-being first and foremost" and "ensure that all children get the basics they need to grow up healthy" but did not state its opposition to block grants, child exclusion proposals, or welfare-to-work policies. Thus in these instances, the diversification of the coalition likely came at the expense of communicating support or opposition to specific policy proposals.

Far from a unitary policy change, this chapter demonstrates that welfare reform involved different issues that varied with respect to their level of salience, uncertainty, and the nature of opposition strength. An analysis of the coalitional activity of organized interests across four issues provides evidence consistent with the premise that groups' coalitional strategies vary alongside such characteristics of the issue. During welfare reform, groups did not pursue the same strategies across welfare-to-work, program structure, child disability and child exclusion issues but rather pursued different strategies in different issue environments. When advocates found themselves in an issue environment characterized by conflict, uncertainty, and salience, they successfully collaborated with diverse partners in pursuit of their policy goal. In the absence of conflict, uncertainty, and salience, diverse partnerships did not form. While the finding that collaborative activity emerges on issues of high conflict and salience is consistent with previous work, the finding that uncertainty is associated with collaborative behavior is an extension to the existing literature. If diverse coalitions function as a signal that reduces legislative uncertainty in the policymaking process, then organized interests will have a greater incentive to collaborate with diverse partners on issues that are characterized by high levels of uncertainty.

9

Interest Group Coalitions and American Social Policy: Implications and Extensions

INTRODUCTION

In the United States, poverty remains a pressing national concern. More than 46 million Americans – including 15 million children – lived below the federal poverty line in 2014. The poverty rate for single women with children, for whom welfare assistance historically provided an important means of support, is nearly double the national average (DeNavas-Walt et al. 2015). Moreover, the cash assistance program created under the Personal Responsibility and Work Opportunity and Reconciliation Act of 1996 (PRWORA) provides benefits to only a small number of these families. For every 100 poor families, only 27 received assistance through the Temporary Assistance to Needy Families (TANF) program in 2010 (Trisi and Pavetti, 2012). Such statistics affirm the need for national policies to alleviate economic hardship for low-income Americans.

Within and outside Washington, interest groups mobilized around antipoverty issues continue to work tirelessly for progressive policy change. Often, they do not win. After all, the citizen groups, nonprofit organizations, research groups, and intergovernmental actors that advocate on behalf of America's least advantaged lack the large constituent bases and extensive funding of businesses and professional groups. But sometimes, such actors do realize their policy goals. This book represents an attempt to understand the mechanisms through which organizations that advocate for the poor gain influence in a political system that does not favor their success.

I have argued in this book that to understand how organizational advocates for the poor gain policy influence, it is necessary to understand how interest group coalitions gain policy influence. Past research shows that collaborative lobbying is prevalent in national politics, particularly among groups mobilized around social welfare policy issues. Although coalitions encounter resource constraints, this book demonstrates that if coalitions are viewed through an informational lens, it becomes clear that a coalition's influence does not derive from the sheer number of resources brought to a collaborative lobbying effort. Rather, influence stems from the diversity of voices and resources within a coalition. Because influence derives from diversity rather than size, it is possible to understand how groups with limited resources can influence the policy choices of elected leaders.

In this chapter, I review the key insights and extensions of the theoretical and empirical analyses. I begin by describing advocates' policy successes during welfare reform on the four issues discussed in the previous chapter. Although the analysis is not designed to test the independent impact of diverse collaboration, the evidence is consistent with the premise that diverse coalitions are associated with influence in the legislative policymaking process, warranting future research on the subject. In the second part of the chapter, I review the central components of the theory of diverse coalitions and describe how the empirical analysis supports the theoretical predictions and refines these predictions for future research. The third part of the chapter discusses the generalizability of the theory beyond the social policy domain, and the fourth part of the chapter describes the implications for research on social policy and interest group influence. In the final part of the chapter, I elaborate on the extensions and implications of the research and conclude.

DIVERSE COLLABORATION AND THE PERSONAL RESPONSIBILITY AND WORK OPPORTUNITY RECONCILIATION ACT OF 1996

The PRWORA undoubtedly represents a conservative turn in American social welfare policy. In addition to ending the long-standing entitlement to cash assistance, the policy imposed strict behavioral requirements as a condition for receiving benefits. Under the PRWORA, low-income individuals faced a lifetime limit on benefit receipt and could be denied assistance for failing to comply with work requirements. States were permitted to deny additional cash benefits to mothers who had an additional child while receiving welfare. And states gained considerable discretion in a wide range of program areas including time limits, eligibility requirements and exemptions, and sanctioning policies.

While the PRWORA is appropriately regarded as an overall policy loss for low-income populations, differences between the legislation that was introduced into the House of Representatives in early 1995 and the bill signed by President Clinton in August 1996 are significant. The final legislation eliminated several of the most extreme behavioral mandates, instituted exemptions and provided additional supports for working parents, and included rules that would discourage states from under-providing welfare assistance. Given the larger political context, in which advocates for the poor were forced to lobby against conservative changes to an unpopular program in a Republican-controlled Congress, these differences represent important policy victories for advocates, who are cited by both participants and scholars as influential in securing such changes (Haskins 2006; Weaver 2000; Winston 2002).

In this section, I describe how the program structure, welfare-to-work, child exclusion, and child disability policies contained within the PRWORA differ from the legislation that was introduced in the House of Representatives in early 1995. In addition, I discuss the relationship between diverse coalitions and the differences between the House legislation and the final welfare reform bill. While the discussion does not constitute a test of the independent impact of diverse collaboration, the evidence is consistent with such a hypothesis. I argue that together with the empirical support for the posited mechanisms of coalitional influence, such evidence warrants future investigation of the relationship between diverse collaboration and influence in Congress.

Policy Choices in the Personal Responsibility and Work Opportunity Reconciliation Act

H.R. 4, the legislation introduced in the House of Representatives on January 4, 1995, contained a wide array of changes to the American safety net. The original House legislation ended the individual entitlement of needy families to cash assistance and capped federal spending on the welfare program. States were given the option of converting welfare funds into a block grant, in which states would receive considerably more authority to design and operate their own welfare programs.[1]

Under the PRWORA, the cash welfare program was converted into a block grant and the individual entitlement to cash assistance was eliminated. Yet while the structure of the welfare program was changed, "maintenance-of-effort" (MOE) provisions were also included. The MOE provisions required that states maintained at least 80 percent of their historic spending levels on the welfare program to receive the full assistance grant. These provisions were designed to discourage states from significantly scaling back their welfare spending after the passage of the PRWORA.[2]

With respect to welfare-to-work provisions, the initial House legislation mandated work activity as a condition of receiving cash assistance. The intent of such provisions, the legislation stated, was to move recipients into employment as quickly as possible. Single-parent recipients were required to work a minimum of 35 hours per week after receiving benefits for two years, and states were required to move 2 percent of the welfare caseload into work

---

[1] *Personal Responsibility Act of 1995*, HR 4, 104th Cong., 1st sess., *congressional Record* 141:1 (January 4, 1995): H122–23; Title III, Sections 302, 201, and Title VI, Section 601.

[2] *Personal Responsibility and Work Opportunity Reconciliation Act of 1996*, Public Law 104–193, *U.S. Statutes at Large* 100 (1996): 2105–355, Part A, Title I; see also Greenberg and Savner (1996).

activity by 1996 and 50 percent by 2003. Individuals who had received cash assistance for 60 months, or 24 months at state option, would be ineligible for further welfare assistance.[3]

The PWROWA contained provisions that were similar to many of the work provisions contained within the original House legislation, but it also included special rules for some recipients. Such rules moderated the work requirements and time limits for young parents, parents with young children, and recipients experiencing violence or other forms of hardship. Under the PRWORA, single-parent families were required to work at least 20 hours per week on receiving benefits for two years and states were required to have 25 percent of the welfare caseload in work activities by 1997 and 50 percent by 2002. The legislation contained special work-related provisions for teen heads of household and single parents with young children, some of which were not mandated but rather available as state options. Welfare benefits remained time limited at 60 months, but states were permitted to exempt up to 20 percent of their caseload from time limits for reasons of hardship or domestic violence.[4]

With respect to child exclusion provisions, H.R. 4 denied cash benefits to children born to teen mothers (teen mother exclusion) and children born to mothers currently receiving welfare (family cap).[5] Under the PRWORA, neither the teen mother exclusion nor the family cap were mandated but rather were permitted as state options. This meant that states were allowed to adopt policies denying assistance to teens and mothers currently on welfare but were not required to do so.[6]

Finally, the initial changes to the child disability provisions in the Supplemental Security Income (SSI) program, which were contained within the legislation that passed the House in March 1995, restricted cash SSI benefits to those children with the most severe physical and mental impairments. The individual functional assessment (IFA), which established disability diagnoses for children with impairments not listed in the Code of Federal Regulations, was eliminated. Children with impairments that were relatively less severe were not eligible for cash assistance but were to receive vouchers for services, which would be provided to states through a block grant.[7] Under the PRWORA, the definition of disability was narrowed and the IFA was eliminated. The program was not converted into a block grant structure,

[3] *Personal Responsibility Act of 1995*, Title 11.
[4] *Personal Responsibility and Work Opportunity Act of 1996*, Part A, Title 1.
[5] *Personal Responsibility Act of 1995*, Title 1.
[6] *Personal Responsibility and Work Opportunity Reconciliation Act of 1996*, Part A, Title I.
[7] To be eligible for cash assistance in the House-passed legislation, a child had to possess an impairment listed in the Code of Federal Regulations, and that impairment (or set of impairments) had to be severe enough to necessitate care in a hospital or residential treatment center. Those children with impairments that were not severe enough to require hospitalization would be eligible to receive funding for services but not cash assistance (See *Personal Responsibility Act of 1995* [*Engrossed House*], Title VI Section 602 and Title VI Part C).

thereby ensuring that all children who met eligibility criteria would continue to receive cash assistance.[8]

The MOE provisions, exemptions and special provisions of welfare-to-work policies, removal of child exclusion mandates, and continuation of the entitlement of disabled children to SSI benefits, represented important victories for advocates for the poor. MOE provisions prevented against a "race to the bottom" in state welfare spending, in which states would potentially under-provide welfare assistance to avoid attracting poor families to the states. The welfare-to-work exemptions assured that young mothers, mothers of young children, and victims of hardship or violence would be subject to a less restrictive set of requirements than other recipients. The removal of child exclusion mandates meant that states would not be required (though they were still permitted) to deny assistance to certain children. And the continuation of SSI entitlements meant that the federal government would continue to provide assistance to children with disabilities. Thus while the PRWORA contained many provisions that advocates for the poor did not support, the final legislation was far less severe than the original House legislation in several key program areas.

These policy changes may seem minor when measured against the overall loss of welfare entitlement, the conditioning of welfare receipt on work activity, the enhanced discretion given to state governments to impose child exclusion policies, and the limits placed on the disability determinations process for children. Yet each of the changes represented a protection or support for low-income families that did not exist in the original House legislation. Such changes demonstrate that, contrary to the established wisdom that the interests of low-income populations are entirely absent in the legislative policymaking process, advocates for low-income populations were able to secure at least some gains during welfare reform policymaking in the 104th Congress.

Diverse Collaboration and Policy Influence during Welfare Reform

As noted in the introduction to this chapter, it is challenging to disentangle the independent effect of diverse coalitions on legislative policy outcomes because organized interests engaged in a wide range of lobbying strategies during welfare reform, on many issues. Groups lobbied independently, mobilized constituents to write letters and call congressional offices, released media advertisements, and met individually with congressional staff. Thus it is difficult to isolate the independent effect of diverse collaboration on the final legislative policy choices.

Yet the evidence does suggest that the groups that mobilized collaboratively in opposition to the family cap and teen mother exclusion

---

[8] *Personal Responsibility and Work Opportunity Reconciliation Act of 1996*, Part A, Title II, Subtitle B.

were effective in their efforts to prevent the adoption of child exclusion mandates. Recall that child exclusion issues were the only issues to witness the formation of an ad hoc and diverse policy coalition: the Child Exclusion Task Force (CETF). This coalition united groups with varying professional identities, from different policy domains, and with diverse ideological positions on the issue of abortion. As the previous chapters illustrate, the CETF used the unique resources of its diverse partners to gain access to Republican legislators, engage in phone campaigns and visits to congressional offices, and distribute packets of information. Much of the activity of the CETF focused on the Senate, where advocates perceived their influence to be stronger. Indeed, participants explicitly attributed the defeat of child exclusion mandates in the Senate to the activities of antipoverty advocates (Haskins 2006: 220).

Moreover, it is noteworthy that the defeat of the family cap and teen mother exclusion mandates occurred against the preferences of powerful constituency groups. Child exclusion mandates were energetically supported by conservative membership-based organizations including the Christian Coalition, the Concerned Women for America, and the Eagle Forum. Such provisions were intended in part to reward conservative groups for supporting Republican candidates in the 1994 elections. Thus it is not simply the case that advocates' successes occurred on issues involving limited conflict or weak opponents. On child exclusion issues, legislators scaled back some of the most extreme behavioral mandates against the wishes of constituents who were mobilized and politically active. Such evidence, while not determinative, is nevertheless consistent with the hypothesis that diverse coalitions help groups gain influence in the policy process. Together with the analysis presented in previous chapters, this evidence warrants future research on the influence of diverse coalitions in the policy process.

DIVERSE COALITIONS AS A STRATEGY OF POLITICAL INFLUENCE

The analysis of interest group collaboration during welfare reform provides support for the three parts of the theory of diverse coalitions and refines the theoretical predictions in several ways. During welfare reform, organized interests on all sides of the policy debate engaged in collaboration with diverse partners. Diverse coalitions brought a broad range of resources to partner organizations and allowed them to engage in varied lobbying tactics. In addition, diverse coalitions communicated information about the underlying support for policy change and were used selectively across issues within welfare reform. In this section, I review the central insights of the theory of diverse coalitions and elaborate on the key findings of the empirical analysis. I also discuss how the analysis of the welfare reform case helps refine the theory's predictions.

Diverse Coalitions and Resource Mobilization

The theory proposed two sets of mechanisms through which diversity leads to influence. The first mechanism is called the resource mobilization mechanism. This mechanism holds that diversity helps a set of organizations gain influence by drawing different types of informational resources to a collaborative lobbying effort and by allowing partners to engage in varied strategies for communicating this information. Diverse informational resources and lobbying tactics are important for several reasons, including that many legislators are involved in the policymaking process and that these legislators are accountable to assorted interests and constituents. Policies are also inherently multidimensional, with the potential to affect a wide range of outcomes. Information from different sources is therefore important when attempting to assess the many electoral, substantive, and political impacts of policy change.

The analysis of organizational activity during welfare reform provides considerable support for the resource mobilization mechanism. On both sides of the policy debate, collaboration allowed groups to pool varied informational resources. Coalitions between groups with different professional identities and diverse ideological leanings and from different policy domains allowed coalitions to draw on multiple forms of electoral and policy information in their lobbying efforts. For example, advocates worked through the Coalition on Human Needs, which drew together citizen groups from varying policy domains with institutional actors with specialized expertise, thereby uniting information about constituents with information about policy. Advocates for low-income children drew varied forms of electoral information to their lobbying activities by allying with children's groups from different policy domains, such as health and education. On the opposite policy side, a set of conservative citizen groups worked informally with Robert Rector of the Heritage Foundation and, in doing so, drew both electoral information and policy expertise to a collaborative lobbying effort.

Coalitions containing partners that differed with respect to their professional identity, policy domain, and ideology also utilized the differential resources of member organizations to engage in varying types of lobbying strategies. The CETF relied on its membership-based organizations, many of which were citizen groups, to engage in outside lobbying activities during the Senate debate on welfare reform. The CETF also utilized the partisan contacts of its pro-life members to gain access to Republican legislators. National children's organizations including the National Association of Child Advocates and the Coalition for America's Children relied on the contacts of regional partners to mobilize organizational opposition to the welfare reform bill at the state and local levels. Informal partnerships between conservative organizations allowed citizen groups with limited expertise on welfare reform, such as the Christian Coalition and Concerned Women for America, access to policy expertise while providing research organizations such as the Heritage Foundation with an active constituent base that would mobilize in support of the organization's policy recommendations.

The analysis of collaborative activity during welfare reform clearly illustrates that diversity within coalitions helped organizations enhance their involvement in the policymaking process. By uniting diverse forms of electoral and policy information, coalitions were able to draw varied forms of information to a collaborative lobbying effort while engaging in a wide range of lobbying tactics. Diversity within coalitions mattered in the sense that it helped groups mobilize the different resources necessary to participate in policymaking. The welfare reform case thus provides support for the resource mobilization mechanism of the theory of diverse coalitions.

In addition, while the theory proposed a broad definition of diversity, three types of diversity emerge as particularly important in the welfare reform case. Diversity with respect to professional identity allowed groups to unite the electoral information of citizen and professional groups with the expertise of research organizations and service providers. Diversity with respect to policy domain drew multiple types of electoral information to collaborative lobbying efforts and allowed groups to enhance outside lobbying activities. Finally, diversity with respect to partisan and ideological identity drew varied forms of electoral and policy information to lobbying efforts. Such resources were particularly useful in helping groups gain access to legislators otherwise unresponsive to their concerns.

Diverse Coalitions and Political Signaling

The theory also proposed that diversity within coalitions leads to influence by providing a credible and informative signal of the underlying support for policy change. Diversity enhances credibility, I argued, by offering heterogeneous informational cues that point to the same policy recommendation (the heterogeneous signaling mechanism) and by providing evidence of costly lobbying efforts (the costly lobbying mechanism). Such insights are based on a body of formal theoretic work that concludes that heterogeneous signals and costly lobbying activities enhance the credibility of information offered in Congress, thereby helping groups gain influence in the legislative process. I referred to these posited mechanisms of influence as the political signaling mechanisms.

As was the case with the resource mobilization mechanism, the empirical analysis provides considerable support for the political signaling mechanisms. Consistent with theoretical expectations, coalitions that united partners from diverse policy domains and with diverse ideologies communicated their diversity to legislators, thereby providing support for the heterogeneous signaling mechanism. Groups communicated diversity by referencing the diversity of coalition members directly, as in the statements by representatives from the National Governors Association and the CETF, or by drawing on a range of arguments to support a given policy position, as advocates did during a news conference opposing Republican welfare reform efforts. Moreover, the heterogeneity of the coalition behind the Stand for Children March was directly challenged by proponents of conservative policy change, providing further support for the argument that heterogeneity of partners within a coalition functions as an important mechanism of influence

With respect to costly lobbying, the analysis explored four types of costs associated with collaborative lobbying: opportunity costs, resource costs, reputational costs, and policy costs. Although the empirical focus on coalitions obscures some of the individual group costs associated with collaborative activity, the analysis provides considerable evidence of resource costs and policy costs for at least some groups.

For example, founders of the CETF experienced resource costs in the form of staff time spent coordinating with partners and multiple subgroups, meeting space, and material resources associated with compiling packets of information to distribute to Senate offices. Policy costs were also present for some coalitions in a variety of forms. In one instance, policy costs took the form of a diluted policy recommendation, as was the case for children's advocates. In another instance, policy costs essentially represented a trade between coalition members, as when Democratic and Republican governors negotiated a welfare policy compromise to restart congressional welfare reform policymaking. Finally, evidence indicates that organizations engaged in activities that may have prevented opportunity and reputational costs. For instance, groups mitigated opportunity costs by lobbying independently as well as collaboratively and may have lessened reputational costs by carefully specifying the terms of collaborative lobbying efforts.

Consistent with both past research and theoretical expectations, coalitions during welfare reform were used in a signaling capacity. In an extension to existing research, the analysis of collaborative activity during welfare reform demonstrates that an important component of that signal was the heterogeneity of voices contained within the coalition. In addition, while the research design is limited in its capacity to uncover costs, evidence shows that organizations engaged in diverse collaboration experienced considerable costs, particularly in the form of resources (the CETF) and policy costs (the Stand for Children March and the National Governors Association). Both the heterogeneity of informational cues and the high costs of collaborating with diverse partners were likely evident to legislators, thereby providing support for the argument that diversity works to enhance credibility by providing evidence of heterogeneous cues and costly lobbying efforts.

Diverse Coalitions and Issue Context

The third part of the theory identified a set of predictions regarding the emergence and activity of diverse coalitions in the policymaking process.

The political context predictions hold that coalitions uniting diverse partners will emerge on issues that are salient to a wide range of interests, uncertain in their implications, and on which policy opponents are perceived as strong. To examine the support for these predictions, the final empirical chapter analyzed diverse collaboration across four issues within welfare reform: program structure, welfare-to-work, child disability, and child exclusion issues.

The chapter provides evidence that coalitional activity varied across issues in ways consistent with the expectations of the theory. Among advocates for the poor, diverse coalitions – particularly those uniting groups from diverse policy domains or with diverse ideologies – were relatively less active on welfare-to-work issues, which were salient and involved strong opponents but were characterized by a high level of certainty. Diverse coalitions were also less likely to materialize among advocates for the poor on child disability issues, which involved high levels of uncertainty and strong opponents but lacked salience to a wide range of organizations. In addition, proponents of conservative reform did not engage in diverse collaboration on either welfare-to-work or child disability issues, as such groups did not encounter strong opponents on either issue.

Both program structure and child exclusion issues were characterized by high levels of salience, uncertainty, and for advocates, strong opponents. Consistent with theoretical expectations, such issues witnessed diverse collaboration among advocates for the poor. Formal diverse coalitions such as the Coalition on Human Needs objected to ending the entitlement to cash assistance (program structure) and mandating the family cap and teen mother exclusion (child exclusion issues). Coalitions uniting groups from different policy domains lobbied against program structure issues in press conferences, media advertisements, and hearings testimony. The CETF, a coalition characterized by domain and ideological diversity, formed in opposition to child exclusion provisions. In addition, it was only on the issue of child exclusion mandates that advocates for the poor were relatively strong. This issue was also the only one to witness informal collaboration between conservative groups that differed with respect to the professional identity of partner organizations.

While both program structure and child exclusion issues saw the emergence or activity of diverse coalitions among advocates for the poor, it is important to note that there were differences in the nature of diverse collaboration on these two issues. Most notably, an ad hoc formal coalition (the CETF) emerged on the issue of child exclusion provisions but not on the issue of structural changes to the welfare program. The analysis suggests that collaboration on program structure issues was in part hindered by a shift in legislative position over the course of the welfare reform debate. Once it was clear that the Clinton administration would not oppose ending the entitlement to cash assistance, structural changes to the welfare program became likely to pass, providing limited incentives for advocates to engage in costly diverse collaboration on this issue.

In providing support for the political signaling predictions, the analysis of collaborative activity during welfare reform expands on findings from existing work in several ways. Previous research finds that collaboration is highly context dependent, with collaboration more likely on issues that involve conflict and issues that are broad in scope. This study is consistent with existing work that finds that groups are more likely to work in partnership when opponents are perceived as strong (Hojnacki 1997). Because broad issues are likely to be salient to a wide range of actors, the finding that salience is associated with diverse collaboration also complements findings from previous research. However, this study suggests that it is salience rather than breadth alone that is the important characteristic shaping collaborative activity.

In addition, scholars have not previously identified uncertainty as a determinant of coalitional activity. Indeed, it is only when coalitions are viewed through an informational lens that the role of uncertainty becomes clear. In the case of welfare reform, diverse coalitions failed to materialize on an issue that was characterized by high salience and strong opponents, but low levels of uncertainty. The analysis of welfare reform thus offers evidence that the level of uncertainty on an issue may create differential incentives for groups to lobby collaboratively with diverse partners.

The Importance of Collaboration

Finally, the theory as a whole prioritizes the role of coalitions in the policymaking process. I argue that to understand the circumstances of interest group lobbying and influence, it is necessary to recognize that many lobbying efforts are characterized by organizations acting collaboratively rather than autonomously. Although focusing on individual group activity is important and yields numerous insights about lobbying and influence, such a focus necessarily obscures a great deal of lobbying activity. By focusing on coalitions and collaborative lobbying activity, scholars may be better able to identify the mechanisms linking interest group lobbying with legislative influence and understand the circumstances under which such influence occurs.

The analysis of organizational activity during welfare reform draws into focus the importance of coalitions in the social policymaking process. Both informal and formal coalitions were common in the two years preceding the passage of the PRWORA, especially among advocates for the poor. The priority given to coalitions in this project also draws into view previously unrecognized aspects of the well-studied case of welfare reform. For example, the focus on coalitions illustrates how advocates were able to gain access to Republican legislators on child exclusion issues and how conservative policy experts were able to mobilize electoral support for their policy recommendations. By drawing attention to *collections* of organizations rather than individual groups, the analysis highlights a critical set of activities and demonstrates how these activities allowed groups to enhance their role in the policymaking process.

Finally, the empirical analysis demonstrates that coalitions were important for all types of groups during welfare reform. Coalitions formed between groups that advocated on behalf of poor women and children, but also between groups that supported conservative Republican proposals. Thus while diverse coalitions were undoubtedly more common among advocates for the poor, it is not the case that diverse partnerships are a strategy utilized exclusively by interest groups with limited financial and electoral resources. Even groups with large membership bases were aided by collaboration with groups that possessed resources that they did not. As I discuss in the fourth section of this chapter, this finding bolsters the argument that the theory's implications may extend to policy domains not dominated by under-resourced organizations.

DIVERSE COLLABORATION BEYOND THE SOCIAL POLICY DOMAIN

This project was motivated by an interest in understanding organizational influence on behalf of the poor. Reflecting this focus, the empirical analysis drew on a case involving lobbying in the social policy domain. As I discussed in the Chapter 3, because the types of interest groups active on social welfare issues tend to differ from the types of groups active on other issues, the empirical findings are intended only to generalize to cases of interest group lobbying in the social policy domain. Yet there are strong *theoretical* reasons to suspect that the theory itself may be applicable to other policy domains because the factors that incline groups toward collaboration are not unique to social welfare policy issues. In addition, the mechanisms that underlie a coalition's influence are likely to apply in multiple issue areas. In this section, I elaborate on the wider generalizability of the theory of diverse coalitions.

First, the institutional factors that incline groups toward collaboration are not exclusive to groups that lobby on behalf of the poor but rather extend across populations and interests. For example, the expansion and decentralization of Congress has affected numerous policy domains (Deering and Smith 1997), creating strong incentives for groups of all types to pool disparate resources to reach the large number of legislators with authority on any given issue. In addition, the size of the interest group population has increased across economic sectors (Schlozman, Verba, and Brady 2012), creating opportunities for groups to partner with the many other organizations active on related issues. Thus while it is true that limited resources create strong incentives for advocates for the poor to collaborate, it is also true that the decentralized nature of legislative policymaking and dense interest group population in Washington create strong incentives for groups with ample resources to lobby collaboratively in pursuit of shared policy goals.

Second, across issues, legislators face uncertainty with respect to the electoral, policy, and political consequences of their policy choices. Congressional scholars frequently draw attention to the pervasive uncertainty that characterizes legislative decision making in many policy domains (Arnold 1990; Kingdon 1989; Wright 2003 [1995]). Lobbying tactics that reduce legislators' uncertainty are therefore likely to help interest groups gain influence, whether those groups are resource rich or resource poor. The theory posits that diverse coalitions reduce legislative uncertainty by drawing heterogeneous information to a lobbying effort and providing a credible signal of the underlying support for policy change. Because diverse informational resources and credible signals are important in multiple policy areas, there are strong reasons to suspect that groups across policy domains may be able to enhance their influence by collaborating, either informally or formally, with diverse partners.

Third, empirical research suggests that interest groups across policy domains use alliances to gain influence in the policy process (Hojnack 1997; Hula 1999). As the examples presented in Chapters 1 and 2 suggest, these alliances are often characterized by the diversity of member organizations. Thus there is evidence that diverse coalitions are emerging in various forms across issue areas, providing further evidence that such coalitions may play an important role in the policymaking process. Indeed, the sheer prevalence of collaborative activity across domains suggests that scholars must continue to prioritize coalitions in their research to better understand the mechanisms and circumstances of interest group influence in Congress.

Finally, diversity has been recognized, in various forms, as important in political decision-making processes. In *The Difference*, for example, Scott Page (2007) argues convincingly that cognitive diversity among a set of individuals produces collective benefits. Different ways of viewing the world, categorizing perspectives, generating solutions, and inferring cause and effect, Page argues, can lead to better problem solving and prediction. In much the same way, I argue that when groups that differ with respect to their engagement and information about policy work together, they can reveal information to legislators about the likely success or failure of a policy change. Working collaboratively, diverse groups can draw on multiple sources of information, thereby improving the policymaking process. Because diversity is valuable for political decisions across issues, it seems likely that coalitions that unite diverse actors may play a particularly powerful role across policy domains.

While the ubiquity of coalitions and the value of diversity have been recognized in previous research, this theory is the first to explicitly link diversity within collaborative lobbying efforts and legislative influence in an informational theory of interest group influence. By proposing a general theory of coalition influence, the book offers a theory that may be used to understand coalitional activity and influence across policy domains. While the empirical support in other issue areas remains to be seen, there are both theoretical and empirical reasons to suspect that the theory may be applicable in other domains. By reconciling a rich theoretical literature on interest group influence with the empirical reality that groups increasingly work in partnership across domains, this book offers a theoretical framework that may be used in future research on collaborative lobbying and influence in the policymaking process.

IMPLICATIONS AND EXTENSIONS: SOCIAL POLICY SCHOLARSHIP

The analysis presented in this book has several implications for social policy research. First, while existing social policy research highlights the role of organizational actors in the policymaking process, such research remains largely separated from theories of organizational influence in Congress. Without a theory to explain *how* advocates gain influence, it is difficult to comprehend variation in the influence of advocates across issues and over time. Although scholars have explored the emergence of movements on behalf of the poor as well as the lobbying activities of groups representing the poor, few have sought to reconcile existing tensions between interest group theory and social welfare policy. By merging empirical insights from social policy research and theoretical insights from political science research on interest group influence, this book offers a theory for understanding how and when advocates for the poor gain influence in legislative settings. The fact that the empirical analysis of activity during welfare reform provides considerable support for the theoretical framework suggests that the theory may be used by scholars interested in social policymaking to understand why advocates for the poor are at times influential in the policy process and at other times ineffectual.

Second, the theory of diverse coalitions is intended as a complement to existing research that investigates larger movements on behalf of the poor. To see that this is the case, consider how existing theories of social movement emergence help explain the larger *lack* of mobilization during welfare reform on behalf of preserving the entitlement to cash assistance. Recall from Chapter 1 that a body of scholarship focused on social movement emergence identifies several characteristics of the larger political context as facilitating the formation of movements on behalf of marginalized populations. These characteristics include the presence of elite allies and public support, as well as electoral instability. While features of the political context can facilitate movement emergence, they can also act as constraints. During welfare reform, the absence of electoral instability, elite allies, and public support can be seen as constraining broader mobilization efforts to preserve the entitlement to cash assistance.

Specifically, Republicans surged to power in the 1994 elections, gaining 52 seats in the House, 8 seats in the Senate, and 10 governorships across the United States (Balz and Brownstein 1996). A decisive victory for the Republican Party, the election created limited incentives for the party to reach out to marginalized groups or their allies in an effort to secure more votes and political power. In addition, proponents of preserving the entitlement to welfare lacked the support of key elite allies – most notably, the Clinton administration and the nation's governors. Finally, the ADFC program lacked public support. Nearly two-thirds of Americans believed that too much was being spent on welfare in 1995 and slightly less than half favored preserving the individual entitlement to cash assistance (Weaver 2000).

The fact that efforts to end the entitlement to cash assistance progressed in an environment characterized by limited electoral instability, few elite allies, and limited public support likely hindered broader mobilization efforts to preserve the structure of the welfare program. Although some diverse coalitions emerged on the issue, reflecting the salience, uncertainty, and strength of opponents, efforts to mobilize broad and diverse support beyond the actors already active on the issue were constrained by the larger features of the political context. Thus while the theory of diverse coalitions helps explain lobbying and influence during welfare reform policymaking in the 104th Congress, the political process theory of social movement emergence helps identify the wider lack of mobilization on the issue. Both types of theories are necessary for understanding the activities and influence of actors mobilized on behalf of America's least advantaged citizens. The theory presented in this book is therefore offered as a complement to existing theories that investigate mobilization and influence on a larger scale.

Finally, beyond scholarship, the analysis has implications for those engaged in the practice of social policy. Because diverse coalitions allow group to pool resources while offering a credible signal of the consequences of legislative choice, groups that advocate on behalf of the poor must consider partnerships with diverse actors as a mechanism for enhancing influence in legislative settings. Collaboration with diverse partners will likely require groups to reach beyond traditional allies and networks to identify allies with different political resources but similar policy goals.

IMPLICATIONS AND EXTENSIONS: INTEREST GROUP SCHOLARSHIP

Interest group scholars have long recognized the ubiquity of collaborative lobbying strategies in Washington. Yet most existing research on interest group influence conceives of influence as deriving from an individual group lobbying independently. I have argued in this book that the prevalence of coalitions across policy domains suggests that theories of interest group influence must begin to position the coalition rather than the individual interest group as the entity able to influence legislators' decisions. Elevating the coalition as the theoretical object of inquiry does not negate the rich literature on interest group influence in Congress. Indeed, the theory developed in this book builds entirely from scholarship that conceives of interest groups as autonomous actors. The mechanisms underlying a coalition's influence in this theory are the same as those that generate influence for an individual group: like a group lobbying independently, a coalition gains influence by targeting multiple legislators and by providing information that reduces legislators' uncertainty about the consequences of policy choice. The critical shift is that it is the coalition that influences the legislator, rather than the individual group.

The study of diverse coalitions raises definitional questions that must be answered before moving to the empirical study of coalitions. What is a coalition? How do coalitions differ from individual groups? And how do we measure diversity? In this book, I have argued for a broad definition of coalitions, defining a coalition as a set of organizations working collaboratively, whose members consist of different organizations. This definition includes informal coalitions that emerge for a short period of time around a single issue or vote, as well as formal coalitions that maintain a distinct organizational identity. The definition also includes associations in which the membership base consists of different organizations, such as trade associations, but excludes associations in which members are local or regional subunits of the larger association. In addition, the definition excludes groups that call themselves "coalitions" despite lacking a membership base of organizations.[9]

The definition used in this book was dictated by the theory, which posits that diverse coalitions are influential because they allow groups to pool disparate resources and signal credible political information. Although many partnerships never establish a distinct organizational identity, informal coalitions allow groups to pool resources and communicate political information through cosigned documents or jointly sponsored events, to name just a few examples. In addition, trade associations and peak business associations are not typically viewed as coalitions, yet these organizations draw together distinct member organizations that have different resources and can offer heterogeneous cues about the consequences of policy choice. Thus according to the theory, it is appropriate to adopt a broad definition that views such associations and informal partnerships as coalitions.

Studying coalitions introduces a set of empirical challenges and opportunities. First, scholars must utilize empirical strategies capable of identifying coalitions of varying degrees of formality. Formal coalitions appear in lists of registered lobbyists or campaign contribution records, yet informal coalitions may only be observable through cosponsored advertisements, protests, or letters to members of Congress. In the welfare reform case, many coalitions remained unnamed and some operated exclusively behind the scenes. To identify informal coalitions, scholars may have to move beyond the most easily accessible data on interest group activity in Washington, such lists of registered lobbyists and campaign contribution records, and pursue research designs that prioritize in-depth analysis of a single case or set of cases, particularly in early stages of theory development.

For analyses of coalitional activity across domains, an excellent source of data exists in the Advocacy and Public Policymaking project (Baumgartner and colleagues 2009). This project collected data on the lobbying activities of

---

[9] In the welfare reform case, a surprising number of "coalitions" existed in name only.

organized interests across a random sample of public policy issues in Washington. The publicly available data merge information from the interest groups active across a set of issues with supplementary information on each policy issue, including congressional hearings and media coverage, which may allow researchers to identify informal collaborative activities.[10] Past research using this data has assessed the presence of formal coalitions (Mahoney and Baumgartner 2004), and future analyses can be used to identify both informal and formal coalitions and analyze their impact on legislative outcomes.

Second, with respect to defining and measuring diversity within coalitions, while the theory developed in this book proposed a broad definition of diversity, the empirical analysis refined the definition of diversity by identifying three types of diversity. Specifically, coalitions that united groups with varying professional identities (e.g., citizen groups, service providers, and research organizations), different policy domains (e.g., health and education), and diverse ideological or partisan affiliations (e.g., pro-choice and pro-life groups) appeared particularly important in the welfare reform case. Each type of diversity allowed a coalition to draw different types of information to a lobbying effort and offer heterogeneous cues about the consequences of legislative policy choices. Moreover, coalitions routinely highlighted diversity with respect to policy domain and ideology, suggesting that groups perceived these types of diversity as particularly important characteristics of their collaborative efforts.

There are strong reasons to suspect diversity with respect to professional identity, policy domain, and ideology to be important across policy issues, as the first type of diversity can unite electoral and policy information, the second type provides information about the preferences of different groups of constituents and interests, and the third type communicates bipartisan alignment in policy preferences. Moreover, all three types of diversity are, in general, easily identifiable characteristics of interest groups. Distinguishing groups by their professional identity reflects the standard categorization of organized interests in interest group research (citizen group, professional association, business, etc.). In addition, most groups specialize in a particular policy domain or economic sector, and some are clearly aligned with particular partisan or ideological interests.

Yet these types of diversity are not exhaustive, and it is possible other types of diversity will emerge as important on other policy issues. Diverse coalitions might unite similar professional organizations that operate in different regions of the country. Regional diversity may be important on issues that have historically divided parts of the country. This speaks both to the applicability of the concept across issues and the importance of political context. While the mechanisms underlying diversity's influence are the same across issues,

[10] See http://lobby.la.psu.edu/ for more information on the Advocacy and Public Policymaking project.

understanding which type is important will likely require attention to the particular issue context. Indeed, identifying additional types of diversity may be a necessary precursor to analyzing the impact of coalitional diversity systematically across issues.

Finally, studying coalitions empirically requires attention to political context. The theory developed in this book posits that coalitional activity is shaped by features of the issue, as well as the involvement of other organized interests. Future empirical research on coalitions must take into account issue-level characteristics, as well as organizational-level characteristics, when assessing the activity and influence of coalitions. Of particular note is the role of uncertainty in shaping collaborative lobbying strategies – an issue-level characteristic not discussed in existing research. Because the incentives to collaborate vary across issues, diverse coalitions are unlikely to emerge (or participate, in the case of preexisting coalitions) on all issues. Thus the *absence* of diverse partnerships on all issues should not indicate that coalitions are unimportant but rather that some issue contexts create strong incentives for groups to lobby independently, while other contexts create incentives for groups to lobby collaboratively.

CONCLUSION

To answer the question that motivated this project, advocates for the poor strategically ally with diverse partners to influence policy choices in Congress. Though they lack the large budgets and membership bases of other interest groups, advocates collaborate to pool the diverse resources necessary for reaching multiple legislators while providing credible information that reduces uncertainty about the consequences of legislative choice. By increasing access to legislators and reducing legislators' uncertainty, diverse coalitions enhance advocates' role in the policymaking process in Congress. Diverse coalitions therefore represent an important tool for communicating the political interests of an under-represented population.

The theoretical and empirical analyses presented in this book have important normative implications. Diverse coalitions draw together distinct voices in support of a single policy choice. In a country composed of disparate and often conflicting interests, diverse coalitions communicate that a policy has the support of a broad rather than a narrow band of society. In doing so, such coalitions enhance the democratic responsiveness of interest groups across issues and policy domains. Moreover, to the extent that they are influential across policy domains, diverse coalitions may also help mitigate resource inequities across interest groups – providing a tool that groups with fewer political resources can use to counter the influence of groups with plentiful resources.

At the same time, the findings may be interpreted as normatively troubling. Diverse collaboration depends on the preferences and interest of potential coalition partners. In the social policy realm, advocates must rely on the activities of organizations with shared policy goals, rather than their own political lobbying activities. If no other interests share their policy goals or consider an issue to be salient, then the obstacles to gaining influence in Congress persist.

For scholars of political science and public policy, this book draws into focus an increasingly common strategy of political influence. Together, the theoretical and empirical analyses demonstrate how advocates for the poor work to gain influence in Congress, thereby resolving the apparent disconnect between political science and public policy scholarship. Moreover, the theory has implications for interest group scholarship more broadly. Across policy domains, interest groups have strong incentives to collaborate with diverse partners to reach legislators accountable to different interests and provide information about the consequences of policy change. The ubiquity of coalitional strategies across policy domains suggests that scholars must begin to think more systematically about coalitional influence to better understand the extent and circumstances of interest group influence in the American political system.

APPENDIX

List of Congressional Hearings

The following is the list of the congressional welfare reform hearings analyzed in the main empirical chapters (Chapters 5–8). These hearings took place between January 1995, when the welfare reform legislation was introduced in the House of Representatives, and August 1996, when the welfare reform legislation was signed into law. Six committees in the House of Representatives and Senate shared primary jurisdiction over the programs targeted by welfare reform efforts. These committees include the Ways and Means, Education and Economic Opportunities, and Agriculture Committees in the House of Representatives and the Finance, Labor and Human Resources, and Agriculture, Nutrition, and Forestry Committees in the Senate. The list of welfare reform hearings is drawn from House and Senate reports of welfare reform legislation in 1995 and 1996 and supplemented with Winston's (2002) list of congressional welfare reform hearings in the 104th Congress. The hearings subject to the in-depth coding and analysis presented in Chapter 5 are denoted by an asterisk (*).

U.S. HOUSE OF REPRESENTATIVES

Committee on Agriculture

Subcommittee on Department Operations, Nutrition, and Foreign Agriculture
"Reforming the Present Welfare System," February 7–9 and 14, 1995

Committee on Economic and Educational Opportunities

Full Committee
"Contract with America: Hearing on Welfare Reform," January 18, 1995

"Hearing on the Contract with America: Nutrition, the Local Perspective,"
  February 1, 1995
Subcommittee on Early Childhood Youth and Families
"Hearing on Contract with America: Child Welfare and Childcare,"
  January 31, 1995
"Child Welfare and Childcare" (Joint with the Committee on Ways and
  Means) February 3, 1995
Subcommittee on Postsecondary Education and Life-Long Learning
"Hearing on Job Opportunities and Basic Skills Act," January 19, 1995

Committee on Ways and Means

Subcommittee on Human Resources
"Contract with America – Welfare Reform," January 13, 20, 23, 27, and 30,
  and February 2, 1995*
"Child Welfare and Childcare" (Joint with the Committee on Economic and
  Educational Opportunities, Subcommittee on Early Childhood Youth and
  Families) February 3, 1995
"Child Support Enforcement Provisions Included in the Personal
  Responsibility Act as Part of the Contract with America," February 6,
  1995
"The National Governors' Association Welfare Reform Proposal,"
  February 20, 1996
"Causes of Poverty, with a Focus on Out-of-Wedlock Births," March 12,
  1996
"Welfare Reform," May 22 and 23, 1996

U.S. SENATE

Committee on Agriculture, Nutrition, and Forestry

"Federal Nutrition Programs," May 23, 1995

Committee on Finance

"Governors' Proposal on Welfare Reform and Medicaid," February 22, 28,
  and 29, 1996
"States' Perspectives on Welfare Reform," March 8, 1995*
"Broad Policy Goals of Welfare Reform," March 9, 1995*
"Administration's Views on Welfare Reform," March 10, 1995*
"Teen Parents and Welfare Reform," March 14, 1995*
"Welfare to Work," March 20, 1995*
"Growth of the Supplemental Security Income Program," March 27, 1995*
"Welfare Reform – Views of Interested Organizations," March 29, 1995*

"Child Welfare Programs," April 26, 1995*
"Welfare Reform Wrap-Up," April 27, 1995*
"Welfare and Medicaid Reform," June 13 and 19, 1996

Committee on Labor and Human Relations

Full Committee
"Impact of Welfare Reform on Children and Their Families," February 28
  and March 1, 1995
Subcommittee on Children and Families
"Child Care and Development Block Grant: How Is It Working?"
  February 16, 1995
"Filling the Gap: Can Private Institutions Do It?" March 26, 1995

Bibliography

Abramovitz, Mimi. *Under Attack, Fighting Back: Women and Welfare in the United States*. New York: Monthly Review Press, 2000.

Ainsworth, Scott. "Regulating Lobbyists and Interest Group Influence." *The Journal of Politics* 55, no. 1 (1993): 41–56.

Almong-Bar M., and H. Schmid. "Advocacy Activities of Nonprofit Human Service Organizations: A Critical Review." *Nonprofit and Voluntary Sector Quarterly* 43, no. 1 (2014): 11–35.

Amenta, Edwin, and Neal Caren. "Social Movements, Political Consequences Of." *Blackwell Encyclopedia of Sociology*, edited by George Ritzer. Malden, MA: Blackwell Publishing, 2007.

Amenta, Edwin, Neal Caren, Elizabeth Chiarello, and Su Yang. "The Political Consequences of Social Movements." *Annual Review of Sociology* 36 (2010): 287–307.

American Tort Reform Association. "About ATRA." Accessed December 10, 2013. www.atra.org/about.

Appelbaum, Lauren D. "The Influence of Perceived Deservingness on Policy Decisions Regarding Aid to the Poor." Political Psychology 22, no. 3 (2001): 419–42.

Arnold, R. Douglas. *The Logic of Congressional Action*. New Haven: Yale University Press, 1992.

Austen-Smith, David, and John R. Wright. "Competitive Lobbying for a Legislator's Vote." *Social Choice and Welfare* 9 (1992): 229–57.

"Counteractive Lobbying." *American Journal of Political Science* 38, no. 1 (1994): 25–44.

Austin-Smith, David, and Jeffrey S. Banks. "Costly Signaling and Cheap Talk in Models of Political Influence." *European Journal of Political Economy* 18, no. 2 (2002): 263–80.

Balz, Dan. "A Historic Republican Triumph: GOP Captures Congress; Party Controls Both Houses for First Time since '50s." *The Washington Post*, November 9, 1994, A1.

Balz, Dan, and Ronald Brownstein. *Storming the Gates: Protest Politics and the Republican Revival*. Waltham, MA: Little, Brown, 1996.

Banks, Jeffrey S. *Signaling Games in Political Science*, edited by John Ferejohn, Fundamentals of Pure and Applied Economics: Political Science and Economics Section. London: Routledge, 1991.

Barreto, Matt A., Stephen A. Nuno, and Gabriel R. Sanchez. "The Disproportionate Impact of Voter-ID Requirements on the Electorate – New Evidence from Indiana." *PS: Political Science & Politics* 42, no. 1 (2009): 111–16.

Bartels, Larry. *Unequal Democracy: The Political Economy of the New Gilded Age.* New York: Russell Sage Foundation, and Princeton, NJ: Princeton University Press, 2008.

Bass, Gary D., Alan J. Abramson, and Emily Dewey. "Effective Advocacy: Lessons for Nonprofit Leaders from Research." In *Nonprofits and Advocacy: Engaging Community and Government in an Era of Retrenchment*, edited by Robert J. Pekkanen, Steven Rathgeb Smith, and Yutaka Tsukinaka. Baltimore: Johns Hopkins University Press, 2014. 254–94.

Baumgartner, Frank R., and Beth L. Leech. *Basic Interests: The Importance of Groups in Politics and Political Science*. Princeton, NJ: Princeton University Press, 1998.

Baumgartner, Frank R., Jeffrey M. Berry, Marie Hojnacki, David C. Kimball, and Beth L. Leech. *Lobbying and Policy Change: Who Wins, Who Loses, and Why*. Chicago: University of Chicago Press, 2009.

Bennett, William J. "The Best Welfare Reform: End It," *Wall Street Journal*, March 30, 1994: A19.

Berry, Jeffrey M. *Lobbying for the People: The Political Behavior of Public Interest Groups*. Princeton, NJ: Princeton University Press, 1977.

The New Liberalism: The Rising Power of Citizen Groups. Washington, DC: Brookings Institution Press, 1999.

Berry, Jeffrey M., and David F. Arons. *A Voice for Nonprofits*. Washington, DC: Brookings Institution Press, 2003.

Blank, Rebecca. *It Takes a Nation: A New Agenda for Fighting Poverty*. Princeton, NJ: Princeton University Press, 1997.

Blank, Rebecca M., and Lucie Schmidt. "Work, Wages, and Welfare." In *The New World of Welfare*, edited by Rebecca Blank and Ron Haskins. Washington, DC: Brookings University Press, 2001. 70–102.

Blee, Kathleen M., and Kimberly A. Creasap. "Conservative and Right-Wing Movements." *Annual Review of Sociology* 36 (2010): 269–86.

Brady, Henry E., Sidney Verba, and Kay Lehman Schlozman. "Beyond SES: A Resource Model of Political Participation." *American Political Science Review* 89, no. 2 (1995): 271–94.

Brooks-Gunn, Jeanne, and Frank F. Furstenberg. "The Children of Adolescent Mothers: Physical, Academic, and Psychological Outcomes." *Developmental Review* 6, no. 3 (1986): 224–51.

Browne, William P. "Organized Interests and Their Issue Niches: A Search for Pluralism in a Policy Domain." *The Journal of Politics* 52, no. 2 (1990): 477–509.

Brownstein, Ronald. "GOP Welfare Proposals Becoming More Conservative." *Los Angeles Times*. March 9, 1994, A20.

Cammisa, Anne Marie. *Governments as Interest Groups*. Westport, CT: Prager, 1995.

Catholic Charities USA. "About Catholic Charities USA." Accessed July 1, 2012. https://catholiccharitiesusa.org/about.

Child Welfare League of America. "Welcome to CWLA." Accessed July 1, 2012. www
.cwla.org/pubs/welcome.htm.
CNN. "Conservatives Criticize 'Stand for Children' March." May 31, 1996. Accessed
July 5, 2011. LexisNexis Academic.
Children's Defense Fund. "An Invitation to Stand for Children." 1996. Available at
http://diglib.lib.utk.edu/cdf/main.php?bid=214&cat2id=2.
Coalition for America's Children. "Who's for Kids and Who's Just Kidding," 1995.
Legacy Tobacco Documents Library. University of California–San Francisco.
Accessed May 4, 2010. Available at www.industrydocumentslibrary.ucsf.edu/
tobacco/docs/#id=xmgn0039
Coalition on Human Needs. "About CHN." Accessed January 10, 2010. www.chn.org/
about-chn/.
Consortium for Citizens with Disabilities. "About CCD." Accessed July 1, 2012. www
.c-c-d.org/about/about.htm.
"Contract with America's Children." C-SPAN Video Library, December 15, 1994.
Accessed May 15, 2013. Available at www.c-spanvideo.org/event/47827.
CQ Weekly. "Section Notes: As Expected, Clinton Vetoes Welfare Overhaul Bill."
January 13, 1996: 95. Available at http://library.cqpress.com/cqweekly/WR409769.
Daly, Mary, and Richard V. Burkhauser. "The Supplemental Security Income Program."
In *Means-Tested Transfer Programs in the United States*, edited by Robert A.
Moffit. Chicago: University of Chicago Press, 2003. 79–140.
Daly, Sharon M., and Deborah Lewis. "Unlikely Allies Oppose Welfare Reform Policy."
Chicago Tribune, November 30, 1994. Accessed October 20, 2009. Available via
LexisNexis Academic.
Danziger, Sheldon H. "Welfare Reform Policy from Nixon to Clinton." In *Social Science
and Policy Making*, edited by D. Featherman and M. Vinovskis. Ann Arbor:
University of Michigan Press, 2001. 137–64.
Dao, James. "Odd Allies Seek Changes for Welfare." *New York Times*, November 13,
1995. B1.
Delgado, Gary. *Organizing the Movement: The Roots and Growth of ACORN.*
Philadelphia: Temple University Press, 1986.
DeNavas-Walt, Carmen, and Bernadette D. Proctor. "Current Population Reports, P60–
252, Income and Poverty in the United States: 2014." Washington, DC: U.S. Census
Bureau, 2015.
Denzau, Arthur T., and Michael C. Munger. "Legislators and Interest Groups: How
Unorganized Interests Get Represented." *American Political Science Review* 80, no.
1 (1986): 89–106.
DeParle, Jason. "Clinton Planners Facing a Quiet Fight on Welfare." *New York Times*,
March 18, 1994a. A18.
"From Pledge to Plan: The Campaign to End Welfare – A Special Report; the Clinton
Welfare Bill: A Long, Stormy Journey." *New York Times*, July 15, 1994b. A1
"The Nation Despising Welfare, Pitying Its Young "*New York Times*, December 18,
1994c. Accessed September 5, 2009. Available via LexisNexis Academic.
De Vita, Carol J., Rachel Mosher-Williams, and Nicholas A. Stengel. "Nonprofit
Organizations Engaged in Child Advocacy." In *Who Speaks for America's
Children: The Role of Child Advocates in Public Policy*, edited by Carol J. De
Vita and Rachel Mosher-Williams. Washington, DC: The Urban Institute Press,
2001: 3–38.

De Vita, Carol J., Milena Nokolova, and Katie L. Roeger. "Nonprofit Advocacy in the Nation's Capital." In *Nonprofits and Advocacy: Engaging Community and Government in an Era of Retrenchment*, edited by Robert J. Pekkanen, Steven Rathgeb Smith, and Yutaka Tsukinaka. Baltimore: Johns Hopkins University Press, 2014.

Deering, Christopher J., and Steven S. Smith. *Committees in Congress*, 3rd ed. Washington, DC: CQ Press, 1997.

Denzau, Arthur T., and Michael C. Munger. "Legislators and Interest Groups: How Unorganized Interests get Represented." *The American Political Science Review* (1986): 89–106.

Dixon, Jennifer. "Group: Welfare Reform Must Put Children First." *Moscow-Pullaman Daily News*, 16 December 1994.

Epstein, David. "Legislating from Both Sides of the Aisle: Information and the Value of Bipartisan Consensus." *Public Choice* 101, no. 1–2 (1999): 1–22.

Erkulwater, Jennifer L. *Disability Rights and the American Social Safety Net*. Ithaca, NY: Cornell University Press, 2006.

Esterling, Kevin M. *The Political Economy of Expertise*. Ann Arbor: University of Michigan Press, 2004.

Feldman, Stanley, and John Zaller. "The Political Culture of Ambivalence: Ideological Responses to the Welfare State." *American Journal of Political Science* 36, no. 1 (1992): 268–307.

Fenno, Richard F. *Home Style: House Members in Their Districts*: Boston: Little, Brown and Company, 1978.

Focus. "The Family Support Act of 1988." *University of Wisconsin-Madison Institute for Research on Poverty* 11, no. 4 (Winter 1988–1989): 15–18.

Furstenberg Jr, Frank F., Jeanne Brooks-Gunn, and Lindsay Chase-Lansdale. "Teenaged Pregnancy and Childbearing." *American Psychologist* 44, no. 2 (1989): 313.

Gais, Thomas L., and Jack L. Walker. "Pathways to Influence in American Politics." In *Mobilizing Interest Groups in America: Patrons, Professions, and Social Movements*. Ann Arbor: University of Michigan Press, 1991. 103–21.

Gais, Thomas L., Richard P. Nathan, Irene Lurie, and Thomas Kaplan. "Implementation of the Personal Responsibility Act of 1996." In *The New World of Welfare*, edited by Rebecca Blank and Ron Haskins. Washington, DC: Brookings Institution Press, 2001. 35–69.

Gardner, Marilyn. "'Stand for Children' – Can a Weekend Rally Make a Difference?" *Christian Science Monitor*, May 30, 1996.

George, Alexander L., and Andrew Bennett. *Case Studies and Theory Development in the Social Sciences*. Cambridge, MA: Mit Press, 2005.

Georges, Christopher. "A Media Crusade Gone Haywire," *Forbes Media Critic*, September 1995.

Gerring, John. "What Is a Case Study and What Is It Good For?" *American Political Science Review* 98, no. 2 (2004): 341–54.

  Case Study Research: Principles and Practices. New York: Cambridge University Press, 2006.

Gibbons, Robert. *Game Theory for Applied Economists*. Princeton, NJ: Princeton University Press, 1992.

Gilens, Martin. *Why Americans Hate Welfare: Race, Media, and the Politics of Anti-Poverty Policy*. Chicago: University of Chicago Press, 1999.

Affluence and Influence: Economic Inequality and Political Power in America. Princeton, NJ: Princeton University Press, 2014.

Gilligan, Thomas W., and Keith Krehbiel. "Asymmetric Information and Legislative Rules with a Heterogeneous Committee." *American Journal of Political Science* 33, no. 2 (1989): 459–90.

Gingrich, Newt. et al., eds. *Contract with America: The Bold Plan by Rep. Newt Gingrich, Rep. Dick Armey and the House Republicans to Change the Nation.* New York: Three Rivers Press, 1994.

Giugni, Marco G. "Was It Worth the Effort? The Outcomes and Consequences of Social Movements." *Annual Review of Sociology* (1998): 371–93.

Goldstein, Kenneth M. *Interest Groups, Lobbying, and Participation in America.* Cambridge, UK: Cambridge University Press, 1999.

Gray, Jerry. "The 104th Congress: Issues and Agendas – Liberal Anger, Stats' Hope and a Technology Debate; Welfare: G.O.P. Governors Make Their Pitch. *New York Times.* January 7, 1995. Section 1, p. 8, 1995.

Gray, Virginia, and David Lowery. *The Population Ecology of Interest Representation: Interest Communities in the American States.* Ann Arbor: University of Michigan Press, 1996

Greenberg, Mark, and Steve Savner. "A Brief Summary of the Key Provisions of the Temporary Assistance for Needy Families Block Grant of H.R. 3734," 1996. Accessed March 5, 2014. www.clasp.org/resources-and-publications/archive/0005.pdf.

Greenhouse, Steven. "Labor and Clergy Are Reunited to Help the Underdogs of Society." *New York Times* August 18, 1996, 1.

Grossman, Gene M., and Elhanan Helpman. *Special Interest Politics.* Cambridge, MA: MIT Press, 2001.

Hacker, Jacob. *The Divided Welfare State: The Battle over Public and Private Social Benefits in the United States.* New York: Cambridge University Press, 2002.

Hall, Richard L., and Alan Deardorff. "Lobbying as Legislative Subsidy." *American Political Science Review* 100, no. 1 (2006): 69–84.

Hall, Richard L., and Frank W. Wayman. "Buying Time: Moneyed Interests and the Mobilization of Bias in Congressional Committees." *The American Political Science Review* (1990): 797–820.

Halperin, Mark. "Coalition Calls for Health Reform." *Time Magazine*, May 8, 2007. Accessed December 10, 2013, http://content.time.com/time/nation/article/0,8599,1618705,00.html.

Hansen, John Mark. *Gaining Access: Congress and the Farm Lobby, 1919–1981.* Chicago: The University of Chicago Press, 1991.

Haskins, Ron. "Liberal and Conservative Influences on the Welfare Reform Legislation of 1996." In *For Better and for Worse: State Welfare Reform and the Well-Being of Low-Income Families and Children*, edited by P. Lindsay Chase-Lansdale and Greg Duncan. New York: Russell Sage, 2002.

  Work over Welfare: The Inside Story of the 1996 Welfare Reform Act. Washington, DC: Brookings Institution Press, 2006.

Haveman, Robert, Rebecca Blank, Robert Moffitt, Timothy Smeeding, and Geoffrey Wallace. "The War on Poverty: Measurement, Trends, and Policy." *Journal of Policy Analysis and Management* 34, no. 3 (2015): 593–638.

Havemann, Judith. "Liberal Advocacy Groups Urge Veto of Welfare Bill." *The Houston Chronicle*, October 6, 1995, P7.

Havemann, Judith, and Barbara Vobejda. "Moderates Kill 'Family Cap' in Senate Welfare Measure." *Washington Post*, September 14, 1995, A1.

Hays, R. Allen. *Who Speaks for the Poor?* New York: Routledge, 2001.

Heaney, Michael T. "Issue Networks, Information, and Interest Group Alliances: The Case of Wisconsin Welfare Politics, 1993–99." *State Politics and Policy Quarterly* 4, no. 3 (2004): 237–70.

Heaney, Michael T. "Brokering Health Policy: Coalitions, Parties, and Interest Group Influence." *Journal of Health Politics, Policy and Law* 31, no. 5 (2006): 887–944.

Heaney, Michael T., and Geoffrey M. Lorenz. "Coalition Portfolios and Interest Group Influence over the Policy Process." *Interest Groups & Advocacy* 2, no. 3 (2013): 251–77.

Heclo, Hugh. "The Politics of Welfare Reform." In *The New World of Welfare*, edited by Rebecca Blank and Ron Haskins. Washington, DC: Brookings Institution Press, 2001. 169–200.

Heinz, John P., Edward O. Laumann, Robert L. Nelsom, and Robert H. Salisbury. *The Hollow Core: Private Interests in National Policymaking*. Cambridge, MA: Harvard University Press, 1993.

Helpman, Elhanan, and Torsten Persson. "Lobbying and Legislative Bargaining." *Advances in Economic Analysis & Policy* 1, no. 1 (2001): 1–31.

Hinckley, Barbara. "Twenty-One Variables Beyond the Size of Winning Coalitions." *The Journal of Politics* 41, no. 1 (1979): 61–87.

Hochschild, Jennifer L. *What's Fair?: American Beliefs about Distributive Justice*. Cambridge, MA: Harvard University Press, 1986.

Hojnacki, Marie. "Interest Groups' Decisions to Join Alliances or Work Alone." *American Journal of Political Science* 41, no. 1 (1997): 61–87.

Hojnacki, Marie, and David C. Kimball. "Organized Interests and the Decision of Whom to Lobby in Congress." *American Political Science Review* 92, no. 4 (1998): 775–90.

Hojnacki, Marie, David C. Kimball, Frank R. Baumgartner, Jeffrey M. Berry, and Beth L. Leech. "Studying Organizational Advocacy and Influence: Reexamining Interest Group Research." *Annual Review of Political Science* 15 (2012): 379–99.

Holyoke, Thomas T. *Competitive Interests: Competition and Compromise in American Interest Group Politics*. Washington, DC: Georgetown University Press, 2011.

"Interest Group Competition and Coalition Formation." *American Journal of Political Science* 53, no. 2 (2009): 360–75.

Hula, Kevin W. *Lobbying Together: Interest Group Coalitions in Legislative Politics*. Washington, DC: Georgetown University Press, 1999.

Hume, Sandy. "Christian Coalition Touts Its Electoral Clout." *Hill*, March 13, 1996.

Imig, Douglas R. *Poverty and Power: The Political Representation of Poor Americans*. Lincoln: University of Nebraska Press, 1996.

"Building a Social Movement for America's Children." *Journal of Children and Poverty* 12, no. 1 (2006): 21–37.

"Resource Mobilization and Survival Tactics of Poverty Advocacy Groups." *The Western Political Quarterly* 45, no. 2 (1992): 501–20.

Jones, Rachel L. "200,000 Rally for Children's Causes: While Some Spoke against GOP Budget Cuts, Some Conservatives Criticized a "Big Government" Emphasis." *Philadelphia Inquirer*, June 2, 1996, A01.

Katz, Jeffrey L. "Welfare Bill Reshapes Cash Programs Reduces Eligibility for SSI." *CQ Weekly*, February 18, 1995a.

"House Passes Welfare Bill; Senate Likely to Alter It." *CQ Weekly*, March 25, 1995b.

"Governors Group Sidelined in Welfare Debate." *CQ Weekly*, May 20, 1995c.

"Human Services: GOP Rift Delays Action on Welfare." *CQ Weekly*, June 17, 1995d.

"Welfare: Dole Bill Aims to Clear Obstacles for Snarled Welfare Overhaul." *CQ Weekly*, August 5, 1995e.

"Reconciliation: GOP Produces Welfare Agreement, Urges Clinton to Sign On." *CQ Weekly*, November 11, 1995f.

Katz, Jeffrey L., and David Hosansky. "Provisions of House Welfare Bill." *CQ Weekly*, March 18, 1995.

Katz, Michael B. *The Price of Citizenship: Redefining the American Welfare State*. New York: Metropolitan Books, 2001.

The Undeserving Poor. New York: Pantheon Books, 1989.

Kersh, Rogan. "The Well-Informed Lobbyist: Information and Interest Group Lobbying." In *Interest Group Politics*, 7th ed., edited by Allan J. Cigler and Burdett A. Loomis. Washington, DC: CQ Press, 2007. 389–411.

Kingdon, John W. *Congressmen's Voting Decisions*. Ann Arbor: University of Michigan Press, 1989.

Kollman, Ken. *Outside Lobbying: Public Opinion and Interest Group Strategies*. Princeton, NJ: Princeton University Press, 1998.

Krehbiel, Keith. *Information and Legislative Organization*. Ann Arbor: University of Michigan Press, 1992.

Lanpher, Katherine. "Standing for Children." *St. Paul Pioneer Press*, May 26, 1996, 1B.

LaPira, Timothy M., and Herschel F. Thomas. "Revolving Door Lobbyists and Interest Representation." *Interest Groups & Advocacy* 3, no. 1 (2014): 4–29.

Levi, Margaret, and Gillian H. Murphy. "Coalitions of Contention: The Case of the WTO Protests in Seattle." *Political Studies* 54, no. 4 (2006): 651–70.

Lewin, Tamar. "The Nation; Abortion Foes Worry About Welfare Cutoffs." *New York Times*, March 19, 1995, 4.

Lohmann, Suzanne. "A Signaling Model of Informative and Manipulative Political Action." *American Political Science Review* 87 (1993): 319–33.

Loomis, Burdett A. "Coalitions of Interests: Building Bridges in the Balkanized State." In *Interest Group Politics*, 2nd ed., edited by Allan J. Cigler and Burdett A. Loomis. Washington, DC: Congressional Quarterly Press, 1986.

Loose, Cindy. "Children's March Mum on Crowd; Organizers Avoid Time-Honored Tactic of Trumpeting Attendance Figures." *Washington Post*, May 31, 1996, F3.

Lowi, Theodore. *The End of Liberalism*. New York: Norton, 1969.

Mahoney, Christine. "Networking vs. Allying: The Decision of Interest Groups to Join Coalitions in the US and the EU." *Journal of European Public Policy* 14, no. 2 (2007): 366–83.

Mahoney, Christine, and Frank R. Baumgartner. "Partners in Advocacy: Lobbyists and Government Officials in Washington." *The Journal of Politics* 77, no. 1 (2015): 202–15.

"The Determinants and Effects of Interest Group Coalitions." Presented at the *Annual Meeting of the American Political Science Association*, Chicago, 2004.

Manza, Jeff, and Christopher Uggen. *Locked Out: Felon Disenfranchisement and American Democracy*. New York: Oxford University Press, 2006.

Mathis, Nancy. "Religious Right Crusades for the Soul of the GOP in State and States, Mainsteam and Moderate Republicans Are Losing Control." *The Times Union*, September 4, 1994, A1.

Mayhew, David R. *Congress: The Electoral Connection*. New Haven: Yale University Press, 1974.

McAdam, Doug. *Political Process and the Development of Black Insurgency, 1930–1970*. Chicago: University of Chicago Press, 1982.

Mead, Lawrence M. *Beyond Entitlement: The Social Obligations of Citizenship*. New York: Free Press, 1986.

 The New Politics of Poverty: The Non Working Poor in America. New York: Basic Books, 1992.

Melnick, R. Shep. *Between the Lines: Interpreting Welfare Rights*. Washington, DC: Brookings Institution Press, 1994.

Mitchell, William C., and Michael C. Munger. "Economic Models of Interest Groups: An Introductory Survey." *American Journal of Political Science* 35, no. 2 (1991): 512.

Mosley, Jennifer E. "Collaboration, Public-Private Intermediary Organizations, and the Transformation of Advocacy in the Field of Homeless Services." *American Review of Public Administration* 44, no. 3 (2014): 291–308.

Murray, Charles. *Losing Ground: American Social Policy, 1950–1980*. New York: Basic Books, 1984.

 "Organizational Resources and Environmental Incentives: Understanding the Policy Advocacy Involvement of Human Service Nonprofits." *Social Service Review* 84, no.1 (2010): 57–67.

Nathan, Richard P. *Social Science in Government: The Role of Policy Researchers*. Albany: Rockefeller Institute Press, 2000.

National Commission on Childhood Disability. "Supplemental Security Income for Children with Disabilities," Report to Congress of the National Commission on Childhood Disability. October 1995.

National Conference of State Legislatures (NCSL). *Voter Identification Laws in Effect in 2015*. Accessed January 10, 2014. Available at www.ncsl.org/research/elections-and-campaigns/voter-id.aspx.

Nelson, David, and Susan Webb Yackee. "Lobbying Coalitions and Government Policy Change: An Analysis of Federal Agency Rulemaking." *The Journal of Politics* 74, no. 2 (2012): 339–53.

New York Times, "How Much Will All This Cost Our Kids?" 1995a.

New York Times, "Why Every Woman in America Should Beware of Welfare Cuts," August 8, 1995b.

Nownes, Anthony J. *Total Lobbying: What Lobbyists Want (and How They Try to Get It)*. New York: Cambridge University Press, 2006.

O'Donnell, John B., and Jim Haner. "America's Most Wanted Welfare Plan." *Baltimore Sun*, January 22, 1995.

Ornstein, Allan C., Daniel U. Levine, and Gerry Gutek. *Foundations of Education*. Bellmont, CA: Wadsworth Publishing, 2010.

Page, Benjamin I., and Robert Y. Shapiro. *The Rational Public: Fifty Years of Trends in Americans' Policy Preferences*. Chicago: University of Chicago Press, 2010.

Page, Scott E. *The Difference: How the Power of Diversity Creates Better Groups, Firms, Schools, and Societies*. Princeton, NJ: Princeton University Press, 2007.

Patterson, James T. *America's Struggle against Poverty, 1900–1994*. Cambridge, MA: Harvard University Press, 2000.

Pear, Robert. "The 104th Congress: Welfare: Republicans' Philosophical Discord Stalls Plan for Change." *New York Times*, January 12, 1995, A20.

"Governors Deadlocked on Replacing Welfare Programs with Grants to States." *New York Times*, January 31, 1995, A14.

"Thousands to Rally in Capital on Children's Behalf." *New York Times*, June 1, 1996, 10.

Pekkanen, Robert J., Steven Rathgen Smith, and Yutaka Tsujinaka (eds.). *Nonprofit Advocacy: Engaging Community and Government in an Era of Retrenchment*. Baltimore: Johns Hopkins Press, 2014.

Perez-Pena, Richard. "Stronger Aid Urged to Ease Move from Welfare to Work." *New York Times*, April 1, 1997, B6.

Persson, Torsten, and Guido Tabellini. *Political Economics: Explaining Economic Policy*. Cambridge, MA: The MIT Press, 2000.

Piven, Frances Fox, and Richard Andrew Cloward. *Poor People's Movements: Why They Succeed, How They Fail*. New York: Random House, 1979.

Potters, Jan, and Frans Van Winden. "Lobbying and Asymmetric Information." *Public Choice* 74, no. 3 (1992): 269–92.

Preston, Jennifer. "Births Fall and Abortions Rise under New Jersey Family Cap." *New York Times*, November 3, 1998.

Price, Joyce. "Children's Fund Founder Enjoys First-Family Ties." *Washington Times*, February 21, 1993, A1.

Proctor, Bernadette D., Jessica L. Semega, and Melissa A. Kollar. *Income and Poverty in the United States: 2015*. U.S. Census Bureau, Current Population Reports P60-256(RV). Washington DC: U.S. Government Printing Office, 2016.

"Pro-Life and Pro-Choice Groups Schedule Joint Press Briefing Wednesday on Child Exclusion Policies." US Newswire, June 13, 1995. Accessed September 5, 2009. LexisNexis Academic.

Rector, Robert. "The Impact of New Jersey's Family Cap on Out-of-Wedlock Births and Abortions." September 6, 1995. The Heritage Foundation. Accessed September 5, 2009. www.heritage.org/marriage-and-family/report/the-impact-new-jerseys-family-cap-out-wedlock-births-and-abortions.

Reese, Ellen. *Backlash against Welfare Mothers: Past and Present*. Berkeley: University of California Press, 2005.

Responsibility and Empowerment Support Program Providing Employment, Child Care, and Training Act of 1993. HR 3500. 103rd Cong., 1st sess., *Congressional Record* 139: H9563.

Rich, Andrew. *Think Tanks, Public Policy, and the Politics of Expertise*. New York: Cambridge University Press, 2004.

Rich, Spencer. "GOP Plan for Disabled Children Draws Fire." *Washington Post*, February 25, 1995, A12.

Rosenfeld, Megan. "Faith, Politics and Charity; They All Call Themselves Christians. But in the Battle over Welfare Reform They're Preaching Two Gospels." *Washington Post*, August 9, 1995, D01.

Rosenstone, Steven J., and John Mark Hansen. *Mobilization, Participation, and Democracy in America*. New York: Macmillan, 1993.

Rubin, Alissa J. "The Budget: Governors Hope Welfare, Medicaid Plan Will Lead to Overall Budget Deal." *CQ Weekly*, February 10, 1996, 352–53. March 25, 2014. library. cqpress.com/cqweekly/toc.php?mode=weekly-date&level=3&values=1996%7E02l February#.

Salamon, L. M., and S. L. Geller. "Nonprofit America: A Force for Democracy? (Communique No. 9)." John Hopkins University Center for Civil Society Studies (2008). Accessed July 15, 2015. http://ccss.jhu.edu/wp-content/uploads/downloads/2011/09/LP_Communique9_2008.pdf.

Salisbury, Robert H. "Interest Representation: The Dominance of Institutions." *American Political Science Review* 78, no. 1 (1984): 64–76.

"The Paradox of Interest Groups in Washington: More Groups, Less Clout." In *The New American Political System*, 2nd ed., edited by Anthony King. Washington, DC: AEI Press, 1990.

Salisbury, Robert H., John P. Heinz, Edward O. Laumann, and Robert L. Nelson. "Who Works with Whom? Interest Group Alliances and Opposition." *American Political Science Review* 81, no. 4 (1987): 1217–34.

Sandfort, Jodi. "Analyzing the Practice of Nonprofit Advocacy: Comparing Two Human Service Networks." In *Nonprofits and Advocacy: Engaging Community and Government in an Era of Retrenchment*, edited by Robert J. Pekkanen, Steven Rathgeb Smith, and Yutaka Tsukinaka. Baltimore: Johns Hopkins University Press, 2014.

Schattschneider, E. E. *The Semisovereign People: A Realist's View of Democracy in America*. Fort Worth, TX: Harcourt Brace Jovanovich College Publishers, 1975.

Schlozman, Kay Lehman, and John T. Tierney. *Organized Interests and American Democracy*. Boston: HarperCollins Publishers, 1986.

Schlozman, Kay Lehman, Sidney Verba, and Henry E. Brady. *The Unheavenly Chorus: Unequal Political Voice and the Broken Promise of American Democracy*. Princeton, NJ: Princeton University Press, 2012.

Shaw, Clay, Nancy Johnson, and Fred Grandy. "Moving Ahead: How America Can Reduce Poverty Through Work." Washington, DC: U.S. House of Representatives, Committee on Ways and Means, 1992.

Smith, Richard A. "Interest Group Influence in the U.S. Congress." *Legislative Studies Quarterly* (1995): 89–139.

Snyder, James. "Long-Term Investing in Politicians; or, Give Early, Give Often." *Journal of Law and Economics* 35 (1992): 15–43.

Social Security Administration (SSA). 1997. *The Definition of Disability for Children*. SSA Publication no. 05–11053. Washington, DC: U.S. General Printing Office

"Some Antiabortion Activists Question Consequences of GOP Welfare Reform." *Washington Post*, February 1, 1995, A4.

Spence, Michael. "Job Market Signaling." *The Quarterly Journal of Economics* (1973): 355–74.

Staggenborg, Suzanne. "Coalition Work in the Pro-Choice Movement: Organizational and Environmental Opportunities and Obstacles." *Social Problems* 33, no. 5 (1986): 374–90.

Stand for Children Rally. C-SPAN video. June 1, 1996. www.c-span.org/video/?72650-1/
    stand-children-rally
State Legislative Leaders Foundation. "State Legislative Leaders: Keys to Effective
    Legislation for Children and Families." Centerville, MA: State Legislative Leaders
    Foundation, 1995.
Stepp, Laura Sessions. "A Lobby for Youth: A Broad-Based Coalition Pushes Its
    'Contract with America's Children.'" *Washington Post*, January 3, 1995, C5.
Strolovitch, Dara Z. *Affirmative Advocacy: Race, Class, and Gender in Interest Group
    Politics.* Chicago: University of Chicago Press, 2007.
Stout, Hilary. "GOP's Welfare Stance Owes a Lot to Prodding from Robert Rector."
    Wall Street Journal, January 23, 1995, A1.
Superville, Darlene. "Rally to Look for Answers." *Salina Journal*, May 27, 1996. A1.
Swarns, Rachel L. "Welfare Family Advocates, Once Allies, Become Rivals." *New York
    Times*, March 29, 1997, 1.1.
Szerlag, Heather. "Building a Children's 'Movement': Florida's Savvy Children's
    Campaign." *Youth Today*, July/August 1996, 27.
Tanner, Michael. "Welfare State has Failed Our Kids." *San Jose Mercury News*, June 2,
    1996, 6C.
Tarrow, Sidney. *Struggle, Politics, and Reform: Collective Action, Social Movements,
    and Cycles of Protest.* Ithaca: Cornell University, 1991.
    "States and Opportunities: The Political Structuring of Social Movements."
    Comparative Perspectives on Social Movements (1996): 41–61.
Taylor, Paul. "Nonprofits Boost Advocacy in the Interest of Children; Changes in Policy,
    Attitudes Seen Necessary." *Washington Post*, January 13, 1992, A1.
Teles, Steven M. *Whose Welfare? AFDC and Elite Politics.* Lawrence: University Press of
    Kansas, 1998.
Tilly, Charles. *From Mobilization to Revolution.* New York: McGraw-Hill, 1978.
Toner, Robin. "The Right Thinkers: Some Voices in the New Political Conversation."
    New York Times, November 11, 1994, B7.
    "The 104th Congress: Welfare; War over an Overhaul Appears to Be No Contest."
    New York Times, January 13, 1995, A22.
Trattner, Walter. *From Poor Laws the Welfare State: The History of Social Policy in
    America*, 5th ed. New York: Free Press, 1998.
Trisi, Danilo, and LaDonna Pavetti. "TANF Weakening as a Safety Net for Poor
    Families." The Center on Budget and Policy Priorities, 2012. Accessed January 20,
    2016. www.cbpp.org/research/tanf-weakening-as-a-safety-net-for-poor-families.
United States General Accounting Office. "Social Security: Rapid Rise in Children on SSI
    Disability Rolls Follows New Regulations." September 1994 (GAO/HEHS-
    94–225).
Van Winden, Frans. "Interest Group Behavior and Influence." In *The Encyclopedia of
    Public Choice*, edited by Charles K. Rowley and Friedrich Schneider. New York:
    Kluwer Academic Publishers, 2004.
Verba, Sidney, Kay Lehman Schlozman, and Henry E. Brady. *Voice and Equality: Civic
    Voluntarism and American Politics.* Cambridge, MA: Harvard University Press,
    1995.
Verba, Sidney, Kay Lehman Schlozman, Henry E. Brady, and Norman H. Nie. "Citizen
    Activity: Who Participates? What Do They Say?" *American Political Science
    Review* 87, no. 2 (1993): 303–18.

Vobejda, Barbara. "Conservative Welfare Idea Criticized; Bills Would Cut Funds for Unwed Mothers." *Washington Post*, June 24, 1994, A18.

"GOP Outlines Broad Welfare Reform. *Washington Post*, January 7, 1995, A1.

"Controversy Hits March for Children; Critics Say Backers Seek More Welfare." *Washington Post*, May 31, 1996, A1.

"Welfare Bill Opponents Turn Up Pressure." *Washington Post*, July 27, 1996, A04.

Vrazo, Fawn. "Old Foes Find Each Other on Same Side; Abortion-Rights Forces and Anti-Abortionists Make Unlikely Allies. Both, However, See Proposed Welfare Cuts as Hurting the Cause." *Philadelphia Inquirer*, March 26, 1995, E01.

Walker, Jack. *Mobilizing Interest Groups in America: Patrons, Professions, and Social Movements*. Ann Arbor: University of Michigan Press, 1991.

Warren, Dorian T., and Cathy J. Cohen. "Organizing at the Intersection of Labor and Civil Rights: A Case Study of New Haven." *University of Pennsylvania Journal of Labor and Employment Law* 2(4) (2000): 629–55.

Weaver, R. Kent. "The Changing World of Think Tanks." *PS: Political Science and Politics* 22, no. 3 (1989): 563–78.

Ending Welfare as We Know It. Wasington, DC: Brookings Institution Press, 2000.

Weaver, R. Kent, Robert Y. Shapiro, and Lawrence R. Jacobs. "Trends: Welfare." *Public Opinion Quarterly* (1995): 606–27.

Wednesday Group. "*Moving Ahead: Initiatives for Expanding Opportunity in America*." Washington, DC: House of Representatives, 1991.

Weiner, Tim. "A Capital Rally Attracts Groups from across the Nation to Focus on Children's Needs." *New York Times*, June 2, 1996.

"Welfare Reform, 1987–1988 Legislative Chronology." In *Congress and the Nation, 1985–1988* (Vol. 7). Washington DC: CQ Press, 1989.

"Welfare Reform, 1995–1996 Legislative Chronology." In *Congress and the Nation, 1993–1996* (Vol. 9). Washington DC: CQ Press, 1997.

Western, Bruce, and Becky Pettit. "Incarceration & Social Inequality." *Daedalus* 139, no. 3 (2010): 8–19.

Wetzstein, Cheryl. "CDF March Aims to Stem Cutbacks on Youth: Stand for Children Hopes for 200,000." *Washington Times*, May 30, 1996, A2.

"Senate Drops 'Family Cap' as GOP Splits." *Washington Times*, September 14, 1995, A2.

Whitford, Andrew B. "The Structures of Interest Coalitions: Evidence from Environmental Litigation." *Business and Politics* 5, no. 1 (2003): 45–64.

Who Stands for Children? C-SPAN video. May 31, 1996 www.c-span.org/video/? 72623-1/stands-children.

Williams, Amy E. "Odd Coalition Lines up against Curbs in Welfare-Reform Bill." *The State Journal-Register*, February 13, 1995, 1.

Wilson, James Q. *Political Organizations*. New York: Basic Books, 1973.

Winden, Frans. "Interest Group Behavior and Influence." In *Encyclopedia of Public Choice*, edited by C. K. Rowley and F. Schneider. Boston: Kluwer Academic Publishers, 2003.

Winston, Pamela. *Welfare Policymaking in the States: The Devil in Devolution*. Washington, DC: Georgetown University Press, 2002.

Witham, Larry. "Religious Right's Turnout Rises – Republicans Benefit from Evangelical Third of Electorate." *Washington Times*, November 11, 1994.

Wright, John R. *Interest Groups and Congress: Lobbying, Contributions, and Influence.*
    New York: Longman, 2003 [1995].
    "Contributions, Lobbying, and Committee Voting in the U.S. House of
    Representatives." *American Political Science Review* 84 (1990): 417–38.
Yin, Robert K. *Case Studies Research: Design and Methods.* Thousand Oaks: Sage,
    2003.

Index